Appearances of the Good
An Essay on the Nature of Practical Reason

"We desire all and only those things we conceive to be good; we avoid what we conceive to be bad." This slogan, which Kant dubbed "the old formula of the schools," was once the standard view of the relationship between desire or motivation and rational evaluation. Many contemporary critics have rejected this scholastic formula as either trivial or wrong. It appears to be trivial if we just define the good as "what we want" and wrong if we consider apparent conflicts between what we seem to want and what we seem to think is good. In *Appearances of the Good*, Sergio Tenenbaum argues that the old slogan is both significant and exactly right, even in cases of apparent conflict between our desires and our evaluative judgments. Maintaining that the good is the formal end of practical inquiry in much the same way that truth is the formal end of theoretical inquiry, this book provides a fully unified account of motivation and evaluation.

Sergio Tenenbaum is an associate professor of philosophy at the University of Toronto. He has contributed to *Philosophy and Phenomenological Research, Noûs, Philosophical Quarterly*, and *Oxford Studies in Metaethics*, and he is editor of *New Perspectives in Moral Psychology*.

Appearances of the Good

An Essay on the Nature of
Practical Reason

SERGIO TENENBAUM

University of Toronto

CAMBRIDGE
UNIVERSITY PRESS

CAMBRIDGE UNIVERSITY PRESS
Cambridge, New York, Melbourne, Madrid, Cape Town, Singapore, São Paulo

Cambridge University Press
32 Avenue of the Americas, New York, NY 10013-2473, USA

www.cambridge.org
Information on this title: www.cambridge.org/9780521837835

First published 2007

Printed in the United States of America

A catalogue record for this publication is available from the British Library.

Library of Congress Cataloging in Publication Data
Tenenbaum, Sergio, 1964–
Appearances of the good: an essay on the nature of practical reason /
Sergio Tenenbaum.
p. cm.
Includes bibliographical references and index.
ISBN 0-521-83783-9 (hardback)
1. Good and evil. 2. Practical reason. 3. Motivation (Psychology) I. Title.
BJ1401.T46   2007
170′.42–dc22   2006011089

ISBN 978-0-521-83783-5 hardback

Contents

v

Acknowledgments

I came to graduate school certain that I was going to write a dissertation on the philosophy of language. However, as I started my graduate work in Pittsburgh, I suddenly became captivated by issues in ethics, practical reason, and philosophy of action, issues to which I had previously paid very little attention. Doubtless my conversion was due in large measure to the outstanding pool of faculty and fellow graduate students I was lucky to have found in the area at that time. Although a number of years have passed since I wrote my dissertation, many of the ideas in this book were born from my philosophical conversations at Pitt. It would be unforgivable not to take this opportunity to acknowledge the enormous debt I owe to the teachers with whom I first discussed many of the ideas in this book: Bob Brandom, Stephen Engstrom, David Gauthier, the late Tamara Horowitz, John McDowell, Michael Thompson, Jennifer Whiting, and especially my ideal (and real) supervisor, Annette Baier. I also owe thanks to the many friends and colleagues with whom I went on to discuss these ideas in the years that followed. In particular, I would like to express my gratitude to those who provided extensive and valuable comments at various stages of writing this book: Donald Ainslie, Talbot Brewer, Phil Clark, Jimmy Doyle, Joe Heath, Pamela Hieronymi, Tom Hurka, Hans Lottenbach, Arthur Ripstein, Fred Schueler, Amy Schmitter, Gopal Sreenivasan, Aladdin Yaqub, and an anonymous referee at Cambridge University Press.

I had the chance to discuss many of the ideas in this book with a group of very talented students in my graduate seminar at the University of Toronto in the spring of 2003. I am very grateful to all the participants in that seminar: Danielle Bromwich, Michael

Garnett, Marta Jimenez, Julie Kirsch, Sari Kisilevsky, Kaave Lave-jardi, Joe Millum, Jonathan Peterson, and Helga Varden. I am also very grateful to Danielle Bromwich, Sari Kisilevsky, and Jonathan Peterson for helping me to prepare the manuscript for publication. I would also like to thank the Cambridge editors who oversaw the publication of the manuscript, the late Terry Moore and Beatrice Rehl.

Substantial portions of chapter 7 previously appeared in my "Judgment of a Weak Will," and substantial portions of chapter 8 previously appeared in "*Accidie*, Evaluation, and Motivation," my contribution to *Weakness of Will and Practical Irrationality*, edited by Sarah Stroud and Christine Tappolet. I would like to thank *Philosophy and Phenomenological Research* and Oxford University Press for allowing me to use this material. Research on this book was supported by a grant from the Social Sciences and Humanities Research Council of Canada.

In the early stages of the manuscript, Alexander Tenenbaum, and later Leonardo Tenenbaum, kept challenging the views I put forward in chapter 6. I am not sure that I did full justice to the various things they brought to my attention; I do know that my interactions with them have been the source of boundless learning and sheer enjoyment.

I owe so much to Jennifer Nagel, philosophically and in so many other ways, that all words of gratitude that I conjure up seem to fall ridiculously short of expressing my debt. The best I can do is to dedicate this book to her.

Appearances of the Good

An Essay on the Nature of Practical Reason

Introduction

There is an old formula of the schools, *nihil appetimus, nisi sub ratione boni; nihil aversamur, nisi sub ratione mali.* [We desire only what we conceive to be good; we avoid only what we conceive to be bad.]

(Kant, *Critique of Practical Reason*)

It is hardly unfair, if unfair at all, to suggest that the philosophical view is overwhelmingly that the good or only the good attracts.

(Michael Stocker, "Desiring the Bad")

Whether accurate or not, Stocker's description of the philosophical landscape in the late seventies would have rung true to many philosophers at the time. Views that accepted what Kant calls the "old formula of the schools," or, as will call them, "scholastic views," enjoyed widespread acceptance through long periods of the history of philosophy. I would hazard a guess that something like what Kant describes as the "old formula of the schools," and perhaps even stronger versions of it,[1] were widely taken for granted around Kant's time, and they were certainly still very influential when Stocker wrote "Desiring the Bad."[2] But wherever the historical truth lies, the climate has changed significantly. Most philosophers accept that we do not necessarily desire the good. Partly because of the influence of

---

[1] As stated, the old formula of the schools does not say that we always desire what we conceive to be good. However, I do think that Kant holds that those who accept that old formula of the schools would also accept its converse.

[2] For a particularly influential example, see Donald Davidson, "How Is Weakness of the Will Possible?"

1

Stocker and others,[3] the current philosophical "mainstream" position is that evaluative attitudes (such as judging that something is good, valuing, etc.)[4] do not determine and are not to be identified with motivational attitudes (such as desires, wants, etc.).[5] Stocker presented some seemingly straightforward counterexamples to the view that the good and only the good attracts: Cases of *akrasia* (weakness of the will), *accidie* (defection), perversity, and so forth were cases in which evaluation did not correspond to motivation, or motivation did not correspond to evaluation. Other kinds of arguments can be added to these: Children and animals seem to want things or have motivational states, and yet it seems odd to attribute to them complex evaluative judgments to the effect that the object of their desire is good. It seems more in tune with their intellectual capacity to say that they simply want these objects. Moreover, one can argue that if anything like the old formula of the schools is true, the notion of the good employed there would be so general as to be vacuous; in order to make the scholastic view come out true, one would need to define the "good" so broadly that it would end up simply being another word for "possible object of desire."[6]

I will call any view that claims that there are motivational states (such as desires, wants, etc.) that do not imply any kind of evaluation, or that there are evaluative states (such as judging to be good, valuing, etc.) that do not imply any kind of motivation, or even the

---

[3] See also, for instance, David Velleman, "The Guise of the Good."

[4] For the purpose of this introduction, I will treat valuing and judging to be good as equivalent. I revise this claim in chapter 1. See Gary Watson's "Free Action and Free Will" for a different way of drawing this distinction.

[5] It is worth noting that although the position has become mainstream, I am certainly not the first to express misgivings toward separating evaluation from motivation. Warren Quinn raises challenges to this view, even if he is agnostic on the issue of whether there could be desires that involve no evaluation. See his "Putting Rationality in Its Place." Joseph Raz raises similar concerns in "The Moral Point of View." Thomas Scanlon's buck-passing theory of the good prevents him from giving a prominent place to the notion of the good in practical reasoning or intentional explanations, but his concerns about whether desires can serve as reasons are similar to my concerns about separating motivation and evaluation. See his *What We Owe to Each Other*. John McDowell also raises similar concerns in his criticisms of Bernard Williams in "Might There Be External Reasons?"

[6] Peter Railton, "On the Hypothetical and Non-Hypothetical in Reasoning about Belief and Action." See also Velleman, "The Guise of the Good," and Philip Clark's "Velleman's Autonomism," for criticism.

view that the motivational force of a mental state need not match its evaluative content, a "separatist" view.[7] Separatist views raise important challenges to scholastic views by presenting arguments for the claim that evaluation and motivation come apart.

The old formula of the schools is also susceptible to criticisms from a different angle. To the extent that the notion of "good" in the old formula of the schools is a normative notion and refers to something that should guide us in what we should desire, then, one might argue, there is nothing corresponding to it. There is no external criterion for the "fitness" of the objects of our desires. Rational deliberation does not consist in trying to form appropriate desires or trying to "correct" the desires we have but in trying to figure out how to pursue the objects of our existing desires (or perhaps the objects of desires that we would form under certain favorable conditions) in the most efficient way possible. If the expression "good" has any meaning, it is just what we desire, or what we would desire under certain independently specified conditions. I will call any view that does not accept that legitimate criticism of the content of our desires in terms of an independent notion of the good is possible a "subjectivist" position or, for reasons that will become clear in chapter 3, a "contemporary subjectivist" position.[8] Subjectivist positions must thus hold that the old formula of the schools is either trivial or false.

These two different sets of criticisms correspond to the two roles that the notions of "desire" and "good" might play. In the context of practical reasoning, desires can be in the "background" of our reasoning about what to do;[9] they can be the sources of the importance we give to pursuing various outcomes or to engaging in various actions. The fact that I want to play soccer might give me a

---

[7] As we will see when we discuss the notion of valuing and conditioning, this might need some qualification. But the blunt version will do for the purposes of the introduction.

[8] See, for instance, David Gauthier, *Morals by Agreement* (especially chapter 2); and Donald C. Hubin, "What's Special about Humeanism."

[9] One may think that the desires themselves are what we reason *about*; they are the content of our deliberations. I find that position implausible. See, on this issue, Talbot Brewer, "The Real Problem with Internalism about Reasons." The more plausible view is that the desires are in the "background" of the deliberation. See Philip Pettit and Michael Smith, "Backgrounding Desire."

reason to look for soccer leagues, take steps to find my way to the soccer field when a game is being played, make sure that I do not sustain major injuries, and so forth. In the same context, the notion of the good plays the role that we ought to aim for when we reason. Realizing that it would not be good (or good for me) to play soccer, I should give up this end. Because a subjectivist thinks that there is no possible criticism of the content of the agent's basic desires (or of her ultimate ends[10]), there is no independent role for the notion of good to play in the realm of practical reason. The old formula of the schools would at best say that we desire only what we desire. I could at most have realized that I didn't want to play soccer, or that I didn't want to play soccer as much as I wanted some other things.

In the context of intentional explanations, desires explain what motivated the agent in the pursuit of a certain thing. One can explain the fact that I took my umbrella by mentioning, among other things, my desire not to get wet in the rain, and we can understand this desire in dispositional terms, as a disposition to act in certain ways given certain beliefs.[11] The separatist can argue that although our desires are often influenced by our evaluative attitudes, there is no reason to think that our dispositions will always match these evaluative attitudes. What explains the action, the argument continues, are the dispositional states, not the evaluative attitudes, even if at times the evaluative attitudes can be part of the explanation of why we are motivated to act in a certain way – why we desire certain things. Thus a notion of the "good" has no necessary role to play in intentional explanations.

Looking at these subjectivist and separatist objections, one might wonder why the old formula of the schools ever enjoyed such widespread acceptance. Why would anyone find this kind of view appealing? What could be the motivations for such a view?[12] Let us start with the context of practical reason. What is the point, in this context, of arguing that our desires aim at the good? Why shouldn't we just accept that desires do not stand under any further ideal, that we should only pursue what we want? In order to answer this

---

[10] As opposed to their instrumental ends.

[11] See, for instance, Michael Smith, *The Moral Problem*, chapter 4.

[12] Of course, I do not propose to speak for every proponent of a scholastic view.

question, we should reflect on the ways in which one's action can manifest error. According to the subjectivist, the only possible error that can be manifested in one's action is, roughly,[13] lack of consistency in pursuing one's ends – such as pursuing incompatible things, or not pursuing appropriate means to one's ends. However, we ordinarily seem to be committed to the possibility that our actions can manifest a different kind of error: that they pursue the wrong kind of object, an object that one ought not pursue not just because it does not fulfill our desires but because it is not the kind of thing that one should desire. No doubt, examples of immoral ends come to one's mind in these cases, but this commitment also shows itself in choices that are not easily classified as moral choices. I might find that my friend is wasting her life away by spending most of her time playing video games. It is not that I believe she does not want, or that she does not want enough, to play video games; rather, it is the fact that she wants it so much that I find particularly disturbing.

A particularly compelling example of this kind appears in Chekhov's play *Uncle Vanya*. Voitski (Uncle Vanya) looks back at his youth, which was dedicated to making it possible for his brother-in-law to live an academic life in a big city. Voitski realizes when he is forty-seven that his youth has been completely wasted; he now sees that his brother-in-law's work did not have the importance he used to attach to it and thus that it cannot bear the weight of a youth sacrificed for its sake. The problem is not so much that his brother-in-law is a fraud and not really engaged in good academic work (although this is true to some extent and is at the forefront of Voitski's invectives against his brother-in-law) but that the importance of a life of academic excellence had been obviously exaggerated. Moreover, nothing that Voitski can do right now can redeem his lost youth; his life has simply been wasted.[14] The question of whether people have wasted their lives in this way is hard

---

[13] This clause is necessary to include informed desired accounts, considered preferences, and so on.

[14] Of course, I am giving a rather coarse version of the intricacies of the play. Unfortunately, I cannot here (or anywhere for that matter) convey with much precision the poignant way in which *Uncle Vanya* gives us a sense of the characters' lives being, at some level, simply wasted.

to understand as a question about whether they failed to fulfill their desires coherently or failed to pursue adequate means to their ends – part of the problem is that Voitski had done *that* all too well. The issue seems to be whether what one wanted was worth having. Of course, the subjectivist might try to find some way to accommodate this possibility, but it is far from clear how this would work. A scholastic view has a quite uncomplicated way of making room for the possibility of this kind of error. The person who wasted her life in this way was one who desired, and acted in pursuit of, something that was not good; the standard of goodness in this case is not fully determined by one's desires. Our desires express our *stances* toward the good, but there is no guarantee that these stances can serve as appropriate grounds for a correct judgment that their objects are good.

Subjectivism takes the ideal government of action and belief by means of our rational faculties to be radically different. To use Hume's apt metaphor, in the practical realm, reason is the slave of the nonrational parts of the soul, whereas in the theoretical realm it is presumably their master. In other words, whereas no theoretical attitude that is relevant for belief formation escapes rational scrutiny (certainly not the deliverances of our senses), in practical reason, our desires or appetites are beyond the reach of reason and yet provide the standard for the rationality of our actions. The scholastic view, on the other hand, conceives of our rational faculties as a unified whole.[15] They are the same rational faculties employed in two different endeavors: theoretical inquiry and practical inquiry. The inquiries are distinguished not by different cognitive faculties but by their formal ends: the truth in the case of theoretical reason and the good in the case of practical reason. By the 'formal end' of an activity I mean the end one must ascribe to an agent insofar as he or she is engaged in that activity. For instance, the formal end of competitive games is winning; insofar as we describe an agent as engaged in a competitive game, we have ascribed to the agent the end of winning. It is important to be clear on what this ascription

---

[15] The view that our rational faculties are a unified whole contrasts with subjectivism, but it is not an implication of its rejection. Doubtless, one could hold objectivist views that did not have this implication.

amounts to. If I take the agent to be engaged in a competitive game, I can now describe various actions such as, for instance, "adopting a strategy"; it makes sense to assess various moves in light of the end of winning. (I can say, for instance, that a certain move is foolish or brilliant, etc.) This does not mean that an agent playing a game always, or ever, represents her end as the end of winning. A soccer player might just be trying to score a goal or to steal the ball from the opponent, and the thought of winning might not be directly guiding her actions at any point in the game. Moreover, agents might engage in competitive games with other ends in mind; they might play for money or prestige or for any other further ends. However, one may at first say that insofar as the agent is engaged in the activity in question, the constitutive end of the activity places an inescapable normative constraint upon the agent's behavior. The fact that a soccer player displayed impressive ballhandling skills does not contribute to making the play a good move in soccer if the play predictably resulted in wasting an opportunity to score.

Even this admittedly vague characterization of a constitutive end might be just a first approximation. Difficult questions arise when an agent is, or at least seems to be, engaged in a competitive game but is pursuing an end incompatible, and even necessarily incompatible, with pursuing the formal end of winning. So a baseball player might care only about making as much money as possible, and this might require that he extend a playoff series by making sure that his team loses a game. A parent might have as his end losing the game to his child. Even in theoretical inquiry, similar things seem to happen. There is much debate about whether it is possible to believe for pragmatic reasons, but it is hard to deny that even if one cannot believe at will, one can at least form the project of getting oneself to believe, by indirect means, a proposition that one holds dear for nonevidential reasons. And a physicist might go to the lab with the sole aim of publishing in a reputable journal and be ready to fudge data, disregard alternative hypotheses, and so on in a way that is incompatible with at the same time being engaged in the pursuit of truth. Are these agents still playing competitive games or engaged in theoretical inquiry? Does the existence of paradigmatic cases of the activities allow these "defective" cases to count (parasitically) as cases in which one is participating in the relevant activities, or are these agents better described as mimicking those who are engaged in these activities? These are difficult questions. But even if such parasitical cases are possible in the case of competitive games or theoretical reason, it is far from clear that there could be "parasitic cases" of practical reasoning. In the case of competitive games, the baseball player engaged in this activity with an extraneous end in mind; the same goes, mutatis mutandis, for the physicist. If one thinks that belief can be formed for pragmatic reasons, one will thereby concede that there is such a thing as engaging in the activity of belief formation guided directly by an end that is extraneous to theoretical inquiry. But it is not obvious that it is possible to pursue an end that is, in this sense, extraneous to practical reason. Practical reasons ought to guide *all* our actions, and by engaging in any activity, in pursuing *any* end, one has entered the realm of practical reason. In this way, the formal end of practical reason is inescapable in a way that no other formal ends are. For that very reason, one might suspect that the formal end of practical reason cannot demand anything very substantive, for it must be something one aims at in every single action.[16] However, there might be important constraints on what can count as good even at this level of abstraction. Part of the aim of the first few chapters of the book is to show that there are such constraints. But independent of the constraints we can uncover, we can learn quite a lot about the structure of practical reason by focusing on the idea that practical reason employs the same rational faculties as theoretical reason toward a distinct formal end. In fact, we should be able to draw from our

---

[16] Similar reasons have made some philosophers suspicious of attempts to derive substantive moral requirements from constitutive ends of practical reason. See, on this issue, Railton, "On the Hypothetical and Non-Hypothetical in Reasoning about Belief and Action"; and Douglas Lavin, "Practical Reason and the Possibility of Error." I do not mean, however, that this argument should be regarded as conclusive. Philosophers speak of actions being "defective" (Christine M. Korsgaard, *Locke Lectures*; and Tamar Schapiro, "Three Conceptions of Action in Moral Theory") and as being more or less full-blooded (David Velleman, "What Happens When Someone Acts"), and one would have to engage their attempts to show that there are such things before dismissing them out of hand. My only suggestion is that making room for cases of actions that are defective is significantly more problematic than making room for defective cases of engaging in particular practices and activities. (Korsgaard, for instance, tries to draw on the analogy of defective cases of other activities to explain a notion of defective action. See her *Locke Lectures*.)

understanding of theoretical reason resources that will help us clarify the structure of practical reason. Understanding our rational faculties as unified in this way has both theoretical and heuristic advantages. As we said earlier, the "good" in the old formula of the schools can be interpreted as having a function in the practical realm similar to that of the true in the theoretical realm: The good and the true are abstract characterizations of the aim of action and belief, respectively. That is, in saying that we aim at the true and the good, we are saying that we aim to get things right in the theoretical and the practical realm, respectively, but this is not to say anything more particular about which actions and beliefs would constitute getting things right. The author of a nonfiction book who when pressed by a strict word limit decided to shorten the introduction to "In this book, I will assert the truth about these events" would probably not be lying about her intention. However, such an introduction wouldn't help us to say *what* the author thought had happened. If we understand "good" in an analogous manner, the old formula of the schools will not settle for us how, in particular, agents should act.[17] Understood this way, the old formula of the schools will only commit us to the view that rational agents aim to act rightly (in this abstract sense) and that intentional explanations aim to show how actions appear to be correct (or make sense) to the agent.

Suppose we accept this reason to give the scholastic view a hearing in the context of practical reason. A separatist might accept all these points and still think that there is no reason to think that motivation and evaluation could not come apart. Is there anything we can say in favor of the old formula of the schools in the context of intentional explanations? At least under one way of thinking about the nature of intentional explanations, there will be a smooth transition from one point to the other. This will be the case if we think that intentional explanations are in certain respects importantly different from explanations in the natural sciences; that is, if we think of intentional explanations as attempts to *make sense* of the

---

[17] As we will see, this does not mean that there will be no general constraints on what can be intelligibly conceived to be good. See chapters 1 and 2 for some of these constraints.

agent, as aiming not so much to show how the agent's behavior *had to happen* given certain natural laws[18] but to explain and evaluate the extent to which it lives up to the ideal of rationality or to understand the extent to which the life of an imperfectly rational agent goes as it *ought to go*. Intentional explanations understood this way would try to track the agent's reasoning so that we can understand how her actions are an expression of a rational, albeit imperfectly rational, will.[19] Because we are imperfectly rational, intentional explanations will not always display the action as a rational conclusion given the agent's situation.[20] However, what the intentional explanation would show in this account is that the action was *intelligible*, even if one cannot be convinced that it was the (or a) right action given the circumstances, one understands why the agent took it to be so.[21] Of course, the aim of intentional explanations cannot be to show that the agent acted rationally; agents don't always do that. The aim of

[18] This is not to say that folk psychology has no predictive power. Even if we accept that folk psychology is to be understood primarily as providing explanations that display agents as approximating the ideal of rationality, these explanations could not work if our actions did not, by and large, approximate this ideal. But if this is so, insofar as folk psychology provides good explanations, its categories and assumptions should be capable of being put to use to predict the behavior of agents.

[19] The assumption that there is this kind of internal relation between the items that appear in intentional explanations and those that are in the background of practical reasoning is often also exploited by those who oppose the scholastic view. This relation is at the forefront of Williams's argument against the external reason theorist in his "Internal and External Reasons." These arguments tend to demand that practical reason conform to a certain conception of explanations. My proposal is to invert the order of priority: to examine how intentional explanations must look if they are to conform to an intuitive understanding of practical reasoning.

[20] Although I think that the conclusion of practical reasoning is always an action (I argue for this claim in my "The Conclusion of Practical Reason"), nothing in the book hangs on this view. However, often for simplicity's sake, I will just rely on the assumption that the conclusion of practical reason is an action.

[21] The notion of "intelligibility" here is borrowed from G. E. M. Anscombe, even if Anscombe might not have fully agreed with my "rationalist" use of the notion. See her *Intention*. I will discuss this notion of intelligibility further in chapter 1. The idea that the ideal of rationality has a constitutive role to play in intentional explanations comes from Davidson. See his "Mental Events." An understanding of intentional explanations that perhaps comes closer to the one I am proposing here can be found in John McDowell's "Functionalism and Anomalous Monism" and Jennifer Hornsby's *Simple Mindedness: In Defense of Naive Naturalism in the Philosophy of Mind*. Jonathan Dancy goes as far as to argue that normative reality directly explains our actions. See his *Practical Reality*.

intentional explanations, according to this view, is to show how an imperfectly rational agent came to the conclusion that a certain action was worth pursuing, even if the action in fact wasn't or the agent should have known that it wasn't.

Now let us take a quite general notion of desire; let us take "desire" to stand for any favorable attitude of an agent toward an object, or at least any favorable attitude toward an object that the agent believes to be in her power to bring about. If we accept the role of the good in practical reason presented earlier, it will now be hard to escape the view that desires can only render an action intelligible if they express how the agent conceived the end of the action to be good.

A comparison with theoretical reason might be helpful at this point. We can think of contexts in the theoretical realm analogous to contexts of reasoning and intentional explanations in the practical realm. In particular, we can distinguish between the context of deliberation, the context in which the agent reasons about what to believe, and the context in which we explain why a certain agent holds the views that he does. Suppose, for instance, Daniel reasons as follows: The last five times we flipped the coin, it came out heads. Therefore, the next time we flip the coin, it is very likely that it will come out tails.

Suppose Daniel starts giving us betting tips accordingly. If someone asked, "Why does Daniel think it is so likely that the coin will come up tails?" we could give something like the following explanation: Daniel believes that the coin came up heads five times before. He is confused about conditional probabilities, so he thinks that because it is very unlikely that a coin will come up heads six times in a row, he can infer that it is very unlikely that the coin will come up heads again next time.

Here, too, we could say that although this explanation does not show that the agent formed the most warranted belief in this situation, it explains why the agent took it to be the case that the content of this belief would (likely) be true. Note that in other cases it will be hard, if not outright impossible, to give a similar kind of explanation. If someone were to infer from the fact that bananas are yellow, that it is very likely that the coin will come up tails without relying on any intervening inferences, we wouldn't be able to explain in the same way why he believed that the coin would come up tails next time. We could say something of the form "He infers B from A,"[22] but unlike the case of the gambler's fallacy earlier, we would have no idea why an imperfectly rational agent would infer B from A. As we register more inferences of this kind, or more contents such that one can't understand why an agent would hold them to be true, it becomes harder to make the agent intelligible in this sense. At a certain point, we will no longer feel warranted in ascribing beliefs in these contents to the agent in question.[23] At any rate, that beliefs can perform the job that they do in both contexts depends on the fact that beliefs aim at the truth. They are relevant for one's reasoning because we represent their content as true, and so their content can serve as grounds for further inferences. And they help us show how the agent took herself to be warranted in her conclusions because they express what the agent represented as true as she was reasoning to this conclusion.

More generally, if we think of intentional explanations and practical reason in this unified way, we can think of a relatively straightforward way of understanding how the various categories employed in intentional explanation relate to the formal end of practical reason. The good is the formal end of practical inquiry, and practical reasoning aims to arrive at a correct evaluative judgment. We can now say that an action is the conclusion of the agent's practical reasoning (and thus the good is also the formal end of the action), or at least that the action carries out the intention that is the conclusion of practical reasoning. In either case, the agent's intention in action would express the agent's overall evaluative judgment, or what Donald Davidson calls the agent's "unconditional [evaluative] judgment." Finally, desires would be the agent's attitudes that express how the agent takes various objects to be putative objects of an evaluative judgment, the various ways in which objects that appear to be good to the agent serve as building blocks in the agent's practical reasoning. Furthermore, the motivational force

---

[22] Although I doubt we would even say that much in this situation.

[23] This is, of course, similar to Davidson's claim that interpretation requires a commitment to the Principle of Charity. See, inter alia, his "On the Very Idea of a Conceptual Scheme."

of the desire is fully explicated by the evaluative attitudes of the agent. This is in essence how the scholastic view sees these various categories of intentional explanation; it is no doubt a rather straightforward way of understanding intentional explanations as displaying why an imperfectly rational agent undertook a certain course of action.

The scholastic view thus takes each of these "motivation-laden" categories of intentional explanation and matches them to an evaluative attitude. For each of these cases, one could try to find various gaps between the motivation-laden attitude and the evaluative attitude that the scholastic view matches to it. So one could say that an agent can desire what does not appear good to her in any way or that some things appear good to certain agents who have no corresponding desires. One could also reject both these claims but think that desires might have an element of brute motivational force; one can say, for instance, that you can strongly want what appears to be slightly good for you. One also can think that an intention need not correspond to an evaluative judgment, or that there is some form of *akrasia* that implies that the agent acts against her unconditional evaluative judgment. Finally, one might think that the good is not the formal end of action and that action does not necessarily express the conclusion of one's practical inquiries. There might be other ways to carve gaps here, but the aim of the book will be to show that one does not need to postulate any such gaps. I argue that the version of the scholastic view presented here gives a compelling "gapless" account; in this account, one's motivation-laden attitudes are fully accounted for by one's evaluative outlook. This kind of "gapless" account seems to be taken for granted when we explain the agent's beliefs and reasoning in the theoretical realm,[24] and perhaps there is no reason not to proceed in the same way in the practical realm.

---

[24] One might think that cases of self-deception do not fit in this "gapless" conception of how we explain an agent's beliefs. But cases of self-deception are cases in which practical reason interferes in the realm of theoretical reason, not cases that call for an analogous separatist view *within* the theoretical realm. Moreover, many prominent accounts of self-deception explain the phenomenon in terms of general strategies of belief formation. See, for instance, Al Mele's *Self-Deception Unmasked*.

Of course these attractions can add to the plausibility of the scholastic view only if there is a version of the scholastic view that can overcome the problems discussed earlier. And this is one of the central aims of this book: to prevent a version of the scholastic view that is immune to these criticisms. More generally, I will try to present a coherent and compelling version of the scholastic view (henceforth I will call this version simply "the scholastic view") that preserves a nonsubjectivist and nonseparatist view of practical reason and intentional explanations. I will not try to provide in this book a conclusive argument for the superiority of this account of practical reason and intentional explanations over others, but I will try to show that it can survive the objections that seemed to be fatal to this approach and that it can accommodate intuitions that are central to our understanding of practical reason and human action. Moreover, I will also try to show that the scholastic view can do a better job than its main rivals in accommodating some of these intuitions. In fact, if I am correct, it even does a better job of accommodating these intuitions where it would seem the least promising. I will argue, for instance, that the scholastic view does a better job than other contenders in explaining the subjective nature of practical reason and *akrasia*. My aim is relatively modest: I hope by the end of the book to have made the case that the scholastic view is a serious contender in the field and that it is indeed a compelling account of the nature of practical reason.

The version of the scholastic view I defend in this book is a particularly strong one. Desiring is, in my view, simply *identified* with conceiving something to be good from a certain perspective. However, in another way, the scholastic view is weaker than the version that seems to be the target of many of the attacks because the view claims that an agent desiring X is to be identified with X *appearing* to be good to the agent (from a certain perspective), not with the agent *judging* it to be good. This small shift guarantees that the view does not fall prey to the most obvious objections to it; the scholastic view, for instance, does not deny that we can desire what we know is not good.[25]

---

[25] I am not the first to notice that desiring should be understood in terms of "appearing" or "seeming" good rather than in terms of unconditionally taking

A consequence of this version of the scholastic view is that there can be no gap between evaluation and motivation; we cannot strongly desire what we conceive as only a little bit good or be only weakly motivated to pursue what we judge to be to a large extent good.[26] Why should we be tempted to defend this strong interpretation of the old formula of the schools? I think the main initial advantage of this scholastic view is the fact that it is particularly suited to the understanding of practical reason and intentional explanations presented earlier. Intentional explanations aim to display the agent's behavior as aspiring to conform to the norms and ideals of rationality.[27] As we said previously, although intentional explanations cannot always make the agents come out fully *rational*, they should make them at least *intelligible*;[28] we should at least be capable of seeing how an agent could have *taken* a certain kind of behavior to be rationally warranted.

One might protest that these considerations provide support only to weaker versions of scholastic views. Putative "desires" whose objects cannot be understood to be intelligible objects of pursuit (and thus could not be conceived as good) will not be able to throw any light on how the behavior was intelligible, and explanations that cite such "desires" would thus not serve the same explanatory aims as intentional explanations do. But this only supports the claim that one only desires what one conceives to be good. It gives us no reason to think that there cannot be any *gaps* between motivation and evaluation. Even if we accept that the explanation must show how the action was in pursuit of some good, why couldn't the explanation postulate that the agent was motivated to pursue this good in a way that was disproportionate to its value?

---

something to be good. See Dennis Stampe, "The Authority of Desire." This is also, arguably, Davidson's view in "How Is Weakness of Will Possible?"

[26] These claims will need to be made more precise once the scholastic view is presented in more detail. See especially chapters 7 and 8.

[27] Compare John McDowell's claim that "the concepts of propositional attitudes have their proper home in explanations of a special sort: explanations in which things are made intelligible by being revealed to be, or to approximate to being, as they rationally ought to be" in his "Functionalism and Anomalous Monism."

[28] I put the point in this way partly because I think that this Davidsonian picture is not far from Anscombe's understanding of intentional explanations in her *Intention*.

However, it is hard to see what kind of contribution an element of brute motivation could make to an intentional explanation understood this way. Suppose we find that there is an element of brute motivation (or lack thereof) in desire that can work to some extent independently of the agent's evaluations, independently of how the agent conceives or judges things to be good. Because this element would not help to make the behavior intelligible, it would be extraneous to the aims of intentional explanations. Insofar as these elements could cause the agent's body to move, they would be better conceived of as *interfering* with activity that could be the subject of intentional explanations; mentioning those causal influences would be better understood as an explanation for the lack of availability of a proper intentional explanation. Assimilating unintelligible impulses into intentional explanations would be a mistake akin to assimilating body ticks, jerks, and paralyses to those explanations;[29] the mental origin of the behavior would not contribute any further to its intelligibility.[30] Because, in my view, the *point* of intentional explanation is to show how an action appeared reasonable to an agent, it will be difficult to find room there for brute motivation.[31] Indeed, if we hearken back to the two cases of theoretical irrationality, we could see something similar.

Theoretical irrationality is generally not understood in terms of brute dispositions to judge that do not correspond to the agent's conception of how things are. This is not how we explain the mistake of the agent who falls prey to the gambler's fallacy. Rather, we explain his mistakes as the natural result of imprecise or incoherent views about a subject matter, of fallacious but tempting modes of reasoning, and so forth. There is no reason to think that the same should not be true of practical reason, especially if the scholastic

---

[29] However, such impulses can give rise to rather complex behavior (for instance, in those who suffer from obsessive–compulsive disorders), and it would be implausible to claim that no instances of such behavior admit intentional explanation. I discuss this issue in chapter 6.

[30] Anscombe gives examples of other mental causes that do not contribute to making behavior intelligible in the same way. See her *Intention*, pp. 15–16.

[31] To say that it is "difficult" does not mean that it is impossible. One might try to find a way to accommodate this possibility within the Davidsonian framework (perhaps by appealing to a notion of "partial intelligibility"). But I will try to show in this book that there is no need to take this route because apparent counterexamples to the scholastic view can be accommodated within it.

view can show how these cases in which we seem to need a gap between motivation and evaluation can be accounted for without postulating any such gaps. If the scholastic view is correct, there is no reason to suspect that cases of practical and theoretical irrationality will be treated in fundamentally different ways.

The book is divided into eight chapters. The first two chapters lay down the basic elements of the scholastic view. I argue that desires are best conceived of as appearances of the good *from a certain perspective* (just as in the realm of theoretical reason we can talk about certain claims appearing to be true in light of certain evidence or in light of certain perceptual experiences). Appearances of the good so understood do not reduce to any kind of theoretical attitudes, and they are to be distinguished both from one's unconditional judgments of the good as manifested in our intentions and also from one's reflection on these appearances in forming a general conception of the good. The nature of the relation of the latter to our actions will divide actions into three kinds: the merely voluntary, the merely intentional, and the fully deliberated. These kinds of actions, I will argue, ought to be controlled by our general conception of the good in essentially different ways.

Chapter 3 considers the case for subjectivism based on our ordinary conception of value. Doubtless, there is *some sense* in which it is true that values are subjective. This seems to be in itself a reason to favor subjectivist theories of practical reason. More generally, the fact that we need to recognize some sense in which values are subjective might be considered evidence for a nonscholastic view because it seems to imply that our desires give reasons for and explain our actions without aiming at some independent good. Under a common understanding of the claim that values are subjective, we have reason to pursue the objects of our desires simply by virtue of the fact that we are inclined to pursue their objects. As we examine the plausibility of such claims, it turns out that there are indeed two plausible constraints on practical reasoning in this neighborhood: object-subjectivism and authority-subjectivism. Object-subjectivism is a constraint on the objects that can be correctly conceived to be good, and authority-subjectivism is a constraint on the relation between objects that are taken to be good for an agent and the agent's attitudes in viewing these objects as good. Although there have been many arguments against both constraints in the literature, especially against object-subjectivism, I try to show that these arguments are only effective *in conjunction with* some other philosophical positions. If we reject these other philosophical positions, the constraints turn out to be quite plausible. Surprisingly, accepting these constraints is not in tension with the scholastic view. Indeed, quite the opposite is true: It turns out that a scholastic view is not only compatible with these two constraints but does far better at accommodating them than "subjectivist" theories of practical reason. Thus, rather than serving as a reason for resistance to scholastic views, the subjective nature of practical reason supports it.

Chapter 4 looks into the kinds of practical objectivity that are possible within the scholastic view. The chapter starts by trying to examine how to move from our understanding of objectivity in theoretical reason to an understanding of objectivity in practical reason. However, with regard to questions of objectivity, the practical realm is not fully analogous with the theoretical realm because of differences in the nature of the formal end of each inquiry; although there can be only one flawless "conception of the true," there can be many flawless conceptions of the good. Nonetheless, two important notions of objectivity turn out to be applicable to the practical realm, and one of them allows us to generate a conception of impersonal goods, defined in this chapter as objects that must figure in every legitimate conception of the good. Making room for the possibility of impersonal goods is essential in showing that the scholastic view can make room for a plausible understanding of morality.

The notion of impersonal good gets a closer look in chapter 5, which investigates in general the possibility of making room for deontological intuitions within the framework of the scholastic view. As presented up to this point, the scholastic view would seem to be necessarily a consequentialist or teleological view, committed to the primacy of the good over the right. However, chapter 5 argues for the possibility of deontological goods, goods that are at least partly constituted by certain rules. Because deontology is most influential at the level of moral theory, the chapter investigates the plausibility of regarding moral rules as constitutive of an *impersonal* good as understood in chapter 4. It turns out that this is actually a particularly plausible way of understanding deontology, one that allows us to solve the "paradox of deontology" – the fact that deontological theories sometimes seem to ask us, rather implausibly, to pursue a lesser over a greater good.

The last three chapters are concerned with putative problems with the scholastic view in the realm of intentional explanation – in particular with the possibility that there will be gaps between evaluation and motivation. Chapter 6 looks into the possibility of motivation without evaluation, or at least without a correspondingly positive evaluation. Cases of obsessive and perverse behavior, and the whole array of apparently intentional behavior displayed by nonhuman animals and small children, seem to be cases in which intentional action is motivated without a corresponding (positive) evaluation. Chapters 7 and 8 look at the possibility of evaluation without corresponding motivation. Chapter 7 looks at *akrasia*. Cases of *akrasia* seem to be cases in which although we evaluate that *A* is better than *B*, we do not seem motivated to pursue *A* at *B*'s expense. Chapter 8 discusses *accidie*, a kind of phenomenon in which motivation is completely absent although one still seems to find value in various objects. It turns out that the scholastic view can not only accommodate the relevant phenomena but often does a better job of accommodating it than the available separatist views. Defending the scholastic view against these objections also gives us the opportunity to refine important aspects of the view.

These chapters do not provide a conclusive defense of the conception of intentional explanations outlined earlier, and no doubt one would be more tempted by this approach if one were already convinced of at least the initial plausibility of this understanding of intentional explanations. As I said, the book does not try to provide a conclusive case for the scholastic view. However, if the arguments succeed, its accomplishment should not be underestimated. If the scholastic view can account for all that I claim it can, and if it seems to be able to do so better than the alternatives, we have a strong case for its plausibility. Moreover, the very fact that the categories of practical reason and intentional explanation receive this unified explanation, and that we can understand our rational faculties in similar ways across the theoretical and the practical realms, should lend support to the scholastic view. So, I hope that, at the end of the book, even those who remain unconvinced that the scholastic view is true will be convinced that it cannot be discarded without much more argument than has ever been provided. Being convinced of *that* amounts to being convinced that the scholastic view still merits a place in the philosophical landscape.

1

The Basic Framework

Desires as Appearances

1.1 INTRODUCTION

In the first two chapters, I present the basic elements of the scholastic view. The first chapter focuses on the notion of desire at the center of the scholastic view. According to the scholastic view, for an agent to desire X is for X to appear to be good to this agent from a certain evaluative perspective. Section 1.2 introduces what Kant calls the "old formula of the schools," the claim that we desire only what we conceive to be good. I define a scholastic view as any view committed to the old formula of the schools. However, I will be interested only in scholastic views that understand the notion of the good in the way presented in the introduction: The good is supposed to be the formal end of practical inquiry in the same way that truth is the formal end of theoretical inquiry. Thus, one can take "conceiving to be good" as analogous to "conceiving to be true." To say that desiring is conceiving something to be good is to say that a desire represents its object, perhaps implicitly, as good – that is, as something that is worth being pursued. Of course, in this sense of "conceiving," the claim that in desiring something I conceive it to be good is not particularly strong. Compare this, for instance, with what can be said about imagining. If I imagine p, I do conceive, at least implicitly, that p is true. One need just note that, at least ordinarily, there is no real difference between imagining p and imagining p to be true. But imagining p does not in any way commit me to the truth of p, not even to the prima facie or *pro tanto* plausibility of *p*. Although even this weak claim will find many opponents, it is important to distinguish the particular version of the scholastic view from the many views that are captured by this definition. Section 1.2 lays down the basic features of the version of the scholastic view that I will defend in this book. The section focuses in particular on how the scholastic view understands the old formula of the schools. The scholastic view understands desires to be what I call "appearances of the good." Because "good" is defined in many ways, we need to explain how the scholastic view understands the notion of good in question, and what an appearance of the good is, when "good" is understood in this manner. These issues are the subject matter of sections 1.3 and 1.4, respectively. According to the scholastic view I defend, desires are appearances of the good *from a certain perspective*. The fact that desires can be grouped together as expressions of the same evaluative perspective plays an important role in distinguishing between objects that can be intelligibly conceived to be good and those that cannot be so conceived. Section 1.5 aims to explain the notion of perspective employed by the scholastic view, as well as the role it plays in our understanding of an agent, and how a perspective can matter to the agent's deliberations.

1.2   THE OLD FORMULA OF THE SCHOOLS

Scholastic views are committed to the claim that we desire (only) what we conceive to be good. This understanding of desire marks an important division between theories of practical reason; a scholastic view is committed to denying that there are purely motivational, nonevaluative elements that do any work in practical reason and in the generation of intentional action. Insofar as a desire of mine motivates me to act in some way, according to the scholastic view, it does so because, by virtue of having this desire, I conceive things to be good from a certain perspective. For a scholastic view, an account of practical reason (and intentional explanation) should appeal to no motivational state that does not have an evaluative counterpart; there are no "brute pushes" in the practical realm. Scholastic views are thus rejected by those contemporary philosophers who accept some version of a "Humean theory of motivation" or of a Humean theory of practical reasons.

Although the view presented and defended here is quite general, it certainly does not intend to range over any possible human movement. Thus, the view is committed to the truth of the formula only in those contexts in which we assume that actions are somehow brought about through practical reasoning;[1] the scholastic notion of desire is applicable only insofar as "desire" appears in the context of free action, intentional explanation, and deliberation.

Commitment to the old formula of the schools is shared by a family of views on the nature of practical reason that diverge significantly on various issues. Indeed, in the sense of "scholastic" employed here, one could apply the term to various forms of Aristotelian and Kantian views.[2] The particular version of the scholastic view defended here will be spelled out in this and subsequent chapters. However, it is important to lay down immediately at least two basic characteristics of the version that I will defend.

First, we can read the old formula of schools in two ways. In one way, the formula merely states a weak necessary condition for desiring something; anything that I desire I must somehow conceive to be good. In this reading, desiring (or motivation) and conceiving to be good (or evaluation) could be out of tune in important respects; for example, I could strongly desire something that I conceive to be slightly good. However, the formula can also be understood to state a stronger claim that the desire for a certain thing should be *identified* with a positive evaluation of this thing.[3] This strong reading rules out the disparity between motivation and evaluation, and it is this sense of the claim that I will defend.[4]

---

[1] This is rather vague because I do not at this moment want to settle any questions about the nature of the connection between practical reasoning and an action (such as "Is an action a conclusion of practical reasoning?" or "Are reasons the causes of actions?").

[2] Among such views, or at least under a generously understood label of "congenial views," one could include Thomas Scanlon's *What We Owe to Each Other*, Christine Korsgaard's "The Normativity of Instrumental Reason," and Warren Quinn's "Putting Rationality in Its Place."

[3] No doubt the weak and the strong readings of the old formula of the schools are not exhaustive; there could be "intermediate" views committed to something between the weak and the strong readings. This claim will also be refined and clarified over the course of the book.

[4] Of course, the weaker reading will be discussed and argued for by implication. As we will see in a moment, I think the correct version of the scholastic view identifies

Second, this reading provides a different understanding of a popular distinction in contemporary philosophy, the distinction between "motivating" and "normative" reasons.[5] As commonly understood, a motivating reason is supposed to be the reason that *disposes* the agent to act in a certain way (and thus explains her actions), whereas a normative reason is a reason that would *justify* certain actions were the agent to act in accordance with this reason.[6] In this view, one distinguishes between the fact that an agent might be inclined to eat sandwiches and the fact that it might be good or valuable for the agent to eat a sandwich. Presumably, the first kind of reason will be appealed to when we *explain* the agent's behavior, and the second kind of reason will be appealed to when we *assess* its rationality. But, for the scholastic view, the distinction is not between two different kinds of reasons but between two different evaluative standpoints that can be roughly characterized as "first-person" and "third-person" standpoints. Because a desire is just the agent's conceiving something to be good in a certain way, a desire is already a "stance" on a normative reason (i.e., it is the representation of a normative reason to act in a particular way). So a desire, which would be a motivating reason par excellence, turns out to be just the agent's (partial)[7] take on the status of something as a normative reason.[8] Of course, intentional explanations will still need to mention the agent's own understanding of what "normative reasons"

desire with a positive evaluation *from a certain perspective*. These evaluations might be overridden upon reflection (i.e., from a reflective perspective).

[5] See, for instance, Michael Smith, *The Moral Problem*. The distinction goes back at least as far as Francis Hutcheson's distinction between "exciting reasons" and "justifying reasons." See his *An Essay on the Nature and Conduct of the Passions and Affections: Illustrations upon the Moral Sense.*

[6] This is not exactly Smith's definition, but I think the definition he gives is somewhat problematic. For a discussion of these problems, see G. F. Schueler, "How Can Reason Be Practical?"

[7] Why we need this qualification will become clear in the sections that follow. It is again related to the fact that a desire conceives something to be good from a certain perspective.

[8] For interesting discussions of how the distinction between motivational and normative reasons should be understood, and whether it should be preserved at all, within an understanding of the relation between practical reasons and intentional explanations similar to the one I am presenting here, see Jonathan Dancy, *Practical Reality*, especially chapters 4 and 5, and Jay Wallace, "Explanation, Deliberation, and Reasons."

there are or, in our language, the agent's conceptions and judgments of the good. Thus, the scholastic view distinguishes between what the agent conceives of and judges to be good and what is actually good (between the agent's views on the landscape of normative reasons and what normative reasons are actually there), and intentional explanations will typically be more concerned with the former. However, the scholastic view does not simply substitute the distinction between the agent's judgments and the things that are actually good (or the actual "normative reasons") for the distinction between motivating and normative reasons. Even those who postulate a distinction between motivating and normative reasons must also employ the distinction between the agent's judgments and the things that are actually good and explain the relation between this distinction and the motivating/normative reasons distinction. For the scholastic view, there is only one distinction: between what appears to the agent to be good and what is actually good.[9]

Third, if an agent's desiring is her *conceiving* something to be good, it is not her *judging* something to be good. An unqualified judgment that something is good is one's final position on how the evaluative world matters, and if I am correct, such judgment always issues in action; in fact, I would say more precisely that these judgments are *expressed* in intentional actions.[10] Although we could not judge something to be good if we did not conceive it to be good from some perspective (thus for every action there must be something that the agent desires), the converse is obviously not the case. There would also be little to be said in favor of the scholastic view if it held that judging something to be good followed immediately from the fact that something appeared to be good – that is, if action arose immediately from the (strongest) desire. Such a view would be just a cumbersome restatement of the view that an agent acts on her strongest current desire. According to the version of the scholastic view I defend, an unconditional evaluative judgment ought to be formed in accordance with a *general conception of the good*, a reflective

[9] Of course, questions of what the agent ought to do in light of what is actually good, and in light of what the agent conceives to be good, are not an easy matter to settle. On some complications, see Niko Kolodny, "Why Be Rational?"

[10] See section 1.7. See also Davidson's "How Is Weakness of the Will Possible?" and my "The Conclusion of Practical Reason."

view on the good formed in light of the various *perspectives on the good* manifested in the various desires of a particular agent. This is not to say that an agent *will* always form an unconditional evaluative judgment in accordance with her conception of the good but only that whenever this does not happen her actions fall short of the ideal of rational action.[11]

It is also worth stating a relatively minor clarification. The sense of "desire" covered in the scholastic formula is the weak sense in which whenever I have something as my aim, or would have it as my aim if it were not for some countervailing considerations,[12] I desire it.[13] "Desire" in this sense need not be passionate, warm, or even felt in any way. I will also allow that a desire might simply be the consequence of practical reasoning, or, to use Thomas Nagel's vocabulary, that there are motivated desires that are not ultimately grounded on unmotivated desires.[14] I am certainly not claiming that this way of understanding "desire" will best fit ordinary usage, but as far as philosophical usage goes, it is certainly quite standard.

A more important clarification concerns the relation between desiring and the good. The old formula of the schools would not be particularly interesting if we simply defined the "good" as whatever is the object of a desire or preference, or of desire or preference under independently specifiable conditions (such as conditions of "full information," for example). Of course, one could simply define "good for X" in terms of what X desires, but this would be a rejection rather than an endorsement of the scholastic view.[15] According to a scholastic view, the good is the goal of desires, and actual desires might be improper conceptions of the good. To use the terminology

---

[11] This is not to commit myself to accepting the view that it is always better to follow one's most reflective judgment. For criticism of this view, see Nomi Arpaly's *Unprincipled Virtue*, chapter 2.

[12] This explication will have to be slightly modified later when I make the case that desires are essentially perspectival.

[13] Nagel distinguishes between motivated and unmotivated desire, and Schueler distinguishes between a desire proper and a pro-attitude. In their terminology, my notion of desire is supposed to cover both motivated and unmotivated desires, and I am using the "pro-attitude" sense of desire. See Thomas Nagel, *The Possibility of Altruism*; and G. F. Schueler, *Desire: Its Role in Practical Reason and the Explanation of Action*.

[14] Nagel, *The Possibility of Altruism*.

[15] A classic instance of this view is Hobbes's *Leviathan*.

I will develop here, desires are *appearances* of the good, and these appearances might turn out to be wholly illusory. But to understand better what it is for a desire to aim at the good, we need to examine the notion of the good employed by the scholastic view in more detail.

1.3 INTELLIGIBILITY AND THE GOOD

The scholastic view might at first seem to conflict with some of the most ordinary things we would like to say about the relationship between desiring (or wanting) and the good. We often say that something is good but not what we want, that we want something even though we know it is bad, or even that we do not know what is good but know what we want.

But the scholastic view actually meets some commonsense expectations about the relationship between motivation and evaluation. Indeed, if I *want* something, there is a sense in which I seem to be making a judgment (or at least putting forth the content of a putative judgment): I take it that what I want has some value, at least from a certain perspective. I might regret that I wanted something, and one may say in such a case that I judge that my want involved an illusory presentation of something as good; the wanting seems to have the structure of a judgment. I might regret having wanted something if it turned out to be incapable of bringing me any satisfaction (the cake was stale) or if for any reason it turned out that there wasn't much value in the object of my desire (eating cake is not that satisfying after all and could not justify my having wanted it so badly). A separatist, of course, would not be without words to account for such common occurrences. A separatist who wanted to deny that this particular desire was for an object conceived to be good might first say that the agent did not intrinsically desire the cake but pleasure that was brought about by the cake. This, however, would not be particularly plausible. It would then be very hard to avoid the unpalatable conclusion that all desires are for some unspecified form of pleasure and all the objects of pursuit are simply means to pleasure.[16] The separatist could alternatively say that the

---

[16] More plausible here would be Elijah Millgram's view that the lack of pleasure is to be taken as some kind of *evidence* in practical reasoning. See his *Practical Induction*.

judgments of these kinds of regrets do not represent a failure internal to the desire but a separate evaluative judgment. Whereas for the scholastic view the failure is internal to the desire, for the externalist the failure is external. But this analysis seems appropriate only for certain cases; it might seem to be a plausible way to think about how I regret having eaten a delicious cake while dieting. Here it seems appropriate to say that there was nothing amiss with respect to the satisfaction of the desire to eat the cake; the evaluative judgment comes from a completely different perspective. But in the case in which one simply finds the experience of eating the cake unsatisfying independently of any other interest one might have in not eating cake, the failure seems internal to the desire.[17] As we will see later, the scholastic view distinguishes between these two cases of regret as, on the one hand, a case in which one's evaluative judgment was the wrong judgment from within the perspective in which eating cake appears to be good and, on the other hand, a case in which the perspective of the desire to eat cake is judged to be illusory or overridden upon reflection.

In the normal cases, there is no problem identifying a want with conceiving something to be good that might or might not in fact be so. Typically, wants and desires are not blind impulses or incomprehensible yens that push me somewhere. When dumbfounded about someone's behavior or even by the fact that someone is tempted to do something, it seems natural to ask, "What does he see in X?" And when finding an activity incomprehensible, we often say something like "And what's the point of that?" Thus it seems that, in the normal course of events, my actions aim at some good, and the desires that can explain these actions could be identified with conceiving something to be good. Except for some moments of insanity, my desires and wants seem to be always directed toward certain objects, projects, and aims whose point I can see.

Of course, one could acknowledge that I must see the point of what I desire in order to desire it without conceding that I also need to conceive of the object of my desire as good; there seems to be

---

[17] Of course, this is not supposed to be a conclusive argument against separatism. The separatist could no doubt try to find other ways to distinguish the cases. Again, the point was just that some features of our ordinary understanding of desire seem to mesh well with the scholastic view.

some distance between the two claims. However, if we see the good merely as the most abstract characterization of the aim of any practical judgment, the distance shortens considerably. To see some point in what I desire (even if the point is just something I can express by the sentence "I felt like doing it") is to see that what I desire at least appears to be worth pursuing; that is, it at least appears to be a fitting object of a conclusion of a piece of reasoning about what one has reason to do. But this *is* to conceive it to be good in this abstract sense of "good."

It might be worth comparing the scholastic understanding of desire with subjectivist theories of practical reason. According to subjectivism, certain attitudes of the agent, if held under certain ideal (but independently specifiable) conditions, suffice to confer value on the objects of the attitudes.[18] According to these views, if I desire to be a caring parent, my *desire* can generate a reason to take my daughter to the doctor this afternoon, but *the fact that my daughter needs to see a doctor* can't by itself be rational grounds for my taking her to the doctor.[19] A subjectivist view takes it that desires cannot be rationally criticized in terms of their content, whereas a scholastic view takes it to be constitutive of desire to aim at an appropriate object (the good). Thus, according to the scholastic view, if the subjectivist contention that the *contents* of desires do not in themselves provide reasons for action is true, then every desire of the agent embodies an illusion.[20]

If the scholastic view allows for criticism of the content of the agent's desires, it is not yet clear *how* it does so. Worse yet, it may appear that if the scholastic view presents the good just as a formal aim of practical reason, then it is vacuous. Just to postulate an aim of practical reason and then be silent about it might seem to make scholastic views into trivial variants of nonscholastic ones. As Peter

---

[18] For a representative statement of this view, see David Gauthier, *Morals by Agreement*, chapter 2.

[19] This is not to say that subjectivism requires that the agent deliberate about her desire rather than the content of her desire.

[20] Of course, this is not to deny that if the agent did not desire X, then X could not be a reason for any of her actions. But, in the same way, the fact that if the agent did not believe p, it could not be a reason for his belief that q, does not impinge on the claim that it is p itself, not the belief that p, that is a reason for q.

Railton points out, "Unless a certain amount of substance is built into the idea of goodness, it will be rather too easy (and uninformative) to think of any sort of desiring as 'deeming to be good'."[21]

Indeed, given the teleological character of a desire, a desire will always have a certain aim. If the old formula of the schools is to have any substance, it must advocate something beyond this obvious point. One way to add substance to this claim would be just to postulate an object, however complex, as the good.[22] This way of making the scholastic view more substantive would put its advocate in the unenviable position of settling what the good for a human being is by means of general considerations of the nature of practical reason. However, our assumption is that "good" functions in practical reason in a manner analogous to "true" in theoretical reason. It is then worth asking whether a similar concern faces theories of truth in the theoretical realm. Interestingly enough, Kant discusses a similar concern about definitions of "true," and what he has to say on this subject is illuminating:

To know what questions may reasonably be asked is already a great and necessary proof of sagacity and insight. For if a question is absurd in itself and calls for an answer where none is required, it not only brings shame on the proponent of the question, but may betray an incautious listener into absurd answers, thus presenting, as the ancients said, the ludicrous spectacle of one man milking a he-goat and the other holding a sieve underneath.... A general criterion of truth must be such as would be valid in each and every instance of knowledge, however their objects may vary. It is obvious however that such a criterion [being general] cannot take account of the [varying] content of knowledge.... But since truth concerns just this very content, it is quite impossible, and indeed absurd, to ask for a general test of the truth of such content.[23]

---

[21] Railton, "On the Hypothetical and Non-Hypothetical in Reasoning about Belief and Action."

[22] One could have an "inclusive" notion of the good, just as some interpreters claim that Aristotle held an "inclusive" conception of *eudaimonia* (see, for instance, J. L. Ackrill, "Aristotle on Eudaimonia"). This is also how Railton suggests that we specify a "high brow" view, a view similar to the scholastic view, in his "On the Hypothetical and Non-Hypothetical in Reasoning about Belief and Action."

[23] Kant, *Critique of Pure Reason*, pp. 97–98 (B 83).

What Kant is saying here about truth is relatively uncontroversial; indeed, so uncontroversial that it inspires him to a rare moment of humor in an otherwise rather sober work. A theory of truth will not have much to say about how we should proceed in the special sciences, and it is certainly no substitute for *engaging* in the special sciences. Kant considered logic to be a theory of truth, and if we follow him on this point, a theory of truth will indeed be of *some* help to the special sciences, but this kind of help cannot go beyond identifying some limiting conditions on what can be thought of as true. Thus no one expects that a philosophical theory of truth will come up with a standard of truth in the sense that seems to be required for a philosophical theory of the "good" – or a theory of practical reason that takes the good to be the aim of practical reason. Although philosophers freely say that belief aims at truth, they do not feel compelled to provide a procedure by which one can distinguish true beliefs from false ones or to dictate procedures that chemists, physicists, and the whole array of researchers who doubtless aim at the truth should follow in order to uncover it. Even the most substantive theories of truth, such as the correspondence theory of truth, would not provide any substantive criteria in this sense.[24] Minimally, characterizing the end of inquiry as "truth" indicates a commitment to the impropriety of inferring p directly from the fact that anyone or any group of people believe p. Somewhat more contentiously, one can say that the aim of truth plays at least a limiting role in determining what can count as a good reason to believe a claim.[25] If these claims are correct, then the claim that belief aims at truth puts substantive constraints on what one can or

---

[24] No doubt there could be "substantive" theories of the good in the same sense that a correspondence theory of truth is a "substantive" theory that would not determine in any particular way the objects that are good. So one could say, for example, that "X is good if and only if X is worthy of being desired." This of course is not the kind of substance in the "idea of goodness" that Railton is after.

[25] One could think, for instance, that formal logic gives us some of the limiting conditions under which claims can be true in any area. Ideas such as truth-preserving and truth-conducive, for example, serve to specify what we expect from good inferences. These thoughts are not, of course, wholly uncontroversial. If one thinks that the notion of truth is fully explained in terms of goodness of inference, one will not think that truth has any such role. Robert Brandom defends a view of this kind in *Making it Explicit* (see p. 113, inter alia, for a statement of the view).

ought to believe whether or not one can give a more precise determination of which propositions are actually true.

Of course, the analogy with truth can only take us so far. Not only might one have doubts about whether truth really places any constraints on our conception of theoretical inquiry or the world,[26] but one needs to say more about how the scholastic conception of the relation between desire and the good places any constraints on our understanding of what one can and ought to desire. For the moment, I just want to establish that the conceptual space is there, or at least that it is not obviously absent: To say that there is no substantive characterization of the good itself in the sense that one cannot have a nontrivial criterion of goodness is not to say that there are no general principles that apply to all objects that are good. Thus, such claims in themselves do not show that the scholastic view is not a substantive thesis. Just as denying that there is a general criterion of truth does not commit us to denying that there are general necessary conditions for any statement, or a set of statements, to be true (such as the laws of logic), denying that there is a general criterion of the good does not involve denying that there are general necessary conditions on the good (such as, perhaps, the Categorical Imperative and the Principle of Instrumental Reasoning). More importantly, however, various structural claims might be consequences of postulating a formal end of inquiry. Demands for coherence that otherwise might have been groundless, demands on how "evidence" (or what we will call "prima facie attitudes") ought to relate to "judgments" (or what we will call "all-out attitudes"), distinctions about different kinds of errors, and successful employments of one's practical employment can be illuminated by understanding practical reason as related to the good in this manner, or so the book will endeavor to show.

We can see better what is involved in saying that to have a desire is to conceive of something as good (from a certain perspective) if we look at pathological cases of behavior. In these cases, the agent often aims at something that seemingly has no point (and in some cases the agent herself will admit that the behavior does not have an intelligible aim). Suppose someone obsessively reordered a pile of

---

[26] For more on this issue, see chapter 4.

books every five minutes. When asked why she was doing it, rather than attempting to justify her actions, she would simply say, "I don't know; I just find myself doing it." Suppose we press further and are convinced that the agent sees no point in the action. (We ask questions such as "Do you keep feeling you can improve on the aesthetic quality of the bookshelf?" and the agent keeps saying that this is not the point of the action.) In this case, no doubt, the agent aims at something (ordering the books) but does not conceive of it as good. And, indeed, as the scholastic view would predict, we would even be reluctant to ascribe to the agent a desire to reorder the books (let alone a desire to organize the books); our having an aim is not a sufficient condition for us to have a desire.[27]

So the first substantive requirement that the scholastic view imposes is what can be called a general "intelligibility requirement." Anscombe makes a similar point in *Intention*. She characterizes intentional actions as those "to which a certain sense of the question 'Why?' is given an application."[28] The sense that Anscombe has in mind is the sense in which we are asked not to find the causal antecedents of a certain action but to make sense of *the agent*. So "Because a certain muscle contracted, causing the finger to bend in its joints with sufficient momentum to move the trigger backward" would not be an appropriate answer to this sense of the question "Why?" but "Because he killed her brother" would. The latter, but not the former, can make intelligible not only a movement but *an action*. We can understand that an agent might find revenge worth pursuing, and we can find intelligible an agent who would leave much behind for the sake of avenging her brother (even if we do not feel inclined to pursue revenge ourselves) in a way that we cannot find an agent who dedicates his life to howling to the moon intelligible. Although it is true that an intelligible aim is susceptible to many flaws because of the obstinate way in which the real refuses to live up to the ideal (it can, for example, be imprudent, immoral, or something that is not fit for a human being to want), insofar as an aim is intelligible, we must be capable of grasping how someone could see the point of pursuing this aim despite its flaws. We can see

[27] I consider this kind of case in detail in chapter 6.
[28] Anscombe, *Intention*, p. 9.

how, from the agent's perspective, this course of action could count as a worthwhile pursuit.

I will propose the following initial understanding of the intelligibility requirement: An end or aim is intelligible when it can be seen as part of a life that aspires to the ideals of rationality,[29] and an agent is intelligible if her life can be understood as aspiring to the ideals of rationality.[30] The notion of having a life that aspires to the ideals of rationality should not be seen as positing an explicit end for the agent. It would no doubt be ludicrous to think that an agent at every step in her life or even often enough asks herself the question "Is this the rational thing to do?" One aspires to be a good parent, a good worker, to have some fun, and so on but one rarely seems to aspire to be rational as such. However, insofar as it makes sense to ask of all these specific aspirations whether the agent ought to have them or whether the agent is justified in giving them that much importance, and insofar as it makes sense to think of the agent as someone who is subject to the normative standards implied by these questions, we can say that the agent's life aspires to the ideals of rationality. The notion of "rationality" here is supposed to cover any legitimate normative standard, any norm to which the life of a rational agent ought to conform. This is, to some extent, reading Anscombe's requirement with Davidsonian spectacles, but I do not think that this perspective takes us very far from Anscombe's understanding of the requirement. Although the Davidsonian spectacles should bring to mind requirements such as the Principle of Charity, one should not overlook the fact that in ascribing desires to agents and providing explanations for their actions, one often aims to reveal the agent as *falling short* of this ideal. Actions, aims,

---

[29] Compare John McDowell's claim in his "Functionalism and Anomalous Monism" that "the concepts of propositional attitudes have their proper home in explanations of a special sort: explanations in which things are made intelligible by being revealed to be, or to approximate to being, as they rationally ought to be." See also Davidson's "Mental Events."

[30] John Rawls distinguishes between reasonable and rational, where the latter is a more formal notion of consistency and the former a more substantive notion. See his "Kantian Constructivism in Moral Theory" in his *Collected Papers*. Scanlon makes a similar distinction in *What We Owe to Each Other*. Although this distinction has some foothold in common usage, the need for repeating "reasonable or rational" or, worse, "reasonableness or rationality" makes for some cumbersome prose. Thus I will use "rational" to cover both "reasonable" and "rational."

projects, and so on can be foolish, frivolous, or cruel, for example.
And the commitment of the agent, and of those who endeavor to
understand her actions, to answer this particular version of the
question "Why?" is a commitment to being able to make sense of
one's actions in the context not only of the norms of rationality but
also of the various excusing conditions and failings of an imperfectly
rational being. It is important to note that the commitment to
answer this question, in the case of the explanations that the agent
herself gives of her actions, is also a commitment to respond to
further challenges to one's answers, especially challenges that imply
that a behavior has fallen far short of those ideals of rationality (if
one's behavior is, for instance, accused of being "foolish" or
"pointless"). Although politeness often prevents such blunt
exchanges, answering the question "Why?" commits me to being
able to head off these accusations unless, through regret or remorse,
I acknowledge that I no longer endorse those reasons or motives
that issued in action. But actions that are flawed in these ways are
flawed in ways that only the movement of rational beings can be;
tables, mountains, ants, and perhaps even higher mammals and
babies can't be foolish, frivolous, or cruel. Thus, even regrettable
actions can find a "home" only in what can be characterized as the
life of a rational agent. This view treats intentional explanations as
attempts to show how the action appeared reasonable to the agent
from his point of view, how they were the outcome of his exercise of
practical reasoning. This might seem too optimistic, as if one
thought that an agent's behavior always cleared high thresholds of
rationality. Obviously, any version of the Principle of Charity will
require that *some* threshold of rationality be cleared before we can
ascribe to anyone intentional explanations. But the view that
intentional explanations should show how the action was the outcome of an agent's reasoning that aimed at the good only requires
that intentional explanations somehow reproduce the agent's reasoning aiming at the good; there's no further requirement that the
agent turn out to be particularly excellent at the task.

Of course, there is more to be said about what makes action
intelligible, and I will be expanding on this notion of intelligibility at
various points in what follows. But I am here especially interested in
one feature of Anscombe's account of intentional actions. Anscombe

correctly points out that the answer "for no particular reason" (or, more precisely, "I just feel like it") can be a perfectly intelligible answer to this form of "Why?" question. If asked "Why are you doodling?" it would be perfectly appropriate for me to answer "for no particular reason" or "I just felt like it." Indeed, if I were to start tapping my fingers on the table during a long, boring wait for my number to be called in a government agency, it would be surprising if I could cite an elaborate reason for tapping my fingers on the table in response to the question "Why?"[31] Note, however, that if the answer "for no particular reason" were always appropriate, the intelligibility constraint would be an empty one. Anything could be made intelligible if one just "felt like doing it" or did it for no particular reason. But that this is the kind of thing that can be done when we feel like doing it, or that we can right away act on this occasion as we feel, must itself be intelligible – it must be capable of being conceived as good. Not everything can be intelligibly done just because one feels like doing it. Indeed, Anscombe notes that the answer "for no particular reason" is *not* always appropriate: "If someone hunted out all the green books in his house and spread them out carefully on the roof, and gave one of these answers to the question 'Why?' his words would be unintelligible unless as joking and mystification."[32]

This marks out the sense in which the intelligibility requirement is a substantive constraint. It marks the fact that not everything could be what Thomas Nagel calls an "unmotivated desire," a desire that is not grounded on other desires or other sources of motivation. Not just any sort of aim can be an intelligible aim, and to say that, in the context of practical reason and intentional explanations, desire can be identified with conceiving something as good is at least to say that anything that is aimed at in action must be an intelligible aim. But even here we should be careful to notice that failure to satisfy the intelligibility requirement can rarely be ascribed by looking solely at a "snapshot" in the life of the agent. A reasonable life can make intelligible behavior that would otherwise be unintelligible,

---

[31] It is important to note that tapping one's finger would probably in most cases be voluntary but not intentional action according to Anscombe. See her *Intention*, pp. 89–90. See also section 2.5.

[32] Anscombe, *Intention*, pp. 26–27.

and we allow that the typically rational agent has eccentricities, oddities, and moments of inscrutability. Perhaps an otherwise intelligible agent could be allowed this sort of eccentricity: Sometimes she just feels like spreading books on the roof.[33] One could say that leading an intelligible life earns us the right to moments of unintelligibility.[34] However, to accept this point is not to concede that the life of an agent could be filled only with projects of this kind that are incapable of receiving any further justification or explanation.

At any rate, if Anscombe is correct here, this would seem to be enough to establish that a scholastic view of practical reason could not be just a notational variant of subjectivism. Subjectivism is committed to the view that there are no constraints of intelligibility on our aims; we could desire anything, and anything we could desire would be intelligible as an aim as long as we desire in a well-informed and consistent manner. This is not to say that Anscombe's examples suffice to refute these views; one could argue that Anscombe's bizarre agents strike us as unintelligible not because their ends are intrinsically unintelligible but because given what we know about human beings, we cannot believe that such agents are indeed well informed and consistent. For instance, one could claim that we know enough about human beings to know that a life dedicated to howling to the moon is not what they would choose if they were choosing under ideal conditions; or the subjectivist could try to construct a similar notion out of the materials from which she starts. But here we need only note that the intelligibility requirement cannot *obviously* be satisfied by any object of a desire; Anscombe's examples do establish at least a presumption that this criterion is a substantive one.

So, although the intelligibility requirement does not single out any specific object as the good, and to this extent could be considered a formal characterization of the good, it is not an empty one. Only the *actual* exercise of practical reason could determine what the good is, in much the same way that only actual theoretical

---

[33] More on this issue in chapter 4.

[34] Even in this case we might expect a smile as the person confesses such bizarre delight, or some acknowledgment that she recognizes that this action is not easily understood.

inquiry could determine the truth. The intelligibility requirement, for instance, constrains the scholastic understanding of deliberation. According to the scholastic view, a desire that did not present its object as being good from a certain perspective could not be an attitude whose object would have positive weight in deliberation or a putative item in an intentional explanation. That I find myself craving something or being moved in a certain direction is not yet a reason to do anything. Suppose I wake up in the morning and find that I am somehow inclined to rearrange the dishes, although I can't see any point in doing it because they are perfectly well arranged and there is nothing pleasant or interesting about moving cups and plates around. When deliberating about what to do, this inexplicable craving could not give me, directly, a reason to do anything. Of course, I might find that the craving is taking my attention away from more important tasks and decide that I had better indulge this craving. I may decide to reorder the dishes so that the craving will go away and I can move on with my life. But it is not the craving that is the source of these reasons for the pursuit of its object but the desire to engage in whatever tasks would make my craving go away – what I want is not to reorder the dishes but to get rid of the craving. Indeed, if I could make the craving go away by taking a deep breath and counting to five, I'd probably prefer this alternative because I do not conceive reordering the dishes to be good in any way.

1.4   APPEARANCES OF THE GOOD

Desires are often treated as if they were the "practical analog" of beliefs, playing roles in practical reason similar to those played by beliefs in theoretical reason. Perhaps a nonstandard notion of desire, according to which desires are "all-things-considered" attitudes, could render this analogy plausible. But the analogy is extremely misleading if we stick to the way that desire is typically understood in the philosophical literature because belief certainly is an "all-out" attitude in the sense that I cannot, insofar as I am rational, have contradictory beliefs. But desires are "prima facie" attitudes in the sense that we *could* have desires for incompatible objects; many want to eat voraciously and stay thin at the same time. This is why the formula of the schools is expressed in terms of what we *conceive* to be good. If anything, the analogs of desire in the realm of theoretical reason are *appearances*[35] in the sense that we use "appear" and its cognates in the following sentences:

(a) From far above, the car appears very small.
(b) Looking only at the evidence you gathered, it appears that she is not guilty.
(c) It appears red to me, but you had better ask someone else.
(d) The raccoon appears to be dead.
(e) Presented this way, the argument appears to be valid, but when we formalize it, we see that it is not.

These "appearances" have the characteristic that Descartes attributes to ideas when he says that they are *tanquam rerum imagines*, "as if images of things."[36] That is, they are glimpses of certain things from certain perspectives that present them to us as being thus and so. The raccoon, from the point of view afforded to us by just looking at it, is represented as dead, and this point of view is at least a putative reason to think that the raccoon is dead. As we know all too well, appearances often turn out to be illusory.[37] But as examples (b)–(d) should make clear, sometimes things appear just as they are, and in those cases it might turn out that the appearance gave us good reason to accept that things are as the appearance represented them. It is important, however, not to think of appearances as necessarily perceptual. Examples (a) and (c), and probably (d), are indeed perceptual appearances; this is how things *look* to the person making the statement. But this is not true of the other examples; an appearance in those cases simply indicates what we could call "an inclination to judge." What we *should* learn from perceptual appearance is that, at least in one sense of "appearance," saying that something appears to be such and such makes reference to a perspective.[38] In cases (a) and (c), the perspective is visual, but in cases (b) and (e) the perspective is not perceptual at all. In (b), a perspective is afforded by the analysis of a (probably incomplete)

---

[35] See Dennis Stampe, "The Authority of Desire," for a similar point.
[36] Rene Descartes, *Meditations*, AT 37, in *The Philosophical Writings of Descartes*.
[37] Or overridden. As I will argue, it is important to distinguish between illusory appearances and appearances that are overridden.
[38] More on this notion in section 1.5.

body of evidence, and in (e) the perspective is afforded by how an argument is presented. It is equally important to note that the appearances of (b) and (e) may fall short of the truth for different reasons. The perspective afforded by the evidence you gathered is incomplete but legitimate. That is, the evidence may in fact lend plausibility to a certain hypothesis but may be overridden by stronger evidence for an incompatible hypothesis. In case (e), the "evidence" is not legitimate at all. The perspective afforded by this form of presentation of the argument is merely illusory.

It is with this meaning of "appearance" in mind that I will identify desires, in a way that is in keeping with the scholastic formula, as *appearances of the good*, and just as in the case of theoretical appearances, these can turn out to be illusory. Indeed, this understanding already removes what may appear to be a major obstacle to scholastic views. After all, one might argue, doesn't one often desire what one recognizes to be bad? And isn't it true that no matter how clearly we understand that something is bad, we often can't stop desiring it? This seemingly obvious possibility of desiring the bad has often been taken to show that the traditional conception of desiring as aiming at the good cannot be sustained.[39] However, if we identify a desire with what *appears* to be good, we can see our way out of difficulty. Theoretical appearances can also be illusory, and things might persist in appearing in a certain way even when we know that the appearance is deceptive. The possibility of desiring the bad is thus no more mysterious than the fact that we can know that the raccoon is alive and at the same time think that when we look at and touch him he appears to be dead. Just as in theoretical reason reflection upon available evidence might prevent us from judging wrongly but not from having appearances present themselves to us in a deceptive manner, in practical reason reflection upon the various appearances of the good might allow us to *know* that something is bad without preventing it from appearing to us, from certain perspectives, to be good.

---

[39] See Stocker, "Desiring the Bad"; and Velleman, "The Guise of the Good." This is just a preliminary point; see chapter 6 for a more detailed defense of the scholastic view against these arguments.

These considerations also help us deal with other arguments that have been raised in order to drive a conceptual wedge between motivation and evaluation. Gary Watson argues that there is no sense in which we value the objects of certain desires we have or judge the objects of these desires to be good.[40] Watson gives us the example of a squash player who has a sudden urge to smash a racket on her opponent's head in frustration. It would indeed be highly misleading to say that this person sees some value in smashing the racket on her opponent's head but that this value is overridden by other values. The agent sees *no* value in this action, not even a smidgen of value. Although this point seems correct, we can now see that it does not threaten the scholastic view. This example only shows that such an agent, *upon reflection*, or, from a reflective perspective, does not attribute any value to such a desire. This is not an objection, however, to the claim that desires are *appearances of the good*. In Watson's case, the reflective judgment takes the appearance to be merely illusory. Similarly, in the realm of theoretical reason, we can distinguish between a consideration that *appears* to make a claim plausible and a consideration that *in fact* lends some plausibility to a claim. A consideration pertaining to the former category will not necessarily pertain to the latter. For instance, one often finds appealing the form of reasoning that urges that one is less likely to win the state lottery if one simply chooses the same numbers that were drawn in the previous week, given that it is very unlikely that the same number will be the winning number twice in a row. But the kind of confusion about conditional probabilities typical of these instances of the "gambler's fallacy" does not yield any plausibility to a belief, despite the fact that it is quite hard to free oneself from its illusion of validity. Suppose we want to spell out the conceptual connection between a theoretical appearance, our being inclined to believe a certain judgment, and a notion such as validity or truth. The preceding example shows that one might be inclined

---

[40] See Gary Watson, "Free Agency." I do not mean to imply that Watson himself is committed to a separatist view. In his "Free Action and Free Will," Watson distinguishes between valuing a certain thing and judging it to be good. For the moment, I will just use the two expressions interchangeably. I will be distinguishing between "valuing" and "judging to be good" in a quite different manner in the next chapter.

to believe a form of reasoning that one (reflectively) judges to be invalid. But one should not therefore conclude that there is no conceptual connection in this area; we merely placed it at the wrong location. It is only insofar as the gambler's fallacy *appears* valid to me that I am inclined to believe it. The same goes for the conceptual connection between desiring and conceiving to be good. It is only insofar as something appears to be good that one desires it.

1.5 PERSPECTIVES

Before we say more about the nature of practical reasoning, it is worth outlining how the scholastic view sees the relation between practical reasoning and intentional explanations. In the ideal case, an intentional explanation will simply describe an instance of practical reasoning so that:

(a) The action is described in such a way to make manifest the evaluative judgment it embodies. (It is described as it was intended.)
(b) The action is a sound conclusion from the premises.[41]

So, "He didn't drink because he was going to drive" would be a case of an intentional explanation of this kind.[42] However, intentional explanations often aim to explain actions that the explainer does not think are fully warranted. So these explanations must allow for inferential steps that are invalid and yet, to some extent, intelligible. They must show the agent as making a mistake that is characteristic of a limited rational agent. Thus, intentional explanations partly aim to provide us with a view of why a certain

---

[41] If one thinks that an intention, not an action, is the conclusion of practical reason, one would have to replace "intention" with "action" here. For an argument that the conclusion of practical reason must be an action, see my "The Conclusion of Practical Reason."

[42] From what I said earlier, it should be clear that I do not think that every intentional explanation must cite a belief and a desire for the agent. But I do think the belief–desire theory gets the following correct: It follows from the fact that a certain intentional explanation is correct that the agent has the relevant beliefs and desires. This is similar to the point Nagel and McDowell make when they invoke the idea of motivated or consequential desires. See Nagel, *The Possibility of Altruism*; and McDowell, "Are Moral Requirements Hypothetical Imperatives?"

conclusion seems warranted from the point of view of a less than fully rational agent. Of course, if the agent simply "blundered" an inference, was misinformed, or overlooked an option, it would be quite simple to add this to the explanation, something typically accomplished by spelling out the agent's beliefs and other cognitive attitudes. "He wasn't drinking because he thought he was going to drive home" or "He walked all this way because he didn't think about calling a cab" would be explanations of this kind. When it comes to a person's proper orientation toward the good, we need to look at two cases. First, intentional explanations will often mark attitudes that the explainer or other agents would not endorse but find permissible. So, for instance, "He traveled to Nepal because he wanted to climb a mountain" could be an explanation of this kind.[43] Even in cases in which one finds a certain attitude unwarranted, the mention of a desire might be enough to explain the action, but if the scholastic view is correct, this could not always be the case: Not just anything can be intelligibly desired for its own sake. So let us say that Sue is throwing stones at a certain boat and the following explanation is given to us:

(E1) Sue wants to cause damage to Ms. S's boat.

Without further explanation, it's hardly intelligible that Sue finds anything good in damaging Ms. S's boat. The situation improves somewhat if one adds to the explanation the following:

(E2) Sue wants to cause damage to Ms. S's boat out of envy. (She wishes she had a nice boat like Ms. S's.)

What does the expression "out of envy" do in this explanation? The scholastic view contends that it expresses a certain evaluative perspective that the explainer might not share but can understand. Attributing an evaluative perspective to someone involves attributing a *certain way in which things appear good to her*. An evaluative perspective clusters various desires that share a "point" or whose objects are found good for similar reasons. Thus, by attributing an evaluative perspective to the agent, we not only clarify why the agent

---

[43] In chapter 4, it will become clear that I can endorse the inference even if I have no desire to climb mountains and thus go to Nepal. In section 2.3, I discuss the notion of a permissible inference.

finds a certain object desirable but also commit ourselves to expecting that the agent will find various other objects good as well. If Sue acts out of envy, she will probably find it desirable not only to damage Ms. S's boat but also to acquire a bigger boat for herself or to learn that Ms. S will be prevented from using her boat for various reasons, for example.

For the envious person, undermining the possibility of someone else having a coveted object appears good in a way that it could not appear good to the unenvious person, even if she coveted the object just as much.[44] To place a certain desire within the context of a perspective is to put it in a context in which it is intelligible both that certain things appear good to the agent and that the agent takes certain things to be reasons for certain actions. Placing a desire in the context of its perspective is not, however, to provide a further reason for the agent's action or to describe a further good pursued by the agent. Sue does not cause damage to Ms. S's boat in this manner as a means (not even as a "constitutive" means) of pursuing the end (or the good) of envy, but rather envy makes this action appear good and thus makes her take "damaging the boat" as a reason for action.

One could object that although envy is not a further end, the person who is envious is just someone who has a "grand end" of harming someone and that the various expressions of envy are further specifications of this grand end. In this view, although these actions are not the constitutive means of envy itself – they are not the constitutive means of envy per se – they are the constitutive means of the end that characterizes the envious person, namely the aim of, say, harming the owner of a coveted good. However, there is no reason to think that the grand end can be characterized so that all and only the instantiations of this end will be proper expressions of envy. Of course, one could simply characterize the grand end as an open-ended disjunction of all the possible actions of an envious person, but it is not easy to characterize the grand end of envy in any more informative way. If the end is, for instance, "causing harm to

---

[44] Again, this is not to say that the unenvious person cannot *understand* how things appear from the perspective of envy. See my "Ethical Internalism and Glaucon's Question" for a related point concerning the "amoralist" understanding of moral concepts.

Ms. S," it will fail to classify as expressions of envy Sue's attempt to buy objects that Ms. S owns. If the end were "to make sure that Ms. S. is not better off than Sue," it would include Sue's attempts to excel in her studies (which would have as a consequence that she would be a happier person overall than Ms. S) as a possible expression of envy.[45] One could also argue that expressions of envy are specifications of a vague desire in the same way that going for a dinner at a particular restaurant can be a specification of a vague desire for an entertaining evening.[46] But this also would not work. First, as we pointed out, "performing an envious action" is not Sue's end, but "having an entertaining evening" is an end of the agent who deliberates in this manner. Moreover, the envious agent does not necessarily deliberate from a menu of alternatives of how she is going to express her envy in the way that the agent who asks how he should spend his evening must do. It is true that in some cases the agent who acts out of envy might deliberate in such a way as to specify her end more precisely. If an envious agent wants to hurt the person who got the job she coveted, she might need to deliberate about what would count as hurting the agent in the "appropriate" way in this situation. This kind of deliberation would be much like the deliberation of the person who wants to have an entertaining evening. But it is important to note that there is nothing in the nature of having a perspective such as envy that rules out the possibility that the envious agent will need no such deliberation; his desires from the perspective of envy might be fully specified. It is even possible that being in a state of envy provides one with an immediate ranking of all actions from this point of view, a ranking that requires no further deliberation. Still, even if this were the case, saying that a certain action was performed out of envy would be explanatory in just the way outlined earlier.[47] The various desires of the envious person share not a common end but a common

---

[45] I am not denying that in certain circumstances this may be an expression of envy. But the qualifier "in certain circumstances" is crucial here; the action could not simply be explained as an expression of envy in the same way that causing harm to the boat could.

[46] This example is from Williams's "Internal and External Reasons."

[47] Indeed, the explanation given does not show in any way *how* the agent deliberated from a more general to a more specific end.

underlying explanation and justification (even if the justification is not fully adequate) of *why* one finds the objects of these desires worth pursuing. Placing an appearance of the good within a certain perspective can be explanatory without thereby describing the agent's deliberation. While the agent is in the grip of envy, the fact that envy calls for a certain action appears nowhere in the agent's deliberation. But even if this is so, the fact that an agent was envious is an essential part of the explanation of the action.

Although I picked a somewhat "nasty" perspective as an example, more praiseworthy perspectives can also be invoked to explain why certain things appear to be good to the agent. Indeed, the list of virtues provides us with a useful list of perspectives. For the generous agent, helping someone in need appears good even when the agent does not profit from this action. For the courageous person, the fact that an action puts her at risk does not make refraining from action appear good, for example. More generally, "Y" in expressions such as "S did X out of Y" will typically describe the perspective from which something appears good to the agent rather than the object of a desire. Indeed, a fact that ethical theorists, especially those sympathetic to virtue ethics, often point to in connection with the virtues turns out on this account to be an instance of a more general phenomenon. Many have noticed that the generous agent does not deliberate as follows: "Helping X here would be the generous action; I am a generous person ..."[48] In fact, there seems to be something untoward about an agent who accounts for her general act in terms such as "I did X because I am a generous person, and this is what a generous person does in such a situation." The generous agent would just conclude the appropriate action from the fact that someone is in need. From my viewpoint, this just means that generosity marks an evaluative perspective. However, there are advantages to understanding this feature of virtue terms as a feature of evaluative perspectives more generally. This understanding also provides an explanation of why such perspectives seldom figure in deliberation: Perspectives are not themselves reasons.[49] It also allows

---

[48] See, for instance, Bernard Williams, "Acting as the Virtuous Person Acts."

[49] Talbot Brewer points out correctly that *vice* terms *can* figure unproblematically in deliberation as things to be avoided. There's nothing untoward about deliberating as follows: "Quitting would be the coward thing to do, so I should

us to see that the phenomenon is more general in two ways. The first way in which the phenomenon is more general is that one need not have the character trait in order to endorse, let alone understand, the perspective. An ungenerous person can perform generous actions, and a cowardly fellow might display courage on occasion. Hume sometimes seems to claim that we hold agents responsible for their actions only when these actions come from a durable character or disposition, but this is not quite true.[50] We do resist attributing responsibility if we cannot see how a particular agent could have intelligibly pursued a certain action (as in cases of "temporary insanity"), but this is not the case for all actions out of character. The coward and selfish person who on one occasion risks his life to save a child from a crocodile pool when he could expect no reward has certainly acted generously and courageously on that occasion; the forgiving person who on one occasion takes advantage of the lack of witnesses to slash the tires of his enemy is vindictive on that occasion.[51] In fact, it would be wrong to think that the character trait is what explains the action in these contexts. The attribution of this action to a character trait simply marks the fact that the agent is someone who not only reliably endorses what she conceives to be good from this perspective but is particularly prone to act from this perspective.[52]

The second way in which the phenomenon is more general is that evaluative perspectives are omnipresent even when we don't use "out of X" to mark them. Let us take our gastronomic enjoyment as an example. This is not an area that is particularly prone to rich

keep going." This is well explained by the scholastic view. "Cowardice" marks an illusory perspective, so the agent in this case is noticing that what seem to be reasons to quit in fact emanate from an illusory perspective, and so they should be discarded. Brewer himself gives a similar explanation of the phenomenon. See his "Virtues We Can Share: Friendship and Aristotelian Ethical Theory," pp. 746–747.

[50] David Hume, *Treatise of Human Nature*, pp. 411–412. At points, Hume seems to be making the weaker claim that we are more forgiving toward actions that are out of character, and this is no doubt correct.

[51] See also on this issue Thomas Hurka, "Virtuous Acts and Virtuous Dispositions."

[52] Schueler, in *Reasons and Purposes: Human Rationality and the Teleological Explanation of Action*, for instance, argues that character traits function as a natural place at which explanations can stop. See also Donald Ainslie, "Character Traits and the Humean Approach to Ethics." If I am correct, character trait is the wrong category to play this explanatory role.

arguments and complex deliberation.[53] However, even here we can
think of our capacities for gastronomic enjoyment and can call the
evaluative perspective that they form "gastronomic sensitivity." We
can say that our gastronomic sensitivity makes certain things appear
good – in particular, certain foods and drinks. Even here, the appeal
to an evaluative perspective is explanatory. First, there is the
obvious commonality among all my gastronomic impulses. One
could, no doubt, try to explain this commonality as an instance of a
grand or vague desire to eat food that tastes good. We do indeed
sometimes have a desire like that; I want to eat well in a foreign
town, and I ask my host to take me to a good restaurant. But
sometimes I just want gumbo or I have a craving for chocolate
pudding. I don't need to deliberate in these cases from the more
general desire, and, in fact, if I did, my conclusion might have been
a completely different action. After all, I know that one can do much
better than gumbo or chocolate pudding when it comes to good
food, and it might even be easier (and cheaper) to get hold of
something else. The good I see in eating gumbo in these cases is no
different from the good I see in gumbo on those occasions that I do
choose gumbo because it is the best food around. We encounter
here something structurally similar to the case of the agent who acts
out of generosity. It is true of the generous agent that he helps
others because it is the generous thing to do, even though the
generous agent is not guided by the end of doing something generous. Similarly, although the desire to eat gumbo is not a mere
specification of the desire to eat foods that taste good, the agent eats
gumbo because it tastes good.

Indeed, one can plausibly put the notion of a perspective to use in
formulating the following more specific intelligibility requirement
on appearances of the good:

(PI) Objects can only appear good from a particular perspective.

In order to ensure that this is not an empty requirement, we put
forth the following requirement on perspectives:

---

[53] One might protest that restaurant reviews, for instance, could be quite
sophisticated in arguing for their conclusions. However, I'll just proceed on the
assumption that gastronomic enjoyment is a quite uncomplicated matter.

(MD) It is never the case that only one object appears to be good from a certain perspective; perspectives always generate multiple desires.

Of course, perspectives do not come clearly delineated. There might be subperspectives within a perspective, perspectives might overlap, and their individuation might be a rather tricky business. However, the main point of bringing this term into our analysis is not to be able to demarcate the various perspectives precisely but rather to register the fact that desires are not isolated psychological entities but are part of complexly structured clusters of evaluation, and these clusters of evaluation make competing claims on a general conception of the good. Although I will not try to individuate perspectives very precisely, I will mark some clear cases in which two different things appear good from the same perspective and some cases in which they appear good from different perspectives.

The scholastic notion of an evaluative perspective not only allows that various desires can share the same perspective but also that desires with the same objects arise from different perspectives. The latter possibility can help explain, for instance, Kant's distinction between the dutiful agent who helps others from duty and the sympathetic agent who helps others from inclination. According to Kant, both agents share the same end, the end of helping someone in distress, and in both cases the end is not adopted in light of any further ends of the agent. However, they differ not in *what* they conceive to be good but in *how* and *why* they conceive it to be good. Put in terms of the scholastic view, they differ in the different perspectives from which their desires arise. If the scholastic view is correct, this marks a difference in how the end in question relates to other ends of the agents, to other things they conceive to be good, and other reasons they see for action.[54] This helps explain why someone like Kant might think that the moral worths of the actions

[54] There is a *New Yorker* cartoon in which separate ticket windows for Graceland tours are labelled "ironic" and "non-ironic." Because people do go to Graceland with these two different mind-sets, one could wonder why there *aren't* two different tours. But obviously there is really no need for two different kinds of tours because the two kinds of tourists differ not in what they desire in this context but in the perspective from which they conceive what they desire to be good.

of the dutiful agent and the sympathetic agent are different. If Kant is correct, only in the case of the dutiful agent does her desire to help others arise from the correct kind of evaluative perspective.

Perspectives are most clearly visible to someone engaged in explaining the behavior of others. Because perspectives often do not show up as *objects* of deliberation, we tend to appeal to them more often when explaining an agent's behavior than when engaged in practical reasoning. This might make it seem like the basic source of an agent's motivation must remain hidden to him; envy is not an object of deliberation for the agent who acts out of envy. It seems then that in this view the deliberative and explanatory perspectives essentially come apart so that we do not explain an action in terms of the reasons for which the agent acted.

This would be a problem, however, if perspectives were necessarily opaque to the agent: if the agent herself couldn't recognize her reasons as being bound up with a certain perspective, or if such recognition would somehow undermine her reasons (if perspectives had to be, in Derek Parfit's terminology, self-effacing).[55] But this is not the case. In fact, it is not even true that perspectives *never* appear in the context of deliberation. After all, in what I will call "fully deliberative actions," one does not act immediately from a desire but from a general conception of the good.[56] In order to form such a general conception of the good, one must *reflect* on various ways in which things appear to be good, and in order to know how one takes in a certain appearance of the good, it will certainly be relevant to assess the evaluative perspective from which a particular desire arises. Thus I may deliberate as follows: "I want to break his boat only because I am envious, but one shouldn't be envious," "I shouldn't put so much effort into getting gumbo; it's just food," or "When one has a chance to be generous with so little effort, one can't just give in to one's selfish desires." Of course, reflection does not imply that a whole perspective is put to examination. I might be concerned with a particular envious action or a particular generous action in a way that does not raise the question of the relative merits of a perspective as such. If, for instance, in order to decide, upon reflection, to refuse to

---

[55] See Parfit, *Reasons and Persons*, section 17.
[56] See section 2.5.

answer inopportune calls to my home phone number from charitable institutions, I need not engage very deeply the question of the importance of generosity as such. Still, trying to understand what kinds of claims a certain perspective makes on one's deliberation is a central aspect of reflection in the practical realm.

A similar phenomenon lurks in the theoretical realm. Much of the time, when I judge that things are just as they appear to me in perception, it would be misleading to say that I am reasoning to a conclusion about the reliability of a sensory perspective. In the "grip of the perceptual perspective," my perceptions just strike me as presenting things precisely as they are. Now suppose I have perceptual evidence for the belief that a pig is flying in my immediate surroundings: I see what appears to me to be a flying pig. When I want to give my final verdict on whether this appearance is veridical, I must consider not only whether this is indeed the content of my visual experience but also the reliability of perceptual appearances, the conditions under which I should accept as true the "evidence of the senses," and so forth. I would need to reflect on the nature of this particular theoretical perspective. The same holds for evaluative perspectives: In forming a conception of the good, we must reflect on the conditions under which one can endorse the content of an appearance of the good. Because, as we will see, only judgments embodied in fully deliberate actions are the immediate consequences of one's general conception of the good, evaluative perspectives will be "visible" to the agent most fully in those actions. However, the consequences of reflection on the nature of these evaluative perspectives can span further; reflection might make me reconsider how much room I should leave in my life for gastronomic desires, sunbathing in my backyard, idle chatting, and other pursuits.

But how does all this happen? How do evaluative perspectives get evaluated? The short answer to this question is "through practical reasoning," as in the various examples given. And because, as noted, the aim here is not to provide a substantive theory of the good, I will not try to say much about which inferences are sound or unsound. However, it is certainly worth saying more about what is meant by "a conception of the good," "an evaluative judgment," and "soundness of inference." This is the subject matter of the next chapter.

2

The Basic Framework

From Desire to Value and Action

2.1 INTRODUCTION

The fact that one desires something does not suffice to establish that one ought to pursue it. The fact that a course of action appears good from a certain perspective does not guarantee that this course of action is in fact good. Insofar as the agent is rational, she evaluates the reliability of various perspectives on reflection and tries to come up with a coherent understanding of what she should pursue. Thus drawing on all particular perspectives, the agent forms a reflective perspective that underwrites what I call the agent's "general conception of the good." Section 2.2 presents, and discusses the importance of, a notion of a general conception of the good.

A perfectly rational agent would always act in accordance with his conception of the good. However, an imperfectly rational agent could have a certain general view of the good and yet act otherwise; an imperfectly rational agent could form an intention at odds with his general conception of the good. According to the scholastic view, what the agent *judges* to be good is the agent's intention in action. Given that the scholastic view identifies desires with *appearances* of the good in part because what makes them *mere appearances* is the fact that they ought to be evaluated from a reflective perspective, it is indeed natural for the scholastic view to identify *intentions* with *judgments* of the good. However, this kind of identification has been the subject of various criticisms. Section 2.3 defends this view of the nature of intentions and replies to various objections.

The move from appearances to judgments, if warranted, will typically rely on various patterns of inference and reasoning. Although this book does not aim to give a general positive account of the validity or soundness of various possible inferences, it does aim to defend the scholastic view from the charge that it is committed to objectionable views on the nature of practical inference. In particular, given the influential status of instrumentalist conceptions of practical reasoning, it is worth asking whether and to what extent the scholastic view is committed to the validity or soundness of noninstrumental forms of practical reasoning. In section 2.4, I examine the extent to which a scholastic view is incompatible with an instrumentalist conception of practical reasoning.

The scholastic view takes our practical thinking to be subject to normative demands that are similar to those that govern our theoretical thinking. How stringent the demands may be, and how directly reason controls or should control our action, will depend on the kind of action in question. Indeed, if the scholastic view were committed to the claim that all actions face the "tribunal of reason" in the same way, it would no doubt be committed to an overly intellectualist conception of the nature of human action. After all, for many, if not most, of our actions, it does not seem that one does or ought to devote much thought to performing them. Often, one seems simply to do things, or to do things simply because one wants to do them. Section 2.5/ distinguishes three kinds of actions and the different ways in which reasoning guides these actions.

2.2 GENERAL CONCEPTIONS OF THE GOOD AND EVALUATION

The agent's conception of the good is the agent's reflective, all-things-considered, practical stance. We can say, as a first approximation, that the agent's general conception of the good contains the agent's views on how the various appearances of the good should be taken into consideration in judging what is good. As such, a general conception of the good should include the agent's views on which practical inferences are appropriate, the relation that holds among various practical commitments, relations between various perspectives, and so on. So, a general conception of the good will include instrumental requirements connecting putative objects of judgments of the good (evaluative judgments) with their necessary means, potential inferences from potential objects of judgments of the good such as "hiking in the woods" and "canoeing," or relations of incompatibility between perspectives such as, perhaps, the "perspective of envy" and the "perspective of self-reliance." Of course, one's general conception of the good will include not only relations, inferences, and conditional judgments but also the various objects that, according to the agent, ought to be judged as good (or better than another object) on the basis of the various appearances of the good available to her. A conception of the good should ideally keep track of the various activities one is and ought to be engaged in, as well as determine which actions should be undertaken in various possible circumstances in light of the practical attitudes available to the agent. As we will see in section 2.5, this does not mean that, even ideally, each action in the agent's life should be the outcome of deliberation over all possible actions. However, the agent's conception of the good should determine when deliberation is or is not appropriate. In an ideal conception of the good, the various items form a coherent harmonic whole. For example, moves from possible judgments of the good to other possible judgments of the good are made only through inferences the agent accepts, perspectives that are deemed to be incompatible are not mutually endorsed, and judgments of the good are properly based on the appearances deemed correct upon reflection. Actual conceptions of the good, however, will probably contain many inconsistencies, and limited rational agents will not have, even implicitly, anything approaching a fully detailed general conception of the good that can prescribe an action on every occasion. Considered dynamically, a general conception of the good may be revised by new experiences, by rethinking a certain issue, by changes in one's sensibilities, and other events. If I am correct, the rational kinematics of one's conception of the good can always be understood in terms of the relation of perspectives on, and appearances of, the good to the conception of the good. A new experience, for instance, can be characterized as making available a new perspective on, or appearance of, the good.

One might take issue with talk of "a conception of the good" as opposed to various inchoate conceptions of the good. After all, it does not seem plausible to think that every time I choose, I have a general conception of how the various things I pursue form a harmonious whole. I walk to work, I eat, I chat, I type, and at each turn it seems that my practical thoughts are wholly focused on the task at hand. One might concede that one can talk of the union of these "local" conceptions of the good as forming a general conception of the good, but it is doubtful that the resulting conception has any kind of coherence.

However, the notion of a general conception of the good must be postulated at least as a normative ideal. The fact that eating now is an activity in which it would not be irrational to engage depends on the fact that eating right now is not incompatible with important aspects of my life. No doubt, in most circumstances a mature human being simply goes ahead and eats lunch; one's conception of the good should allow one to proceed with merely intentional actions of this kind without further deliberation.[1] The idea that we are guided by a general conception of the good is not a claim about the general form of practical deliberation (that it always has, for instance, a general conception of the good life as a major premise). To adapt Kantian terminology, a conception of the good is not simply *given* for an agent but *given as a task* to the agent; rational action can be such only if it can be shown that it would have been warranted by such a conception of the good. The idea also marks the fact that no pursuit in the life of the agent, no voluntary movement, however trivial, is immune from conflict with any other element in the agent's conception of the good. My plans for eating this morning could conflict with my commitment to a good friend (if I choose a restaurant that he has been boycotting because of ill treatment). The claim that we ought to be guided by a general conception of the good simply marks the fact that a rational being is capable of, and committed to, making correct decisions when such conflicts arise.

In order to get a better sense of the importance of a general conception of the good, it is worth examining the importance a similarly general conception of the world might have in theoretical

---

[1] More on this point in section 2.5.

reason. We can perhaps imagine a being for whom the move from an appearance to a judgment was completely unmediated.[2] If the sun appears small, this being judges it to be small, if a piece of reasoning appears cogent, it judges it to be so, and so on. Were we to judge in this manner, our cognitive life would no doubt be unenviable. Beliefs formed in this way would be so chaotic and inconsistent that it would no longer be clear that they aim at truth. We can say that a judgment ideally should be formed only upon reflection guided by a general conception of how things are. We can identify at least two aspects of the process of reflection:

(a) assessing the reliability of certain perspectives as disclosing how things are; and

(b) assessing the impact of adding a certain content to one's general conception of how things are.

For our purposes, we need to note two things. First, both (a) and (b) are guided by a general conception of how things are, which we could even call, trading some awkwardness for a clean parallel, "a conception of the true." Although this is clear in the case of (b), it is also true of (a). For instance, many of us are often tempted by what can be called "the perspective from narrative requirements." That is, it often appears to us that reality will follow the same course as a novel written according to orthodox narrative conventions. One might feel that expressing undue confidence about certain events is evidence against their likelihood. One might unreasonably expect that those who boast will somehow founder or that things will take a wrong turn for those who were assured once too often that they have nothing to worry. If reflection is working properly, it will tell us to discredit these appearances; our understanding of how things are precludes that the world would disclose itself to us in this manner. We do not need to check if judgments formed on the basis of this perspective conflict with some of our beliefs or to compare these appearances with conflicting evidence. These appearances give us no reason to reflectively assent to their content. Certainly some

---

[2] I say "perhaps" because one might want to say that something could appear to a being in a certain way only if this being had some kind of reflective capacity (if, for instance, one thinks that without reflection there is no cognition and that without the possibility of cognition there are no intentional states).

evaluative perspectives are good candidates for being like this. Perspectives in which we are guided by spite and revenge are possible examples.[3]

On the other hand, suppose I see what appears to be a flying pig. I will certainly take this to be a perceptual illusion, not because of the way in which it appears to me that there is a flying pig but because, in light of my existing knowledge of swine behavior, this is not content that I can add to my conception of how things are. The problem here is not about *how* something is being disclosed to me but about *what* is being so disclosed. Indeed, if pigs were to fly, I would expect to learn of the presence of a flying pig in my surroundings through appearances that are indistinguishable from the perceptual illusion. Similarly, someone who believes that sexual impulses disclose an important form of value need not think that everything that appears good from this perspective is indeed good. Just as with appearances from the perspectives of spite and vengeance, some of these may be cases of illusory appearances.

However, these cases of appearances that are rejected from one's conception of the good should be distinguished from the cases that might have no counterpart in theoretical reason. Suppose I only have $100 that I can spare, and I can use it either to support the local library or to provide much-needed medical supplies for a hospital in an economically depressed area. Suppose I provide the medical supplies. It would seem wrong to say that my desire to help the local library involved any kind of illusion or was misleading in any way. The improvement of the local library is indeed a good thing, even if its value was *overridden* by the value of helping those in need of medical supplies. What I judge to be good in the end is helping those in need of medical supplies, but does that mean that I

---

[3] This would be one way of interpreting some of Mill's remarks in chapter 5 of *Utilitarianism*, on the "feeling of justice." Mill's point is that insofar as the feeling of justice is guided by a "thirst for revenge," we have no reason to think that it is a reliable guide to how we ought to behave. His claim is that the feeling of justice aims at the public good *when it does not aim at revenge*. Although I do not think that Mill is correct about this last point, I think he does have the right conception of how to vindicate a utilitarian account of justice. Justin D'Arms and Dan Jacobson argue that envy and all human emotions have instances in which they are felt appropriately, but they would not, as far as I can tell, disagree with Mill on the question of whether such emotions are reliable guides to action. See D'Arms and Jacobson, "Anthropocentric Constraints in Human Value."

judge that supporting the local library is bad? Or even that I do not judge that it is good? This might seem like an absurd conclusion, but it is worth noting that in some sense it is correct. After all, I would consider it wrong of me to have sent the money to the local library. I would consider this kind of action to fall short of an ideal. Because the good should be our aim, falling short of the ideal could not be identified with the good. However, we are obviously missing something if we leave things at that. There is a sense in which I consider improving the library to be a good thing, even if I am unable to help at the moment. What we need to conclude is that a conception of the good includes only a subset of what one considers *valuable* because a conception of the good needs to be fashioned in accordance with the conditions of agency, which do not always permit us to bring about all that we find valuable. Insofar as we take a judgment of the good, an evaluative unconditional judgment, to be a guide to action, the judgment will also need to conform to the contingencies of agency.

But if this is true, what is the notion of "finding something valuable" that we just introduced? Because there are many ways of spelling out this notion that are compatible with the scholastic view, I will provide only a tentative account here. My conjecture is that any refinement or modification would not significantly impact the scholastic view, but to pursue that issue here would take us astray. The most important thing is that "finding something valuable" will not be disconnected from the general evaluative notion of the good. So, if we have reserved the notion of an unconditional evaluative judgment for a judgment that something is good, finding something valuable must be some kind of conditional judgment. The obvious way to go is to think that if we were not already pursuing something more valuable, or if contingent impediments were lifted, we would have pursued what we found valuable. We can hazard a definition as follows:

Value Judgments (VJ)

A judges X to be valuable if for some Y either (a) if he were not judge Y to be good, he would judge X to be good, or (b) he would judge X to be good if A believed it were in his power to bring about X (and he were not, in this case, to judge Y to be good).

We can also say then that X is *in fact* valuable for A just in case X *should* indeed be an element in A's conception of the good if these counterfactual conditions were to obtain and A's current conception of the good is not defective in any way. The basic idea is that there are at least two cases in which despite the fact that an agent does not pursue X, we can still say that the agent finds X to be valuable. The first is a case in which the agent does not pursue X because there is something else (Y) such that the agent judges Y to be better than X.[4] Condition (a) thus allows us to consider as valuable those actions that were not performed because of the performance of something else one deemed to be more important. Recall that we said that one's conception of the good would include not only what we would pursue in certain circumstances but also "contingency plans." Condition (a) turns these contingency plans into judgments of the form "X is valuable." So, in our library example, one could consider contributing to the local library fund valuable even if one prefers to send the money to another charity.[5] Condition (b) allows us to consider valuable things that are in the past or beyond our causal powers, for example. So I might think that playing soccer well is something valuable even though I am not capable of doing it and thus it could not be part of my general conception of the good. Moreover, condition (b) allows us to say that an agent who only drinks tea in the winter still judges the activity of drinking tea in cold weather to be valuable in the middle of the summer. A notion of comparative value can be similarly explained in terms of counterfactual judgments of the good. Although I will not pursue a detailed proposal here, comparative judgments should be understood as questions about, ceteris paribus, what one would choose to

---

[4] Note that it follows from the fact that one judges X to be good that one also judges X to be valuable. All that you need to get this consequence is to substitute any object that one does not actually judge to be good for Y in VJ.

[5] There might be intermediary things that one would do if one were not to contribute to financing the medical supplies. It might be that I would have sent the money to the local museum before I would have sent it to the local library. But because nothing precludes Y from being a disjunction, this would not be a problem. One could also introduce a recursive condition, but this would bring up unnecessary complications for our purposes.

bring about in a situation in which one is forced to bring about one of two or more options.[6]

However, it is important to note that this definition is just an approximation. First, VJ might not provide an exhaustive description of the reasons that one does not pursue something that we can legitimately say that one judges to be valuable. That is, there might be conditions other than (a) and (b) that we would add to a definition of "*X* is valuable," such that if such conditions were to obtain with respect to *X*, we would say that the agent judges *X* to be valuable. In fact, in chapter 8 we will add at least one more way in which contingent impediments can prevent one from judging as good what one considers to be valuable. Secondly, I am leaving unexplained how the counterfactual should be understood in VJ. Finally, some "tweaking" might be necessary to yield the correct results. An agent might think that if she fails to bring about certain things, then she might as well kill herself, but this does not mean that she finds killing herself valuable. Hopefully, however, the approximation will do for our purposes.

We should note a few further complications. In some circumstances, we can only choose the lesser of two evils. If someone has a choice between hurting a friend's feelings or lying to her and chooses the former, we would be reluctant to conclude that this person judged that hurting her friend's feelings was good. Fortunately, we need not embrace this unwelcome consequence. It might help to see this point if we define more precisely what can serve as the content of a judgment of the good. Although the scholastic view does not depend on a particular view about this matter,[7] it is worth stipulating that contents of judgments of the good are that-clauses that can be meaningful complements to the phrase "α brings about that...." The content of evaluative

---

[6] In fact, the proposal here need not be essentially different from the common ways of determining a preference ranking in rational-choice theory. Also, questions about the *correct* comparative judgments will be questions about how one ought to judge under these circumstances.

[7] This is not true, however, of the introduction of deontological goods in chapter 5, in particular the discussion of a deontological, impartial good. There a specific conception of the object of judgments of the good plays a central role.

judgments is thus possible states of affairs,[8] or what Kant would call "possible objects of the will." The notion of "possible states of affairs" or "possible objects of the will" is quite broad, and it could include, for instance, "that I am a kind person," something that could not be accomplished by a single action and that may even be a type of activity that cannot be identified with any particular set of actions. Evaluative judgments are supposed to pick out not only the action in which the agent engages but the description under which the agent intends it. Evaluative judgments create opaque contexts by picking out the aspect under which the agent considered a certain possible state of affairs to be good.

Now we are ready to come back to our agent who found that hurting her friend was the lesser of two evils. We need not say that the content of the agent's judgment was "that her friend is hurt" because this content does not pick out the aspect under which she took this possible state of affairs to be good. We should say that what the agent judged to be good was "being honest to one's friend" (despite the fact that this would hurt her feelings). Often, the best characterization of what an agent judges to be good will be just the avoidance of a certain evil. Moreover, one might need to specify the circumstances in which the agent finds herself in order to know what the agent judges to be good. We cannot generalize from the fact that one finds chastising the children to be good when they misbehave to the conclusion that one simply judges that chastising the children is good.

Although VJ makes the notion of the valuable conceptually dependent on the notion of the good, it is important to note that the notion of the valuable so defined marks important distinctions in the realm of practical reason. The notion of valuable is bound up with a distinction between illusory and overridden desires of the agent. It marks the realm of "veridical" deliverances of practical reason.[9] We might distinguish two ways in which desires can conflict.

---

[8] More precisely, the content is something the *agent considers to be* a possible state of affairs. After all, an agent might try to bring about *p* without realizing that *p* is not a possible state of affairs. For convenience's sake, however, I'll leave this complication aside.

[9] "Veridical" is in quotation marks because it is, properly speaking, an evaluation from the domain of theoretical reason.

Desires can be said to be in *external* conflict if their objects cannot be brought about at the same time or if one cannot reasonably expect that their objects can be brought about at the same time. So, for instance, my desire to be healthy and my desire to eat immoderately are in external conflict because given what I know about the effects of immoderate consumption of food, I cannot expect to satisfy the first desire without putting some restraints on the satisfaction of the second. Thus they are in conflict insofar as I can only incorporate one of these objects in my conception of the good. However, this conflict does not prevent me from judging both to be valuable, from judging that were I capable of bringing about health and immoderate consumption simultaneously, I would choose a life that contained both.[10]

Let us look at a different kind of conflict. Let us take a coarse version of a possible conflict in our desires. Suppose one has desires that arise from what one might call the "proto-Hegelian" perspective, according to which every harm done to us should be avenged. Suppose one also has what we might call "the economist's perspective," according to which losses incurred in the past should count as "sunk costs" and shouldn't influence our deliberation about the future. No doubt, these two perspectives might conflict, but the conflict is interestingly different from the conflict between the pursuit of health and the pursuit of immoderate consumption. Let us say someone endorses the economist's perspective and on that account spends the weekend doing minor repairs in her house rather than executing an elaborate revenge plan. It would not be true that had she not done the minor repairs she would pursue the revenge. Endorsing the economist perspective entails that she can no longer accept the claims of the proto-Hegelian perspective. The conflict in this case is not a conflict generated by our limited resources but rather by incompatible evaluative perspectives – what one sees as valuable from one perspective can only be so if what we see as valuable from another perspective is illusory. Thus, one can

---

[10] There is also nothing that prevents the view that there is something wrong with one of them *irrespective of the conflict with the other*. Kant had this view about gluttony. See his *The Metaphysics of Morals*, Ak. 427. I think that our general hesitation to say that immoderate consumption is valuable is rooted in the fact that we share, to some extent, Kant's negative assessment of gluttony.

say that a desire is illusory if, on reflection, we do not find its object to be valuable.

Note that this kind of conflict has no clear place in a subjectivist framework. It is not clear that there could be internal conflicts among values for the subjectivist. Although the understanding of internal conflicts and illusory desires suggested earlier depends on a definition of "valuable" that relies on the scholastic view, we can easily see how the subjectivist will have problems building a parallel notion. To be sure, if I want both to eat gumbo before I eat anything else and to eat asparagus before I eat anything else, I will not be able to satisfy both desires. But the conflict would be external. If there is no possible criticism of the content of my desires, it seems that only the impossibility of their simultaneous realization could put a rational constraint on acting on both desires at the same time. Suppose I choose gumbo; in this view, the only thing to be said against choosing asparagus is that were I to choose asparagus, I wouldn't be able to have gumbo as the first thing I eat in the morning.

We often seem to deliberate in ways that require the distinction between external and internal conflicts. So, for instance, when asked by the local library to donate money, one could reasonably say, "I wish I could, but I have committed all my spare money to fighting famine." However, tempted by a desire to humiliate someone, a kind person would not say, "I wish I could humiliate Laura, but. . . ." The kind person will think of these impulses as illusory presentations of value. Of course, subjectivists (and others) have noticed similar phenomena and have tried to account for them within the subjectivist framework in various ways, for instance by drawing a distinction between "valuing" and "desiring."[11] One can also appeal in this context to "second-order desires," "identification," "informed desires,"[12] and so on. My aim is not to assess the

---

[11] Michael Smith provides a useful summary and criticism of various positions on the relation between valuing and desiring in his *The Moral Problem*.

[12] "Informed desire," however, couldn't possibly capture the distinction at hand because it cannot distinguish between the desire to contribute to the local library and the desire to humiliate others. Neither of them will be acted on by the fully informed agent (assuming that full information does not lead one to reevaluate one's commitment to the local library or to be more appreciative of humiliating

vast literature on this topic but just to point out that, on the one hand, attempts to accommodate similar distinctions within a subjectivist framework have been, to say the least, controversial,[13] whereas, on the other hand, the scholastic view has a rather straightforward way of distinguishing between these two types of conflicts.

But one might complain that we've missed the basic way in which this account of the valuable is counterintuitive: It seems to invert the order of explanation. After all, it seems that we bring about something because it is valuable rather than making it valuable by bringing it about or even less by wishing that we could bring it about. The scholastic's account of value, one might complain, cannot do justice to this intuition because it claims that our conception of the valuable is constructed from a more basic conception of the good rather than the other way around. However, the scholastic view only postulates a *conceptual* priority of the notion of the good, not a metaphysical or epistemological priority. As for the metaphysical or epistemological order of things, the good does not determine the valuable and the valuable does not determine the good. This point can be made clearer if we start from the epistemological end. A conception of the good is supposed to be arrived at by reflection and reasoning from appearances of the good. And reflection on how appearances of the good would justify different actions in different contexts is what allows us to come up with a conception of the valuable. So, even though the *concept* of the valuable is defined in terms of the *concept* of the good, it is not true to say that the scholastic view grounds the *conception* of the valuable on the *conception* of the good; rather, in the scholastic view, both the conception of the valuable and the conception of the good are grounded on the same foundations. So there is no reason to think that something being valuable needs to be *explained* in terms of something being good; claims about good and valuable are explained by the same things that justify, respectively, a conception of the good and a conception of the valuable.

others), and there is no non–question-begging reason to assume that full information would do away with the *temptation* to be cruel in this manner.

[13] I examine this issue a bit more in the discussion of *akrasia* in chapter 7.

Now it is true that the scholastic view has no place for a notion of value that is detached from the context of action. The scholastic view does not have room for a notion of value such that it does not follow that, ceteris paribus, if X is valuable, then one ought to bring about X if it is within one's power to do so. But there is nothing pretheoretically intuitive about the need for such a notion.

Before we move on, it is worth pointing out that to say that a reflective being need not move directly from an appearance to a judgment does not mean that this being could *never* judge in this manner. First, there could be cases in which one forms judgments that are, what will be called in section 2.5, "intentional" but not "fully deliberated." Indeed, a more cogent description of the formation of perceptual judgments might represent it as, in normal cases, a direct move from perceptual appearances to beliefs (with reflection playing a background role analogous to the role it plays in the production of merely intentional actions).[14] These would be cases in which reflective scrutiny is sidestepped without major violations of rational requirements.[15] However, it seems possible to think that one could move directly from appearance to judgment even in cases in which reflective scrutiny is rationally mandatory. Moreover, so far we have said nothing to rule out the possibility that one moves directly from appearance to judgment *in opposition* to one's reflective assessment of the situation. That is, we seem to have left open the possibility that one considers a certain appearance unreliable on reflection and yet judges on the basis of this appearance. No doubt, neither of these cases would be possible for a perfectly rational being, but because human beings do not fall under this category, this fact gives us no reason to close off these possibilities. However, a more detailed account of these possibilities will be postponed until chapter 7, in which we will try to understand the possibility of *akrasia* in terms of such a direct move from appearance to judgment.

---

[14] See section 2.5.

[15] Of course, to say that reflective scrutiny is sidestepped in these cases is not to say that the belief is not open to revision as a result of reflection.

2.3 INTENTIONS

Intentions are most naturally seen in the scholastic view as unconditional evaluative judgments that either are embodied in or precede action. Just as in the case of desire, we should not think of the judgment as something other than the intention. And here, too, we identify evaluation and motivation by saying that the judgment is the intention. If to desire is to conceive something to be good, to act is to *take* the object of one's intention to be good. As Davidson has argued, the same action can be described in many ways, but only a few of them will describe the action as the agent intended. What the agent judges to be good cannot be inferred from just any accurate description of her actions. On the other hand, the intention need not be something separate from the action. As I move the dial on my old radio, I do it with the intention of tuning in to a different station. However, it need not be the case that the relevant intention was formed prior to my moving my hands.[16]

Ideally, intentions, as unconditional evaluative judgments, are warranted by one's conception of the good. But given that we are not perfectly rational, this is not always true. In practical reason, as in theoretical reason, we can form judgments that are unwarranted by our assessment of the relevant "evidence."[17] And just as in theoretical reason we form beliefs not only by reflecting on all the available evidence but in all kinds of manners (such as directly from perception, directly from testimony, etc.), in practical reason an intention need not be formed by reflection on what is warranted by one's conception of the good. However, one is irrational insofar as one's intention conflicts with one's conception of the good, and one falls short of perfect rationality if one's intention could not be warranted by one's conception of the good.

This conception of an intention is not particularly new; it is not very different from Davidson's view on intention.[18] However, Davidson's view has been much criticized. In particular, some of the

---

[16] In my "The Conclusion of Practical Reason," I argue that the relevant intention never precedes the action.

[17] For more on this issue, see chapter 7.

[18] See Donald Davidson's "Actions, Reasons, and Causes," "How Is Weakness of the Will Possible?" and "Intending."

problems that Michael Bratman[19] identifies with the belief–desire account of intention are supposed to extend to the Davidsonian view and, a fortiori, to the scholastic account. We can understand Bratman as making two independent points. First, he identifies a number of features of intentions that must be accounted for by any plausible view on the nature of intentions. Second, he argues that previous theories of intention fail to account for these features. One might think that the same holds for the scholastic view of intentions; it will leave much of the phenomena of intention unexplained. What I propose to do in this section is to show that the scholastic view can explain these features that Bratman claims to be at the core of our notion of intention.

First, according to Bratman, intentions are "conduct-controlling" rather than "potential influencers of actions."[20] Although desires only "push" us in a certain direction or "suggest" possible ends or actions, intentions are supposed to control one's actions. If I intend to go to the library, the intention will not simply give me an incentive to go to the library but will also result in my taking the necessary means to get to the library and my making sure that I do not engage in activity that will prevent me from getting to the library, for example. This is no doubt correct about intentions, but here the scholastic view faces no problems. If intentions are one's all-out judgments, then one will not only be inclined to engage in the action in question but *will* engage in the action, and, insofar as one is rational, one will try to make sure that one's all-out attitudes do not conflict.

Second, Bratman claims that agents have a disposition to retain their intentions without reconsidering them. This feature can also be easily accounted for in the scholastic view.[21] After all, if I am not aware of any special reason to revise my all-out evaluative judgment, I should take the matter as settled and not spend valuable resources in endless reconsideration. Bratman considers this position, but he thinks that it will not do full justice to the issue. He gives an example of an intention settling between two courses of action that are

---

[19] See Michael Bratman's *Intention, Plans, and Practical Reason* and "Two Faces of Intention."

[20] Bratman, *Intention, Plans, and Practical Reason*, p. 16.

[21] Ibid., p. 17.

equally valuable.[22] Suppose I can get to my destination by going through road A or road B, and I see no reason to prefer one road to the other; I would turn left to take road A and turn right to take road B. Suppose I pick road B and thus form the intention to take road B. When I turn right, my intention explains the rationality of turning right *rather than turning left* in a way that none of my desires, judgments, and so on could do. After all, my view on the matter is that I am indifferent whether to take road A or B and a fortiori to turn left or right. We will momentarily turn to how the scholastic view deals with forming intentions among indifferent actions. However, we can see already that this is not likely to be a problem for any view of intention. As John Broome has been arguing recently, various normative requirements are wide-scope requirements; that is, the requirement is properly rendered as follows:

(a) It is required that (if p then q).

Wide-scope requirements contrast with putative narrow-scope requirements, which should be represented as follows:

(b) If p, then (it is required that q).

If normative requirements are wide-scope requirements, the truth of the antecedent of the conditional does not guarantee that we can "detach" the consequent; one can accept that (a) and p are true and reject that it is required that q, without incoherence.[23] Whatever one thinks about the generality of Broome's treatment of normative requirements, this seems clearly to be a case in which the rational requirement to intend to turn right cannot be detached even if I form the intention to take road B. After all, if just before turning left I revise this intention and then turn left, there's nothing irrational about what I do.[24]

---

[22] Bratman, *Intention, Plans, and Practical Reason*, p. 23. I have changed his argument slightly so that it can be relevant to the scholastic view.

[23] This has to be stated with caution. If further conditions obtain, one might be required to detach the consequent. For a discussion of some of these cases regarding the hypothetical imperative, see Patricia Greenspan, "Conditional Oughts and Hypothetical Imperatives."

[24] Sometimes Bratman seems to suggest that once I form the intention I have some reason to stick to it, and changing it for no particular reason might be irrational. I see no intuitive reason to accept this conclusion. Bratman might be compelled to

But in general one might think that any such notion of intention will have trouble dealing with Buridan situations such as our choice between roads A and B, situations in which the agent must choose between two evaluatively indistinguishable alternatives that are better than all the other alternatives.[25] After all, if both options are really evaluatively indistinguishable, it seems that if I judge one to be good, I ought to judge the other to be good as well. The same reasons to add the state of affairs that I take road A into my conception of the good would also warrant that the addition of the state of affairs that I take road B to my conception of the good, and the same reasons I would have to leave one state of affairs out of my conception of the good would be reasons to leave out the other one. This would result in my having both states of affairs or neither of them in my conception of the good. But both options are unacceptable; by hypothesis, I cannot take both roads A and B, and assuming that I have good reasons to get where I want to be, it would be irrational of me not to take one of the roads. However, this problem arises only in an overly restrictive view about how inferential requirements work in the formation of a conception of the good; in particular, it assumes that rational requirements in the formation of a conception of the good must always be obligatory ones, never permissive ones. More plausibly, one can say that one has a *permissive reason* to incorporate road A into one's conception of the good. In other words, we can think that reflection on the appearances of the good in my case should yield the following requirements:

(a) It is permissible to add "I take road A" into my conception of the good.

this view by his two-stage assessment of the rationality of revising intentions. Because the rationality of a particular revision depends on the rationality of one's policy, and given that one's policy of revising intention should not allow for whimsical revision, it seems to follow that any whimsical revision is irrational. But this shows a limitation of the two-stage account rather than the irrationality of the revision in question. Broome also argues that it's not irrational to change the intention in question. See his "Are Intentions Reasons?" and "How Should We Cope with Incommensurable Values?"

[25] Bratman explicitly uses Buridan cases to argue against Davidson's views on intentions in his "Davidson's Theory of Intention" in his *The Faces of Intention: Selected Essays on Intention and Agency.*

(b) It is permissible to add "I take road B" into my conception of the good.

(c) It is not permissible to add both "I take road A" and "I take road B" into my conception of the good.

(d) My conception of the good must include either "I take road A" or "I take road B."

Of course, this assumes that some inferences can be merely permissible, but I see no reason to deny this.[26] In fact, it is at least arguable that we need to admit the notion of permissible inference even in theoretical reason; it might be that some kind of evidence permits, but does not require, rational agents to form a certain judgment. For instance, the evidence in favor of string theory might be of that kind.

However, one cannot deny that there is something unique about practical reason in these cases, namely the possibility of combining the permissibility of making two inferences with the requirement of making at least one of them. It's certainly not required that I judge one way or another with respect to string theory. And this uncovers a more profound disanalogy between the two cases. In the theoretical realm, there is no question that one of the judgments is correct and the other incorrect. However, with respect to practical reason, this is not so: The claim that certain reasons are merely permissive does not tell us merely about the epistemic status of the agent who might not be in a position to know which of the options are in fact good. It tells us something about the nature of value itself; in particular, that although there is only one unimpeachable "conception of the true," there can be many unimpeachable conceptions of the good.[27] The consequence of this fact is that whereas it is at least plausible to suppose that in theoretical reason an epistemically ideally situated agent would have no merely permissive reasons for belief, an epistemically ideally situated practical agent can have merely permissive reasons for action.

---

[26] In *Brute Rationality*, Joshua Gert distinguishes between justifying and requiring reasons. Although the notion of a justifying reason there is similar to my notion of permissive reason, Gert's notion extends much more widely than cases such as Buridan's ass or the optional pursuits that I discuss in chapter 4.

[27] We will deal with this issue in more detail in chapter 4.

A more serious challenge might come from something that is at the core of Bratman's work on intention. Intentions can be very general, long-ranging states. This in itself does not pose a problem for the scholastic view of intention. However, when we look closely, we see that an implication of the scholastic view might seem to conflict with this aspect of intention. Suppose I have a standing intention to train to run a seven-minute-mile marathon. I am, let us assume, pretty far from this goal, so in order to succeed, I need to follow a long-term rigorous schedule. My training schedule involves a training run every Tuesday afternoon, but this Tuesday, Barcelona is playing Chelsea, and I want to watch the game live. So I decide to give up on the training run on this occasion so I don't miss the soccer match. Of course, this could be a case of *akrasia*, but I want to consider the case where it isn't:[28] I simply came to the correct conclusion that the reasons not to do the training run prevailed on this particular occasion. However, it seems quite obvious that I haven't *abandoned* my intention to train to run for a seven-minute-mile marathon, not even temporarily. It's only that the reasons for acting from that intention were overridden. But how can the scholastic view do justice to the idea that there is still an intention here? We cannot say that my intention to train to run a seven-minute-mile marathon is an unconditional evaluative judgment that preceded or was embodied in my action; after all, the intention, on this occasion, did not result in any action.

This objection depends on a controversial view of the nature of action. It presupposes, roughly, that actions are uninterruptedly extended in time only if, at any point in time through the duration of the action, there is a current bodily movement such that it is an action performed at this time and it is part of the action extended in time. In other words, the objection assumes that if I cannot identify at this moment anything that counts as performing part of a certain activity, then I am not engaged in the activity at this time. However, this seems implausible. Suppose it's a beautiful day and I decide to go for a walk. Having walked a few blocks, I stop to browse some books in the discount bin at the storefront. A friend of mine sees me there, greets me, and asks me "What are you

---

[28] We will discuss the case of *akrasia* in chapter 7.

doing?" It seems that I can answer this question, without stretching the facts, speaking metaphorically, or stopping anywhere short of literal truth, by saying, "I am just taking a walk," even though right now I am not engaged in any part of this activity. If this is true for a paradigmatically continuous activity such as taking a walk, it is all the more so with regard to "choppy" actions such as training to run a seven-minute-mile marathon, studying for an exam, or courting a potential partner, for example. The fact that I am not right now engaged in any part of the activity, even if I could right now be engaged in it, does not mean that I am not engaged in the activity as such. My action has moved to the background, but it is still among the things I am doing right now, and so its object is still something that I judge to be good right now. Of course, at some point, as I keep finding more reasons not to keep my training schedule, it will no longer be true that I am engaged in this activity and thus no longer true that I judge my training for a seven-minute-mile marathon to be good. The border-lines here are difficult to figure out but, whatever they are, it should remain true that I am engaged in various actions at any time, and thus that it is possible that it turns out that I am engaged, simultaneously, in bringing about incompatible or jointly unrealizable ends. In fact, the broader conception of action is essential in explaining some cases of irrationality. One important source of practical irrationality and practical mistakes is the forma-tion of all-out judgments that are either outright incompatible or have as objects states of affairs that could not be jointly brought about given some contingent facts. Without this broader concep-tion of action, one could never pursue jointly unrealizable, or mutually incompatible, ends.

Bratman has suggested that focusing on intention in action leaves aside another important aspect of intention that is characteristic of future-directed intention. Intentions have an important role to play in coordinating and planning that can be lost from sight if we focus on intention in action. However, we can accept Bratman's broader point that this aspect needs to be kept in sharp focus and think that blindness to this aspect of intention did not come from focusing on intention in action but from the narrow view of the nature of action. Once we allow that certain activities can be complex, with many actual and possible parts[29] extended through long stretches of time, we can say that intentions, as judgments of the good embodied in these actions, have exactly this coordinating role at least insofar as engaging in forming a more comprehensive conception of the good requires making sure that all of one's judgments of the good are compatible and can be jointly carried out. Still, this conception of intention does not make room for the possibility that an agent will have new reasons for action that arise solely from forming an intention. Of course, once I start *acting* on an intention, the configuration of my reasons for action will change accordingly. If I have been taking route A for the last twenty minutes, then, ceteris paribus, I have good reason to keep following route A rather than backtracking and trying to reach my destination through route B. But the scholastic view does not allow for new reasons that arise directly from the formation of the intention. However, the best examples of putative new reasons created by merely forming a certain intention are provided by Buridan ass cases,[30] and I suggested earlier that the examples do not really support the view that forming an intention gives rise to a new reason.[31]

There has been some criticism of views that identify desire and belief.[32] The scholastic view does not identify a desire with a belief for the simple reason that beliefs and desires play different roles in theoretical and practical reason, respectively – belief is an all-out attitude but desire isn't. Intentions, on the other hand, are all-out attitudes, and it makes sense to ask whether an intention is a kind of belief according to the scholastic view.[33] In particular, we may ask

[29] For a related point on the nature of action and action explanation, see Michael Thompson, "Naïve Action Theory."

[30] Of course, I do not want to deny that there might be reasons to form a *commitment*. But a commitment is not the same as an intention, and again it's far from clear that forming an intention gives rises to any reason beyond the reasons that one had to be committed to a particular course of action. We'll look at similar issues when we discuss deontological goods in Chapter 5.

[31] For further arguments that intentions do not give rise to reasons in this way, see Broome, "Are Intentions Reasons?" and Govert den Hartogh, "The Authority of Intention."

[32] See, for instance, David Lewis, "Desire as Belief."

[33] Some caveats: If the conclusion of a practical syllogism is an action, then an action, not an intention, is the all-out practical attitude. But because I agree with Davidson et al. that an intentional action must have a description under which an agent intended it, such an intention can be considered the all-out attitude manifested in action. I am thinking here of a broader notion of "intention" than the one used by

whether an intention to pursue X should be identified with a belief that X is good. If "good" is the practical analog of "true," the precise answer cannot be "yes." If α believes that p, then α holds p true, but this does not mean that the content of α's belief is "p is true."[34] But just as theories of truth must have something to say about the difference between believing p and believing "p is true," "theories of the good" must have something to say about the difference between intending X and believing "X is good." First, it might be worth taking a look at the difference between intending X and believing "I hold X to be good." In this case, the distinction is fairly clear; the latter is my opinion of the sort of person I am, one who holds X to be good. Because self-knowledge is fallible, this opinion might turn out to be wrong and I might not be this sort of person, in which case I do not intend X.

When we move to the belief that X is actually good, we are no longer thinking of attributing to me merely a belief that I hold X to be good; rather, we are attributing to me a belief that X is *in fact* good. I will make a simplifying assumption that "X is good" is equivalent to the unqualified "X ought to be held to be good."[35] So the belief "X is good" is the same as the belief "I ought to hold X to be good." In the first case, we could find a gap between my opinions about myself and what I intended. Can we find a similar gap between what I hold to be good and what I believe I ought to hold to be good? It seems that this is at least a possibility because the belief expresses my theoretical views of how practical reason should be conducted, whereas the intention expresses the outcome of my reasoning practically, of actually conducting the exercise of practical reason. Those two things, one would think, could part company. The exercise of practical reason depends on a reflective perspective on the good, a perspective that can compare appearances of the

Bratman. Finally, it might seem that intention cannot be the only all-out form of holding to be good because I might hold to be good things that it is not in my power to do anything about, but see my "The Conclusion of Practical Reason" on this issue.

[34] Velleman makes the same point, but draws quite different conclusions for the fate of scholastic views, in his "The Guise of the Good."

[35] One might think that this is a case of, as it were, equivalence in asserting, of the kind that would generate a version of Moore's paradox if one were to assert one and deny the other.

good that might conflict, check the claim of those appearances, and sometimes deem them to be illusory. A belief that I ought to hold something to be good is a recognition that this is how things appear from the reflective perspective, but my belief that things appear this way from a reflective perspective need not (although it typically will) be accurate, and even when it is accurate, it would still not necessarily be in accordance with any intention of mine. There is no guarantee that all my intentions are in accordance with my reflective perspective even if it is a requirement of practical rationality that they should be.[36]

Now we can apply this discussion to the relation between desiring and seeming to be good.[37] For an agent to desire X is to have X appear to be good for this agent, but this is not the same as having the theoretical attitude that X seems to be good. The latter would be more like having the belief that people desire (or should desire) X rather than having the desire. That is to say it is the attitude one forms after inquiring about what kind of things are such that they appear good to agents and coming to the conclusion that X is one of them. As such, the theoretical attitude is a belief like any other. One could, in principle, have the belief without having X appear good to oneself. One would, in this case, be making a theoretical mistake about one's practical attitudes. I could also form the belief that practically rational agents ought to be such that X appears good to them. In this case, if I form this belief and do not desire X, I should come to the conclusion that I am not a practically rational agent, at least if I am aware of my not having a desire for X. Although the scholastic view requires that one's motivation be in line with one's *practical* attitudes toward the good (that is, one's desires, intentions, and so forth), there is no demand that they also align with one's theoretical attitudes about what one's practical attitudes are or ought to be. The practical realm, in the scholastic view, is one in which the good performs the same role that the true performs in the theoretical realm; practical attitudes are *not* in this view subspecies of theoretical ones.

---

[36] The possibility that my intentions may not follow my reflective perspective is what gives rise to the possibility of *akrasia*. This, too, will be discussed in chapter 7.

[37] Compare Dennis Stampe, "The Authority of Desire."

2.4   REASONING AND PRACTICAL KNOWLEDGE

Appearances of the good cannot, or at least cannot always, simply move us to act immediately; otherwise, one would be incapable of coherently pursuing ends. Because at each moment in our lives we have various incompatible desires and in virtually any choice situation there are always incompatible alternatives that would satisfy different desires, were we always immediately moved by those desires, we would find ourselves always going back and forth in the pursuit of various objects. Thus, we need to distinguish between appearances of the good and the unconditional judgments of the good that immediately precede, or are simply manifested in, action. According to the scholastic view, this is the essential difference that separates desire from intention. But as I said earlier, a judgment of the good ideally should not itself be the immediate consequence of a desire.[38] The move from an appearance to a judgment should be mediated by a more general conception of the good formed on the basis of an evaluation of the various relevant appearances of the good. Practical *reasoning* in this conception would be employed primarily in the reflective formation of a general conception of the good. Upon reflection, we deem appearances illusory or overridden, infer from certain practical judgments to others, and so forth, in such a way as to form a general conception of the good. Let us define as an instance of "practical knowledge" any practical judgment that is both correct and formed on the proper epistemic grounds. In the case of unconditional judgment, I would have practical knowledge if what I judge to be good is in fact good and my judgment that it is good is justified in the proper way. It should be clear that unless one wants to claim that our deliberations and intentional explanations involve deeply mistaken assumptions, the scholastic view is committed to the possibility of our acquiring a vast body of practical knowledge. Because our deliberations aim to form a general conception of the good, they aim to figure out what is good, all things considered. However, a general conception of the good can't simply be determined by the "strongest" desire or "most preferred" object. Because desires are appearances of the good, the

---

[38] This will need some refinement. See section 2.5.

content of a desire should be incorporated into a conception of the good not simply[39] because it appears so to us but because *what* appears to be good is *in fact* good. If this kind of practical knowledge is not possible, then characterizing deliberation as aiming to acquire this kind of knowledge, and intentional explanation as showing the agent as someone who aspires to this kind of knowledge, would be characterizing them as being committed to illusory assumptions.[40]

However, many philosophers seem to be sceptical about the possibility of much practical knowledge. In particular, "instrumentalism," often identified with subjectivist positions, has almost the status of a "default" view of the nature of practical reason.[41] Instrumentalism is a view according to which practical knowledge is limited to what is warranted by the principle of instrumental reasoning.

The scholastic view does not sit well with an instrumental conception of practical reason. But how plausible is instrumentalism? What is the evidence in favor of such a theory of practical reasoning? It is sometimes assumed that instrumentalism wears its plausibility on its sleeve.[42] However, I think that, under close scrutiny, the reasons one might have for making this assumption support only a very weak version of instrumentalism – a version that is actually fully compatible with the scholastic view. There is very little to support

---

[39] As we will see in chapters 3 and 4, this qualification is important because appearances of the good can serve as the grounds for the goodness of their object in certain conditions.

[40] It might seem that in the case of intentional explanations we would only be committed to ascribing this kind of mistake to others. But given the description of intentional explanations in the introduction that guides this project, the explainer herself would be committed to this mistake.

[41] But instrumentalism has also been challenged from various directions. See Korsgaard, "The Normativity of Instrumental Reason"; Stephen Darwall, *Impartial Reason*; and Jean Hampton, "On Instrumental Rationality" and *The Authority of Reason*. I do not imply by "default" position the majoritarian position. Rather, it is often assumed that instrumentalism needs no positive arguments but only be able to withstand refutation. For a defense of an unorthodox version of instrumentalism, see Candace A. Vogler, *Reasonably Vicious*. Vogler calls instrumentalism the "standard" position.

[42] See, for instance, Peter Railton, "Moral Realism"; and David Velleman, "The Possibility of Practical Reason."

stronger versions of instrumentalism, or so I will argue in this section.[43]

Let us start by laying down a version of the Instrumental Principle. We will take the instrumental rule to be a principle of inference that allows us to make the following inference:

(IP)

X is good

Y would promote X

Therefore, Y is good

There are various ways of representing the Instrumental Principle. One might prefer to have the middle premise as (IP$_1$), "Y is the best means to promote X," or (IP$_2$), "Y is the necessary means to promote X." For our purposes, it does not matter how one represents the Instrumental Principle, but I think that there are decided advantages to (IP). We could treat the conclusion of instrumental reasoning as undetachable;[44] we could say that what we conclude through this reasoning is that Y is good insofar as it promotes X. This avoids obvious problems with (IP$_1$) and (IP$_2$). (IP$_2$) makes the Instrumental Principle rarely applicable because it is rarely the case that there is only one means to a particular end.[45] (IP$_1$), on the other hand, would depend for its application on several uses of (IP) because what counts as "best" means depends on the compatibility of a certain course of action with other ends of the agent. In order to determine this compatibility, one would have to employ (IP). Of course, the application of (IP) might lead one to revise the desirability of the original end. If the disjunction of all conclusions of (IP) that have

---

[43] A more detailed examination of a closely related view, subjectivism, will be undertaken in the next chapter. There is, however, one avenue for defending instrumentalism that I do not discuss: the claim that instrumentalism is the only metaphysically "respectful" view of practical reason. For a discussion of such arguments, see Jean Hampton's *The Authority of Reason* and "On Instrumental Rationality."

[44] For a now famous discussion of the undetachable or "wide-scope" nature of the Principle of Instrumental Rationality, see Broome, "Normative Requirements."

[45] Of course, we could always concoct the necessary means by disjoining all possible means. But this loses the main advantage (IP$_2$) could have over (IP): It no longer provides us with grounds to conclude that a specific action is called for. Moreover, as we will see, we can still accept that the disjunction of means plays an important role without rendering the instrumental rule of inference as (IP$_2$).

the same first premise is an unacceptable judgment of the good, one should thus come to the conclusion that X is not good *simpliciter*.

Here it is worth noting an important disanalogy between theoretical and practical reasoning. If one infers q from p, there might be no interesting, nonepistemic sense in which the truth (or plausibility) of q is "derivative." However, there seems to be an important distinction in practical reason between *intrinsic* and *derivative* goods. Moreover, although we can characterize all deductively valid inferences in theoretical reason as "truth-preserving,"[46] in practical reason, "good-preserving" inferences are only a subset of the set of all possible valid inferences. One cannot rule out in advance the possibility that there are inferences in practical reason that contain no premises on which an object is taken to be good. In other words, we cannot rule out in advance the possibility that there will be valid inferences from nonevaluative premises to evaluative conclusions. Thus we may define in practical reason the special class of principles of inference that guide good-preserving inferences. We can say that an inferential principle is a *transfer* principle[47] if it allows inferences from claims of the form "X is (intrinsically) good" to "Y is (derivatively) good" when X and Y are not identical.[48] Instrumental goods are the only kind of derivative goods if and only if the Instrumental Principle is the only transfer principle of practical reasoning.[49] Note

---

[46] Although nondeductive inferences obviously are not truth-preserving, we can say that they are "truth-conducive" or some similar notion. We could also make a similar distinction in practical reason. More on these issues will be presented in chapter 4. Gilbert Harman has reservations about thinking of reasoning in terms borrowed from the evaluation of arguments. See his *Change in View: Principles of Reasoning*.

[47] See Darwall, *Impartial Reason*, for the idea that the Instrumental Principle "transfers" the reasons from end to means.

[48] This is a rough characterization. It will allow as a transfer principle a number of trivial principles. A more precise characterization would rule those out, but the rough characterization is all we need for our purposes.

[49] Jay Wallace has suggested that the rationality of complying with the Principle of Instrumental Rationality is better understood as a demand of theoretical rationality; that is, as a demand of consistency of beliefs. In this case, even the Principle of Instrumental Rationality would not be, properly speaking, a transfer principle. See his "Normativity, Commitment, and Instrumental Reasoning." This is a very interesting suggestion, and I cannot do justice to it here. However, I do want to mention briefly some reason to be skeptical of Wallace's suggestion. Wallace's argument depends on the assumption that one is able to form an intention that p only if one believes that it is possible that p. But it is far from clear

that the notion of a transfer principle can be defined without relying on the notion of the good, so that this notion does not commit one to a scholastic view. One could use, for instance, "original aim" or "original desire" and "derivative end" and "derivative desire" instead of "intrinsic good" and "derivative good."

But is the Instrumental Principle the only transfer principle of practical reason? I tend to be agnostic about this issue, and I do not want to commit myself to one side or the other of the debate. Just to give an example of another possible transfer principle and another correlative set of derivative goods, think about the following putative transfer principle:

> (ES) If one judges X to be good, and if Y would significantly improve one's epistemic standing regarding whether X obtains or not, then, ceteris paribus, one ought to judge Y to be good.

This transfer principle seems quite plausible to me. Suppose I send a birthday present to my nephew in Brazil. A few weeks later, I call my sister, and it occurs to me that not everything that is sent to Brazil by mail arrives there safely. I have now a virtually costless opportunity to check whether my nephew indeed received the gift (assuming that I don't find it awkward or self-congratulatory to ask about the arrival of this token of my generosity). We may assume that there's nothing I can do right now to rectify the situation if the present has not arrived; the Brazilian post office is unmoved by complaints, and my family tradition does not allow for late birthday presents. Even so, it would be bizarre, to say the least, if I were now completely indifferent to the prospect of making sure that the gift had arrived. One can ask, more generally, whether it would be reasonable for someone to care about various things but not care at all about knowing whether they obtain or not (at least in the cases in

---

that this is true. For instance, at the time that Roger Bannister became the first to run a mile in under four minutes, it was a popular opinion among experts that it was not humanly possible to run a four-minute mile. For all we know, in light of this fact, Bannister did not believe that it was possible to run a four-minute mile. He might have thought that the balance of evidence was in favor of the view that it was not humanly possible to run a four-minute mile and so found himself unable to believe that it was possible to do it. But at the same time, not being fully certain that it was impossible, he might have decided that it was worth giving it a shot. I see no reason to deny that even if this were the case, Bannister did intend to run a four-minute mile.

which the agent cannot change the situation in question). If one is tempted to answer "no," one should be tempted to regard (ES), or a similar principle, as a transfer principle.

But whatever one's views are on this matter, it is important to distinguish the claim that the Instrumental Principle is the only transfer principle from various other claims one could make with respect to the Instrumental Principle and to see how the scholastic view stands with respect to those claims. Instrumentalist conceptions of practical reason are immensely popular; subjectivists often take themselves to be instrumentalists or to defend some such conception of rationality, such as a maximizing conception. The claim that the Instrumental Principle is the only transfer principle is not what is generally meant by an instrumentalist conception of practical reason. Someone who accepts this claim but thinks that there are other inferential principles is not typically considered an instrumentalist. Let us take the following inference principle.

Categorical Imperative (CI)

(a) X cannot be consistently pursued by all rational beings at the same time.

(b) Therefore, refraining from pursuing X is good[50] (and all rational beings ought to refrain from pursuing X).

Someone who thought that CI was a valid principle of inference would certainly not be counted among the ranks of the instrumentalists. However, CI is not a transfer principle; it does not have any premise of the form "X is good." Note that even if we understand (a) as implicitly stating that X cannot consistently be conceived to be good by all rational beings at the same time, this would still not be a statement of the form "X is good." Of course, an instrumentalist must deny not only that there are other transfer principles but also that there are any other principles of inference whatsoever. But even this point needs to be clarified. First, one could accept that the Instrumental Principle is the only *formally* valid principle of practical reason

---

[50] As I pointed out, I do not think that evaluative judgments necessarily have "good" in their content (no more than theoretical judgments have "true" necessarily as part of their content). However, it is often less cumbersome to treat them that way in the context of examining these inferences, so I will put forth the judgments in this form, but this should not be taken to be more than an expository device.

but think that there are *materially* valid inferences that do not rely on the Principle of Instrumental Rationality (PIR). For instance, one could think that the following inference is valid but not formally valid:

1. Lying is wrong.
2. Therefore, it is good to refrain from getting your brother to lie.

However, instrumentalism is also *not* the view that all valid practical inferences are applications of PIR. There might be other views that accept that the principle of instrumental reasoning is the only valid inferential principle and yet think that there are some ends that we ought to adopt, whether or not we currently desire them or anything to which they would be conducive. Someone could accept that PIR is the only valid practical principle of inference but also accept, for instance, that our basic ends were set by God and that we knew them by intuition or revelation. In fact, any kind of intuitionism about the good could accept the claim that all valid practical inferences are applications of PIR. Certainly, this kind of intuitionism would not count as an instrumentalist conception of rationality. Instrument-alism, at least in its purest[51] form, accepts a much stronger claim that can be put roughly as follows.

Instrumental Conception of Rationality (ICR)

Every practical mistake (cognitive failure) must be a failure to apply PIR correctly.[52]

[51] I say in its "purest form" because an instrumentalist might accept that our desires or preferences must be considered, fully informed, and so on. The extent to which this should still count as an instrumentalist view is dubious. See Korsgaard, "The Normativity of Instrumental Reason"; and Hampton, *The Authority of Desire*. See, on the other side, Peter Railton, "Naturalism and Prescriptivity"; and Hubin, "What's Special about Humeanism." I discuss this issue in more detail in chapter 3.

[52] Does anyone accept a pure version of instrumentalism? Hampton claims that maximizing conceptions are not instrumentalist. Robert Nozick argues that they are at least very close to instrumentalist conceptions. See his *The Nature of Rationality*. It is not clear that one can build a notion similar to the one of "good-preserving" for maximizing conceptions of rationality, but I hope that much of this discussion would still be relevant for those who favor a maximizing conception of rationality. (My own view is that the maximizing conception is an instrumentalist theory of practical reason but that one needs to make a distinction similar to Rawls's distinction between a concept and a conception. See Aladdin Yaqūb's distinction between an account and a theory in *The Liar Speaks the Truth: A Defense of the Revision Theory of Truth*.)

How far does the scholastic view stray from instrumentalism? The scholastic view is certainly incompatible with ICR, at least if it is not accompanied by some kind of error theory, because if every desire involves an agent's conception of its object as good (indeed, for the scholastic view, desiring *is* just the agent's conceiving something to be good), and given that whether the object is good or not is not fully determined by the fact that it is desired, it should be at least possible that for any desire the agent has conceived of its object in a mistaken way; that is, that the object is not really good. Desiring in this manner would thus, under the scholastic view, mark a cognitive failure. However, for instrumentalists, only derivative desires could mark cognitive failures.

But we should look at how the scholastic view stands with respect to the following weaker theses that we distinguished from instrumentalism:

(a) PIR is the only formally valid transfer principle.
(b) PIR is the only formally valid inferential principle of practical reason.
(c) All valid practical inferences are applications of PIR.

Even Kantians who think of the categorical imperative as a formally valid inferential principle need not conceive of it as a transfer principle, as was suggested by our discussion of CI. There is no reason to think that the scholastic view requires richer resources than these Kantian views in terms of transfer principles.

This kind of Kantianism is no doubt committed to denying (b); CI in this case is presented as a formally valid principle of inference. But there is no reason to think that all scholastic views are committed to (b). Even if a scholastic view requires that we be capable of acquiring substantive practical knowledge, there is no reason to think that this knowledge must be acquired by means of formally valid practical principles.

One could also accept (c) and reject ICR. This view would then be committed to something like an intuitionist epistemology because except for knowledge of what is instrumentally good for what, all practical knowledge would be noninferential. As we will see in chapter 4, the scholastic view has good reasons to reject at least some forms of intuitionism. At any rate, I would not want the plausibility of the scholastic view to depend on the plausibility of an intuitionist epistemology. Thus, if (c) turned out to be true, scholastic views would be in a rather precarious position. So I will try to argue that (c) is not all that plausible, at least if we leave aside for the moment claims that rejection of (c) would result in some kind of metaphysical embarrassment. Although my case for the rejection of ICR will be made in terms of rejecting (c), I hope it will be clear that similar arguments could be made if one would prefer to accept (c) and reject ICR on the basis of an intuitionist framework.[53]

But before I argue against (c), it is worth examining how plausible claims (a) and (b) are. A good case can be made for (a), especially if PIR is broadly conceived. A formally valid transfer principle that allows us to move from X to Y requires a necessary relation between the goodness of X and the goodness of Y that is not based on the content of X or Y. Relations of entailment, constitution, or identity, for example, might be one way in which such necessary relations obtain,[54] but the validity of the inferences based on these relations might be derivable from logical principles that are more properly placed in the domain of theoretical reason.[55] One could think that the goodness of X and the goodness of Y are necessarily related only if X and Y are necessarily related. That is, one could argue that if there is no necessary relation between, say, my taking a walk and my being healthy (such as, for instance, one being the cause of the other), there could be no necessary relation between the goodness of taking a walk and the goodness of being healthy. But if this is the case, a broadly conceived instrumental principle would encompass all of these relations. In all such cases, X is either a necessary or sufficient means for Y. One way of understanding this argument is that practical inconsistency (holding on to two incompatible evaluative judgments, or failure to infer the consequences of one's evaluative judgments) should always be found in the pursuit of incompatible *objects*, pursuing X and at the same time pursuing

---

[53] It is worth emphasizing that although intuitionism is compatible with (c), it obviously does not imply it.

[54] "Necessary" here in the broad sense that would include causal necessity.

[55] I am not sure that this is possible. At any rate, given how the notion of means is expounded in what follows, this assumption will turn out to be unnecessary because it will be possible to cover all such relations under the means–end relationship.

other objects in such a way as to make X unattainable or at least more difficult to attain.

There is much more that can be said about the merits of the argument. Its plausibility depends in part on whether it can accommodate the requirements of rational-choice theory on a broader conception of instrumental rationality and whether one can plausibly reject other transfer principles such as (ES). However, I think it is plausible that the Instrumental Principle, perhaps together with the principles of decision theory,[56] exhausts the formal transfer principles of practical rationality. If it were true that these principles exhaust the evaluative judgments a person might make in light of her current evaluative judgments and other beliefs she might have,[57] these principles would fully explicate practical consistency. That is, all forms of practical inconsistency (failure to comply with formal requirements of what evaluative judgments can be held simultaneously) would be cases of violations of instrumental rationality or the norms of maximizing conceptions of rationality.[58] However, it is important to note that this contention is fully compatible with the scholastic view. This is not a minor result; much of the plausibility of instrumentalism comes from the plausibility of (a). When one makes claims of the form "There is nothing inconsistent about desiring anything as long as one pursues appropriate means to one's ends" or "There is no argument that would force one to accept an end to pain of incoherence," one is in fact defending (a), not (b) or (c).

Wouldn't violating (b) be a case of incoherence? After all, if the inferences that allow moving from nonevaluative to evaluative statements are valid, the person who accepts the premises but rejects the conclusion is guilty of some kind of incoherence. Yet, this would not be *practical inconsistency* because the premises themselves are not

---

[56] Principles of decision theory are better seen as governing comparative judgments rather than absolute judgments of the good. However, the consistency principles of decision theory can be taken to be similar in kind; they determine how one is committed to accepting certain "better than (or equal to) judgments" in light of one's acceptance of other comparative judgments.

[57] One needs this clause because inconsistency is determined in light of what one believes – lack of information does not an irrational agent make.

[58] Compare this with Scanlon's "narrow" view of rationality in *What We Owe to Each Other*.

practical judgments (unconditional evaluative judgments). Such
inferences would be better seen as what, following Wilfrid Sellars, we
could call *entry moves* in the realm of practical reason.[59] And just as
someone who failed to make entry moves that she was warranted to
make in the realm of theoretical reason would not thereby be guilty
of theoretical inconsistency, the same should go for someone who
failed to make some entry moves in the realm of practical reason.
Perhaps it is more perspicuous to put this point in terms of the *ideal
world* that is warranted by the agent's practical judgments. An
agent's practical judgments should yield a (perhaps incomplete)
conception of how the world ought to be – an ideal world for her.
The ideal world is one in which the agent succeeds in bringing about
every object that she deems good. We can say that the practically
inconsistent agent is the agent who cannot form a coherent conception of the ideal world. However, the person who denies the
practical judgment warranted by an inference from nonevaluative
premises is not thereby precluded from willing a coherent ideal
world, even if this ideal world is one that a perfectly rational agent
would not will.[60]

What kinds of consideration can one raise against (b)? There has
been a long tradition of denying that one can infer an "ought" from
an "is," but merely asserting the impossibility of the inference seems
to beg the question against the defender of (b).[61] One could instead
mount an argument against (b) based on the successive failures of
philosophers to come up with any valid principles of inference. One
might point out that philosophers have been trying for centuries to
find such a plausible principle, but unlike the principles of first-
order logic and modal logic, for example, there has never been
much agreement on any such principles. I am not very sympathetic
to this kind of inductive pessimism; it seems that such arguments
would lead us to the conclusion that we should rarely expect radical

---

[59] Wilfrid Sellars, "Some Reflections on Language Games."

[60] I do not wish to deny that one might want to defend a wider notion of practical
inconsistency. My point is that there is an interesting notion of a practical failure
that can be isolated by isolating formally valid transfer principles and that this
might explain the "intuition" that there is something special about the
Instrumental Principle or the axioms of rational choice.

[61] Judith Jarvis Thomson argues that such arguments are question-begging in *The
Realm of Rights*, pp. 4–20.

intellectual innovations.[62] However, I mostly want to take this argument as a backdrop against which to evaluate the plausibility of (c). What the argument gets right is that it's far from clear that ordinary reasoning is committed to any other formally valid principle of inference. Moreover, if there are such principles of inference, they do not seem to be explicitly appealed to in ordinary reason; it would be the job of philosophers to uncover them.

If the argument for (a) can be based on certain intuitions we might have about practical consistency, and perhaps the argument for (b) can be based on some kind of induction with respect to the failure of philosophers to produce the relevant principles, I suspect that (c) cannot be based on anything but metaphysical considerations. That means, other than possible suspicions that there is something metaphysically suspect about practical inferences (perhaps one cannot imagine what in a parsimonious picture of reality could warrant such inferences), I don't know of any effective argument against the possibility of a valid inference that is not an instance of PIR. Let us take the following inferences as examples:

(α_1) Children can't measure their anger properly or stop themselves from being carried away by these feelings.

(α_2) Therefore, it makes no sense to resent a child when she says "I hate you" after being denied some object.

(β_1) I acquired the desire to buy Duff beer only because I watched an advertisement featuring someone drinking Duff beer while relaxing on a beautiful beach. I actually don't particularly like the taste of Duff beer.

(β_2) I shouldn't buy Duff beer.

(χ_1) It's raining very heavily.

(χ_2) I should take an umbrella if I am going on a long walk.[63]

(δ_1) I am going to drive tonight.

(δ_2) I shouldn't drink too much.

---

[62] This kind of argument also seems self-refuting. After all, a similar inductive pessimism seems warranted in the case of philosophical arguments, and this is a philosophical argument.

[63] This is from Robert Brandom. See his "Actions, Norms, and Practical Reasoning." All these inferences need ceteris paribus clauses, or, as Brandom puts it, they are nonmonotonic.

On the face of it, these inferences are sound, though certainly not formally valid. One could, no doubt, challenge them; one could try to argue that one should resent even more those who cannot react appropriately, or one could think that there is no better reason to buy beer than the seductiveness of the advertised images. But this is true also of any piece of reasoning; one can always imagine challenging them. These are not particularly persuasive challenges, and thus we should not abandon our assessment of the soundness of the inferences in the face of these arguments. One could also insist that someone who refused to draw these inferences would be guilty of no incon- sistency, but this would just be repeating a point we have already granted – transfer principles determine the realm of practical con- sistency. Also, these inferences involve ceteris paribus clauses: On an extremely hot and dry day, in the absence of air conditioning, one might not object to getting wet; or I might be intent on killing myself by driving drunk on deserted roads. We could also add premises to these inferences that would make some moves explicit or that would even transform them into formally valid patterns of inference. We could add premises such as "One should never buy beer ..." or "I do not want to get wet, and one gets wet ..." However, even if adding a premise would make an inference more perspicuous, this does not mean that the inference was not sound as it was. Let us suggest the following way to assess the soundness of a material inference: If a reasonable person would not need any further information to draw the inference, then the inference is sound. Let us look, for instance, at the inference from (χ_1) to (χ_2). Would a reasonable person need to add, for instance, "I do not want to get wet?" Assuming that the ceteris paribus condition is not violated,[64] and given that it would be rather imprudent not to take an umbrella on a rainy day, a reasonable person could certainly draw the inference directly from (χ_1) to (χ_2).

Looking at the many examples of apparently sound practical inferences, it seems that one cannot raise against (c) the same kind of objections one could raise against (a) and (b). Someone who is

---

[64] One might complain that this begs the question; if one were to specify this clause, one would get a formally valid inference. However, a reasonable agent does not need to be in any way aware of all that could count as an unusual circumstance in order to be fully warranted in taking the umbrella as the only prudent thing to do.

unsympathetic to the notion of material validity will have problems with this defense of the scholastic view. One would insist in this case that a reasonable agent implicitly accepts some kind of premise that allows her to move, say, from (χ_1) to (χ_2). Moreover, if one also thought that one could be justified in accepting these premises, one would also be contravening instrumentalism. Although I prefer to think of the move from (χ_1) to (χ_2) as an inference, this would be a rather minor variation on the scholastic view. Whether or not we accept this minor revision, we end up with the same conclusion: Any plausible version of instrumentalism is compatible with the scholastic view.

Before we leave this topic, it might be worth pointing out a different kind of inference that often seems to be at work in deliberation and intentional explanations. Suppose a millionaire is asked why she takes such good care of an old, beaten-up quarter and she says, "This is the first coin I ever earned through my labor; my dad gave it to me for helping him herd the sheep." No doubt these actions are made intelligible by the relation of the coin to other goods, perhaps the good of self-reliance and the good of one's relationship with one's parents. It seems hard to think of the relationship between the good that the millionaire finds in the coin and these other goods as warranted by any kind of cognitive operation. They don't stand in the relationship of means to ends, of conditioning and conditioned. We can't even say that a proper appreciation for the evaluative perspective that gives rise to the goods of such personal relations or the goods of self-reliance will force her to think of the good in this manner. The commitment to the coin does not make the millionaire more self-reliant and, arguably, in no way a better daughter. The coin simply *stands for* these goods; it is a merely "symbolic" relation.

On the other hand, the answer she gives is an answer to the question "Why?" in the Anscombean sense, and it is an answer that makes her actions intelligible in the way that only rational beings can be intelligible. And, at least to some degree, her inference, if one may call it that, can be criticized in a manner that the "movements of ideas" in a rational being can be criticized. One can think that she is fetishizing these goods or that she gives too much importance to the coin, for example. On certain occasions, one might think that the object that stands in this relation is inappropriate: if, for instance, one keeps a miniature of one's father's coffin in order to keep his memory alive or if, in a fit of anger, one breaks the picture of one's beloved's sibling instead of the picture of one's beloved. There even seems to be a transfer principle at work here, not a rationally inescapable "good-preserving" transfer principle but a "value-preserving" optional transfer principle; that is, not a principle that would mandate that if I judge an object to be good I must also conceive another object to be good, but a principle that authorizes me to move from finding value in an object to finding value in another object. Because a rational being moves through these symbolic connections from legitimately finding value in one object to legitimately finding value in another object, I see no reason not to treat these moves as inferences, but even if they are in some ways analogous to moves generated by a transfer principle, they seem irrelevant to the question of whether the agent is acting in a manner that is practically consistent.

2.5 VOLUNTARY, MERELY INTENTIONAL, AND FULLY DELIBERATED ACTION

A common complaint against scholastic views is their apparently overintellectualist character. It could be argued that if the scholastic constraints on what counts as desire and how desires figure in our deliberation and in intentional explanations were accepted, then their domain would be considerably narrowed, or a scholastic view might be thought to ascribe to human beings more deliberation and ratiocination than an impartial observer could attribute to us. Most of our actions seem to be things that we just do or that we just wanted to do, and this fact seems to be better explained by postulating merely motivational desires. It seems that at least sometimes my desires just move me to act independently of any evaluative assessment on my part. If desires are indeed just *appearances* of the good, it's unclear that anyone could reasonably act simply because one wanted something – one should at least, probably through deliberation, establish that appearances are not misleading, that there is nothing even better in the neighborhood, and so on. But, the objection goes, the idea that our actions are always or should always be the subject of such deliberation is ludicrous. Many of our actions are just things we do simply because we are motivated to act in such a way. If the identification of desires with conceptions or appearances of the good aims to locate every action as a conclusion of a complex piece of practical reasoning, it seems not to be in tune with the rather "thoughtless" way in which our life progresses. And even if we think that much of the deliberation that the scholastic view postulates is implicit, the view still seems to credit actions with more implicit thought than one would or ought to find in the lives of most human beings.

Of course, a defender of a scholastic view could respond to this objection by restricting the scope of the theory. If we accept that much that goes under the name of "action" cannot be properly accounted for by the scholastic view, we can block off these bodily movements from the purview of the scholastic thesis or claim that these are not, properly speaking, "actions." But this would leave the scholastic thesis applicable only to a refined corner of human behavior. One would be left wondering whether a more satisfactory account of all human behavior, including those instances in which the scholastic view seems to be at its most promising, might not be drawn from a more general theory.

However, I think that the charge seems plausible only if we overlook the resources available to scholastic views, in particular if we do not distinguish the various ways in which one's conceptions of the good might be "in control" of our actions. What we need in order to answer this objection is to draw a distinction between merely voluntary, merely intentional,[65] and fully deliberated actions. Each of these categories will mark a different way in which one's conception of the good relates to one's actions.

When I tap my fingers while waiting for my turn in line or pace back and forth during a lecture, I am no doubt acting. But these are certainly not things I do for a reason; it would even be awkward to say that I tapped my fingers on the table just because I wanted to do it or because I liked doing it. Anscombe also notes that these actions do not seem to be susceptible to any kind of desirability characterization, but she seems happy to leave this as a category of human

---

[65] I will often leave out "the merely" in further discussion of these two categories of action.

behavior isolated from intentional actions. This is not wholly satisfactory. After all, voluntary actions are inside the normative sphere
of intentional explanation. I can be held responsible for my behavior (I'll try to pace less if I see that it is bothering my students, and I
certainly stop short of leaving the room while lecturing), and my
actions seem to a large extent to be under my control. These actions
are also subject to criticism in familiar ways: My pacing can be
annoying, disruptive, and so on, and on that account one might
expect that my behavior should change. (No doubt, a teacher can
tell a student "Your tapping your fingers against the desk is very
disruptive. You must stop doing this.") That an action is merely
voluntary does not take it away from the purview of normative criticism in the way that something that merely happens to me does.
Thus, an account of practical reason should at least explain the
relation of voluntary actions to intentional and deliberative ones.

Merely intentional actions also seem to involve no deliberation
and not be required to be the outcome of deliberation. When one
engages in this kind of action, one simply does something because
she wants to do it. Moreover, if I go out for a walk and come back,
my answer, "I just wanted to go for a walk," seems perfectly reasonable. A demand to explain how this action was the outcome of
deliberation that took into account an array of possible alternatives
would be unreasonable. Of course, there might be deliberation
involved *in* my taking a walk, but I don't need any further justification to go out for a walk. Of course, one could say that the only
difference between intentional and fully deliberated action is
whether thinking is implicit or explicit. Now, I do not want to deny
that, *in a sense*, much thought is implicit in intentional actions, and
in fact any action leaves much of its deliberation implicit.[66] But this
does not distinguish appropriately between these two kinds of cases.
It seems that, in certain cases, "I wanted X" is the full justification of
the action, whereas in fully deliberated actions this is not the case.
Indeed, even if one thinks that this answer is not fully adequate in
the case of my decision to go for a walk, it seems harder to deny that
this is the case when one thinks of the more specific plans involved
in going for a walk, such as the decision to turn right at the next

---

[66] Or in any other action; see my "The Conclusion of Practical Reasoning."

intersection, the decision to go a little bit slower, and so on. I will proceed to explain why I think that this distinction is necessary, but, of course, in a sense by doing this I am making the case for the scholastic view harder. The scholastic view best explains fully deliberated actions, and thus if intentional actions can be simply assimilated to them, this will no doubt make the case for the scholastic view all the easier.

Now suppose I go out for a walk and you ask me why I did it. I can say in reply, "I just wanted to go for a walk." It seems that this, in many circumstances, fully justifies my action. Here in particular the following challenge seems out of place: "You know you could also have taken this time to gaze at the stars (which is also something you like doing). Why did you go for a walk instead?"

Although one might say in this case something like "I prefer walking to gazing at stars," one need not go that far, and one might even reject this thought and still be fully justified in going for a walk instead of stargazing. It seems fine for me to insist that I just wanted to go for a walk and perhaps add that I didn't even consider stargazing. And it is important to note that this is not to say that I *overlooked* this possibility (or that I was distracted or not sufficiently attuned to my environment) or that I had to leave aside this possibility because of the costs of extended deliberation. This claim could amount to no more than the recognition that one's action did not issue from the kind of comparative deliberation in which stargazing could have been one of the options contemplated.

Compare my decision to go for a walk with my decision to go to Paris for my long vacations. If asked the reason for my decision, it would seem rather inadequate if all I had to say about it was, "I simply wanted to go to Paris." First, there is the obvious fact that I probably wouldn't be happy simply setting foot in Paris. Rather, there are a range of activities that I probably want to engage in while I am in Paris, and this is what makes my trip to Paris desirable.[67] But, more importantly, it seems that I could not be justified in going to Paris if I did not engage in the kind of comparative deliberation that was unnecessary in the case of my going for a walk. Indeed,

---

[67] Note that the same is not true for the case in which I just go for a walk because I want to.

suppose you tell me something like "Why didn't you go to London? They also have museums and parks in London, and on top of all that, people speak English there."

Here it seems that a reasonable (and articulate) speaker would have something to say about the choice. Perhaps the fact that people speak English in London actually counted against traveling there, perhaps Paris has a special charm for me, or perhaps I have another reason. The reasons, of course, need not be particularly noble or enlightened, and I need not even be particularly articulate in expressing my reason ("Paris just has a certain *je ne sais quoi* about it"). However, having *overlooked* London is certainly a possible criticism here. If I were to say, "I didn't even think of London," my reasoning would have fallen short. Perhaps it would be excusable, or perhaps I was justified in overlooking certain possibilities given time constraints on deliberation, but unlike in the case of merely intentional actions, in many cases it will be true that I would have deliberated better had I considered London. Of course, the point here is not that a rational being should consider all possible alternatives. This is certainly not feasible, and, in this particular case, given my limited resources, it might not have been in any way blameworthy that I left London out of consideration. All that I am claiming is that because this is a fully deliberated action, my grounds for going to Paris would have been better had I considered an alternative such as going to London (and had good reasons to discard it). The same does not hold for the stargazing case. Of course, the demarcation lines of the two kinds of action are hard to draw. However, this should not prevent us from seeing that there is a difference in principle in two ways that actions can be justified.

We can now put the objection as a question of whether the scholastic view can allow for the possibility of voluntary or intentional actions, or whether the scholastic view must assimilate all actions to fully deliberated actions. But now we can see that the objection can be easily answered. The scholastic view claims that our actions ought to be governed by a general conception of the good. However, this demand that our actions be guided by a general conception of the good manifests itself in different ways depending on the kind of action in question. Fully deliberated actions are actions that ought to be governed directly by one's general conception of the good. Ideally, an agent would perform an action of this kind because the outcome of deliberation determined that, given her general conception of the good, no better action was available at that point. However, given that we are limited agents for whom deliberation is often costly, not all our actions can be determined by deliberation in this manner. However, actions can also be indirectly guided by one's conception of the good. So it could be part of one's conception of the good that, under certain circumstances, deliberation should not or need not take place prior to action. It could be part of one's conception of the good that under certain circumstances, within certain bounds, some of my desires can or should give rise to action directly, without deliberation as to whether a better action is available at this point. This would give rise to merely intentional actions that are nonetheless warranted by one's conception of the good. But also, given that the scope of bodily movements under our control might outrun our desires, our conception of the good may allow or demand that in certain circumstances, within certain bounds, our bodily movements should run more freely without the positive control of deliberation or desire. This would give rise to merely voluntary actions that would also be warranted by one's general conception of the good.

Understanding voluntary and intentional actions as being under the guidance of our general conception of the good has some important advantages. First, as noted, even voluntary actions are subject to normative criticism. We can now see why an agent can fail to do as she ought when performing a voluntary action if either her general conception of the good did not warrant that particular instance of voluntary action or if the general conception of the good should not have warranted that particular instance of voluntary action. Tapping my fingers at a solemn occasion might be something I ought not do, and certainly moving my tapping from the table to my neighbor's shoulder should be something that my conception of the good does not warrant me to do.

More generally, this way of understanding these actions gives a good account of the difference between voluntary and intentional actions on the one hand and instances of behavior that are not at all under the purview of intentional explanations. Consider an instance of merely intentional action: I reach for coffee when wondering about the best format for this document. Let us suppose that the action proceeds without thought or deliberation. This would be a case in which my action was not under the direct control of my general conception of the good. But this is also a case in which my conception of the good warrants the performance of a merely intentional action.

It is worth comparing a case like this with a case in which one instinctively slams the brakes while skidding despite the fact that one knows that one should not slam the brakes in such a situation. At first one might think that there is no difference; in both cases, a certain behavior is brought about directly from an impulse. However, the two cases are different, and their difference can be brought to light with the help of the scholastic formula. First, it is worth noting that I obviously do conceive drinking coffee to be good when acting in this manner. Although I have not deliberated on this particular occasion, I will probably have something to say in response to the question, "What is the point of drinking coffee?" If I am articulate enough, I will probably be able to say, for example, some of the following things: "It keeps me awake"; "I just love coffee"; "I can't live without caffeine"; or "I need to do something with my hands while I am thinking." Moreover, although we are assuming that there was no deliberation even implicit prior to or embodied in my reaching for coffee, there are good grounds for saying that the action was nonetheless indirectly guided by my conception of the good. First, there is the obvious fact that not all actions are allowed to proceed in this way from my desire. A desire to spit might not be indulged in the same way, an urge to scream is fortunately on most occasions checked, and more bizarre urges and desires that could assault me would typically be curbed. Also, my allowing the desire to proceed in this manner is no doubt dependent on my background understanding of the situation. I would not be reaching for the coffee if I were told that it was mixed with ink or if I were to learn that coffee would cause prompt and severe consequences to my health. Furthermore, as I move to a situation in which deliberation is required, I would no longer simply proceed with the action. If it is getting late in the day and I know that coffee might keep me awake beyond reasonable hours, I won't reach for coffee without further deliberation. Moreover, my actions are circumscribed by the bounds of what would be considered acceptable within my general conception of the good: At home, I don't bother to see where I am putting down the coffee; at someone else's place, I want to make sure that the surface will not be marked by cup stains.

But these features mark an important respect in which my reaching for coffee is different from my slamming the brakes at the wrong time. My background understanding of the situation does not have the same control over the relation that holds between my desires and the action. We can say that in the coffee case my action is indeed expressive of what is valuable to me in a way that is not true here. I do, after all, know that slamming on the brakes might result in my death, and I do not think for a moment that the desire to relieve one's impulses to slam the brakes should run amok irrespective of traffic. Here the scholastic view does a good job of accounting for the difference. In the coffee case, that my desire issues directly in action finds a place in my conception of the good. The same is not true of the case of my slamming on the brakes. The scholastic view allows that desires issue in action immediately, but this immediate relation between desire and action must be conceived to be good.[68]

The distinction between merely intentional and fully deliberated actions is also important in distinguishing two ways in which justification of one's actions can come to an end. On the one hand, in the case of merely intentional action, it might come to an end because one has mentioned the fact that one wants it, which in this case suffices to justify an action. Or one's justification might come to an end because at this point one cannot explain further what makes the object of one's pursuit good in this case. Here an explanation runs out either because the agent is convinced that she has shown, beyond any reasonable doubt, that the *object* of her pursuit is in fact good (it is what an agent in her situation ought to pursue) or because

---

[68] Another way to put it is to say that the scholastic view allows "mediated immediacy" for an immediate relation between desires and action, but this relation itself needs to be mediated by the exercise of practical reason. What the scholastic view does not allow for is "pure immediacy," the possibility that desires issue in action immediately independent of a background understanding that allows for this relation.

her capacity to articulate her reasons has run out. If one keeps being pressed, at some point one will probably find it hard to explain further why one thinks that the object of one's pursuit is good. No doubt the latter is more common than the former. It is important to keep this distinction in mind to foreclose another seemingly powerful argument against the scholastic view.

In the absence of infinite powers of "articulation," one will at some point be unable to provide further reasons for what one does or further answers to the question "Why?" in the Anscombean sense of the question. At this point, it would no doubt be natural to say: "This is just what I really wanted" or "This was what was really important to me." These could be the answers that someone would give if asked, for instance, why she spent much of her life trying to find the cure for cancer. Now compare this with the answer that the agent who goes on a stroll gives to the question "Why?" In the example we gave earlier, the agent answers by saying: "I just wanted to go on a stroll." It is tempting to assimilate the account of fully deliberated action to the account of merely intentional action. One would then conclude that these two answers both point to a "founding desire." And it might be tempting then to come to the general conclusion that, for every reason to act that one has, there must be a desire that is beyond the reach of rational criticism.[69] But with the help of the distinction between merely intentional and fully deliberated actions, the scholastic view allows us to see the two termini of an explanation as essentially different. For the intentional action, it is true, to some extent, that acting on a desire cannot be criticized insofar as one has that desire. Assuming that the desire is for an intelligible object and that it is within the bounds of one's correct (or at least reasonable) conception of the good and the circumstances that it allows, there would be no grounds to criticize acting on this desire; for instance, the fact that the agent failed to consider potentially better options would not in itself be grounds for criticizing the action. But the same is not true for fully deliberated actions and thus would not be true for the actions that arise out of the desire to find a cure for cancer. No theory of practical reason

---

[69] Joseph Heath argues that subjectivist views are grounded on a foundationalist view of practical reason in "Foundationalism and Practical Reason."

should postulate that the explanations ought to go on forever, but this is not to say that there is any point at which explanations *must* stop, at least for fully deliberated actions. After all, one *could* legitimately challenge the agent who advances this explanation on the basis, for instance, of options overlooked (or not given enough) consideration. Although it is hard to find fault with someone who dedicates her life to curing cancer, it's not impossible to come up with at least one kind of objection. One could argue that her life didn't leave much time for her family or even for herself. (One could think of a parent saying, "My darling, you have to think more of yourself. You need to go out more and have fun.")[70] One could even think that it is narrow-minded or self-indulgent to worry so much about the cure for cancer when so many more people die of malnutrition; resources used to fight cancer should go into social justice. Of course, imperfectly rational agents will not be articulate enough or wise enough to have answers to all objections and questions that their behavior might raise. The scholastic view does not postulate this kind of rationality as a fact but as an ideal to which we are all bound.

---

[70] Susan Wolf's famous paper "Moral Saints" comes to mind in this context. However, it is not as easy to find "fault" in the life of the cancer research scientist as it is in Mother Teresa's because the life of the research scientist is in many ways well rounded.

3

The Subjective Nature of Practical Reason

The claim that "values are subjective" can be understood in a wide variety of ways, ranging from extremely controversial to nearly trivial interpretations of the claim. Throughout this chapter, I will introduce various versions of the claim and examine what these different versions imply, as well as whether the scholastic view can make sense of the claims that seem the most intuitively plausible. Two constraints, I argue, turn out to be very plausible. The first constraint I call "object-subjectivism." Although this constraint has fallen into some disrepute, I will argue that when properly understood, it is a quite plausible constraint. The other constraint, which I call "authority-subjectivism," is more popular among contemporary philosophers. These two constraints seem to pull in opposite directions. On the one hand, object-subjectivism places constraints on the content of what one ought to desire or what can count as valuable; such content must be suitably related to the agent's mental states. On the other hand, authority-subjectivism makes value depend somehow on the evaluative attitudes of the agent. Something is valuable, according to the constraint, only if it is properly related to the agent's evaluative judgment or to other similar attitudes. It seems perfectly possible (and in fact true) that an agent might judge to be good (or have whatever other evaluative attitude ultimately figures in the constraint) objects other than mental state or fail to judge to be good (or fail to have) whatever other evaluative attitude ultimately figures in the constraint toward any mental state.

Thus, it is far from clear that these two constraints are compatible. I will argue in this chapter that, with the aid of the scholastic view, we can formulate plausible versions of each constraint that are compatible with each other. According to this version of the constraints, object-subjectivism and authority-subjectivism turn out to be two independent, but related, requirements on what can be legitimately conceived to be good. These versions of the constraints cannot be reconciled with the contemporary subjectivist position. In fact, I argue that contemporary subjectivist views[1] of practical reason have problems accommodating each of these constraints. If the argument of this chapter works, the scholastic view will be shown to be able to accommodate the intuitions that lend credibility to contemporary subjectivist positions; indeed, the argument should show that it can do this better than contemporary subjectivism itself. The scholastic view turns out to accommodate the two most plausible features of the claim that values are subjective. It is worth clarifying the argumentative ambitions of the chapter. I will try to show that these constraints are indeed quite plausible and that many of the reasons one seems to have for rejecting them are actually reasons to reject much more demanding versions of the constraints or other views unnecessarily appended to these constraints. In my view, these constraints, when suitably formulated, are plausible enough that if the price of accepting the scholastic view is to reject these constraints, then it's not clear that this is a view that we can afford to have. However, the arguments for these constraints are, admittedly, not fully conclusive. If one found them intuitively very implausible to begin with, one probably would not be fully persuaded by the arguments here. However, if this were one's view, one would also not find them a threat to the scholastic view or find that contemporary subjectivism was a serious contender to the scholastic view. Someone who was unconvinced by the arguments of this chapter for these reasons would still have no reason to reject the scholastic view, or at least the scholastic view minus the constraints defended in this chapter.

[1] I'll present two constraints that I will endorse using the name "subjectivism": authority-subjectivism and object-subjectivism. I'll use the label "contemporary subjectivism" to refer to the theory of practical reason that is incompatible with the scholastic view.

It might also be worth mentioning a side benefit of this chapter. If these are indeed plausible constraints, they will also serve as illustrations of how one can accept substantive, general constraints on what can be good without thereby having a more specific theory that would allow us to determine what is and is not good. This will give us further reason to reject the view that a substantive scholastic view must include a substantive theory of the good conceived in this manner.

3.1 PRELIMINARY REMARKS

Mary avoids pain and pursues pleasure, and she avoids her pain and pursues her pleasure more eagerly than the pain or pleasure of anyone else. She also hates peanut butter but loves pumpkin pies, and she finds dancing boring but enjoys singing along with loud music. She takes secret pleasure in ensuring that she never steps twice on the same slab while walking to work. She pursues and avoids the objects of these attitudes, unconcerned by the fact that many people do not share such attitudes. In fact, not only does this disagreement raise no doubts in her mind about the rationality of her behavior, but she also thinks that those whose behavior is guided by contrary attitudes are perfectly rational. If pressed on this point, Mary answers simply by saying, "That's how I am, and those are the things I like and dislike doing; other people want different things in life."

When Mary acts in accordance with those attitudes, she seems to be, at least in most cases, entirely reasonable. Ceteris paribus, there is really no reason for her to eat peanut butter, avoid pumpkin pies, listen to soft music, go to dance sessions, or even walk in a less idiosyncratic manner. Furthermore, it is in no way surprising that she pursues pleasure and avoids pain or that she shows a greater interest in her own welfare than in the welfare of a complete stranger. It is hard to make the case that any of these facts raise suspicions about her overall rationality.

These observations seem to support some version of the claim that values are subjective or that the correct theory of practical reason is subjectivist. But what forms of subjectivism, if any, are made plausible by these rather uncontroversial claims?[2] Are any of the forms of subjectivism warranted by these facts compatible with the scholastic view? Because I am mostly concerned with the latter question, what I have to say about the former question will be expressed in the terms of the scholastic view. However, most of the issues I discuss with regard to the first question are independent of one's commitment to any particular theory of practical reason.

Before we look into these problems, a clarification is in order. There is a burgeoning body of literature on the issue of well-being.[3] Matters of well-being or prudential good are supposed to form only part of the considerations that an agent takes into account when acting. Although the prospect of peace in the Middle East is something for which I might care deeply, it is plausible to say that it is not part of my well-being because, in some important sense, it is not expected to affect me directly. This notion of well-being is not coextensive with the forms of subjective or relativized good I will be discussing, or at least it would take a great deal of argument to show that it is. Although the exact ways in which they differ will become clearer, it might be worth quickly pointing out an obvious way in which these two notions might separate. The notion of something being merely good for Mary marks those things that only Mary has reason to pursue or at least that only those who happen to care for these same things have reason to pursue.[4] At least prima facie, these things do not necessarily overlap with plausible constituents of Mary's well-being. Even some of the examples given earlier, such as making sure that she does not step twice on the same slab, could be reasonably left out of an account of Mary's well-being. But there seem to be various things that Mary, but not others, might have

---

[2] Not all of these claims are completely uncontroversial. No doubt, some religious sects might dispute that pleasure is, ceteris paribus, to be pursued, or even that pain is, ceteris paribus, to be avoided. Some utilitarians might also think that a perfectly rational person gives equal weight to the pleasure and pain of each person.

[3] For example, see James Griffin, *Well-Being: Its Meaning, Measurement, and Moral Importance*; and L. W. Sumner, *Welfare, Happiness and Ethics*.

[4] A distinction here might be in order. There might be things that other people have no *direct* reason to pursue but have a derivative reason to pursue; that is, things that *in themselves* would give no one else a reason to pursue but that someone else might have reason to pursue simply on account of the fact that they are good *for Mary*. More on this in chapter 4.

reason to pursue, such as making sure that an old friend from her high school has a date for the school reunion, that do not seem to concern her well-being in any reasonable account of this notion. On the other hand, her well-being, at least considered as such, might be something that everyone has at least some reason to pursue.

Mild versions of subjectivism will certainly be innocuous and also compatible with any remotely plausible theory of practical reason. It would be difficult to deny, for instance, the claim that one's sub-jective states can at least be relevant in determining what one ought to do. No doubt, even in the most objectivist theory, one's subjective states might be part of the relevant circumstances that one has to take into account in determining what is valuable and what one ought to do. The fact that performing one action rather than another will cause me pain, or that I am susceptible to pain in certain situations whereas others are not, will be taken into account by any reasonable theory of value or practical rationality. In what follows, I will assume that calling a view or constraint "subjectivist" always implies something stronger than this obvious claim.

However, if we assume that Mary is reasonable, we seem to be justified in accepting stronger versions of subjectivism. First, the fact that she acknowledges that her desiring and avoiding certain things is perfectly compatible with others having the opposite attitudes toward the same objects seems to warrant a kind of subjectivism that is incompatible with the scholastic view. After all, it seems that Mary does not endorse that any of these things are good or bad *simpliciter*, and yet the absence of such endorsement does not make it the case that her behavior is in any way irrational (or wrongheaded). Even if one wants to allow that some values are objective, the claim that some values are subjective seems compelling. How can the scholastic view accommodate the fact that one desires something in this particular way? An obvious proposal is that the scholastic view can distinguish between something appearing to be good and something appearing to be good *for me*. But how exactly would a scholastic view accommodate a relativized notion of the good?

It is worth pointing out some ways in which this could *not* be done. We would certainly not capture what we intended if we relativized an appearance of the good to a particular person as follows:

1. It appears to me that X is good.

What (1) makes relative to the agent is not the good but only its appearance. It opens the possibility that different things will appear good to different persons but not the possibility that different things will *be* good for different persons. Another proposal would be to try to put the first-person pronoun where it seems to belong most naturally:

2. It appears that X is good for me.

Proposal (2) might be our aim, but it cries out for an explanation of the difference between conceiving something to be good *simpliciter* and conceiving something to be good for oneself. Given the formal nature of "good" in the theory, there seems to be no room for another kind of good that can occupy the place of good *simpliciter* in the original expression. Whatever I correctly see as desirable is, according to the theory, good.

One could alternatively claim that conceiving to be good is always conceiving to be good for oneself. But now rather than legislating subjective value out of existence, we seem to be legislating *objective* value out of existence. Why couldn't I conceive something to be good *simpliciter* rather than just good for me? Believers in objective value constitute a sizably smaller sector of the philosophical population than believers in subjective value, but this should not be enough to make us feel comfortable about ruling out objective values on such flimsy theoretical grounds. However, we can accept this proposal and still leave the objectivist some room to maneuver. We can accept that a relativized notion of good is primary and work up the conditions, if any exist, under which we can drop the indexical.

The way we will proceed does not fit either strategy precisely. "Conceiving to be good" is a notion that finds its natural home in action; conceiving something to be good is conceiving something to be an appropriate object of pursuit in action. It might seem then that it is natural to say that when an agent conceives something to be good, she conceives it to be good primarily *for her*; that is, she pursues the object of the representation as one at which *she* should aim in *her* actions. However, this does not show that the relevant notion of the good is indexical. As I argued in the previous chapter, the various particular ways in which we conceive certain things to be good should provide the materials from which one can build a more general, reflective conception of the good, a conception that ought to guide our actions. But insofar as a conception of the good justifies one's actions, it has to find that certain appearances of the good are legitimate or in need of revision and to infer certain evaluative stances from other evaluative stances. It is hard to see how the legitimacy of these moves can depend solely on the fact that this is *my* conception of the good rather than on the perfectly general circumstances of my acting. On the other hand, the various perspectives that the agent has on the good, and the various ways in which things appear to be good to the agent, are among the circumstances of her action. Some of the things that the agent ought to judge to be good might be perspective dependent; they might be good only insofar as the agent has a certain perspective on the good. The idea that some goods are perspective or appearance dependent takes us some distance to the view that acceptable conceptions of the good will have essentially subjective elements. Moreover, nothing rules out the possibility that these subjective elements have a central role to play in forming the conception of the good. Of course, in order to evaluate the cogency of these strategies in capturing our "subjectivist intuitions," we need to spell out both the strategy and the intuitions. This is what the following sections aim to do. I hope that in the end it will be clear that these intuitions are best captured by accepting two independent constraints on what can be legitimately conceived of as good.

3.2 OBJECT-SUBJECTIVISM

It might seem obvious that subjectivism is the claim that values depend somehow on the mental states of the agent for whom something is valuable. But the problem is that without the "somehow" this claim does not characterize any particularly distinctive view of the nature of value. Whatever one's views are about value, it seems fairly reasonable to assume that mental states, including the agent's own mental states, are some of the states that are sources of value, are themselves valuable, or are at least reliably connected to values, and thus it is unclear why anyone would deny such a claim. There seems to be no reason to think that this fact would be hard to accommodate for any theory of practical reason. Let us take for instance a rather simplistic version of Aristotle's position about the supreme good.[5] According to this position, the sole good is contemplation or knowledge. Because knowledge is at least partly a mental state, this theory would qualify as a form of subjectivism. Of course, this view is distinct from a view that does not refer to mental states, such as the view that the good consists in the harmonious course of nature governed by laws, but this seems hardly enough to capture what is distinctive about subjectivist views.[6]

It seems plausible to argue that the problem with this characterization is that it focuses on the characteristics of the *objects* themselves rather than on the *grounds* for our considering the object "good." To the extent that preserving first-person authority is an important aspect of subjectivism, it is neutral on the objects themselves. It is a view about the nature of the grounds for considering objects to be good. According to such a view, certain attitudes of ours (such as desires or preferences) *confer* value on their objects. These value-conferring attitudes are not just any attitudes. Rather, they are themselves judgments about the good or what is valuable.[7] According to this form of subjectivism, something is valuable in part because I *take* it to be valuable. No doubt, one needs to work out which attitudes are value conferring and under which conditions, and which attitudes count as genuine instances of taking something to be valuable (Is it desire, informed desire, preference, or something else?), but in general what makes something valuable is that we take it, under appropriate conditions, to be valuable. A view that is committed to accepting this version of the claim that values are subjective is committed to a form of authority-subjectivism. It is fair to say that most recent subjectivism is committed to authority-subjectivism.[8] For

---

[5] See Aristotle, *Nicomachean Ethics*, Book X.

[6] Although, as will become clear, I actually think that the Aristotelian view does answer the constraint imposed by a plausible form of object-subjectivist view in a way that the latter view does not.

[7] Most subjectivists, of course, will use language of desire, preference, and so forth instead of "judgments of value."

[8] David Gauthier, *Morals by Agreement*, and Richard Brandt, *A Theory of the Good and the Right*, among others.

example, what James Griffin refers to as the "taste model" is a form of authority-subjectivism, but Griffin's own view, in which we move to "informed desire," is also a form of authority-subjectivism.[9] We can contrast authority-subjectivism with what can be called, if somewhat paradoxically, "object-subjectivism," a view according to which whatever is called "good" must itself be a mental state or partly constituted by mental states. As I pointed out, it might seem that authority-subjectivism simply corrects the confusions of object subjectivism.[10] However, there seems to be something plausible about the idea that something can be valuable only if it is an aspect or property of a mental state, or at least appropriately related to an aspect or property of a mental state, which at least contemporary subjectivists would have a hard time accounting for.[11] For instance, consider the intuition that lies behind the commonly held view that if all humans (or if all animals)[12] were wiped out, nothing of value would remain. This is clearly *not* an implication of authority-subjectivism because if today I desire that a million years from now the moon will be perfectly round, and it happens, then there is value in the world at that time whether or not animal life is still present in the universe. Of course, there might be issues about the dating of the value, but if authority-subjectivists do not want to say that the desiring itself is part of the good, then, to the extent that it makes sense to "date" a good at all, the date should be the realization of the object of one's attitudes, not the date of the attitude. Even if all you can say is that X is good for me at t, what is good is X, and the time in which such value is realized is the time that X occurs, not the time in which it is good for me.

---

[9] James Griffin, "Against the Taste Model"; *Well-Being*.

[10] David Gauthier, for instance, explicitly rejects object-subjectivism in favor of authority-subjectivism in *Morals by Agreement*, p. 47.

[11] However, not all contemporary philosophers reject it. Robert Audi, for instance, defends what he calls "axiological experientialism" in his *The Architecture of Reason: The Structure and Substance of Rationality*, pp. 98–100. (See also his *The Good in the Right: A Theory of Intuition and Intrinsic Value*.) Audi's view, like mine, does not rely on the claim that only my own mental states (in his case, my own experiences) can be good for me, but his defense of it, unlike mine, relies on Moore's notion of organic unities (and also on a distinction between intrinsic and inherent value).

[12] Whether one thinks that we should stick to the phrase "all humans" or replace it with "all animals" will depend exactly on whether one thinks that nonhuman animals are capable of having the right kind of mental states.

On the other hand, if we think of many cases in which an agent fails to satisfy the general intelligibility requirement, it seems that the agent fails because the object of his pursuit does not connect to any mental state. For instance, one finds it hard to see the point of having a basic desire that the moon have the shape of an isosceles triangle at noon on March 1, 2110. We can't see why anyone would care about whether this particular state of affairs obtains. Of course, if one is somehow comforted by the thought, there might be some value in it, but the value is the value of being so comforted. One can also see the force of this intuition in our ethical views. One's distaste for pain is given significantly greater weight in deliberating about what we owe to each other than, say, one's distaste for the fact (if it is a fact) that there are more ladybugs than dragonflies in Italy.[13] Let us call preferences or desires whose objects make no reference to any mental states "idle attitudes." We can see the difference in our attitudes if we think about a person who likes to prevent the realization of people's idle attitudes as a hobby. Let us call this character Sam. Sam lives in Seattle, and when Sam hears that someone in France would like there to be dandelions in a garden near Seattle, he goes out and makes sure that there are no dandelions there. When he hears that someone in the 1930s wanted there to be no olive trees in Seattle, he plants one. Sam does not tell anyone he is doing this and does not try to make sure that the relevant persons or their descendants find out that he has frustrated their desires; he just does it. In fact, we can further stipulate that Sam does these things only when he is certain that the relevant person will *not* find out about it. Unlike someone who would prevent the realization of people's nonidle attitudes, Sam strikes us as more capricious than cruel.[14]

Object-subjectivism will seem quite implausible if we unwittingly saddle it with controversial addenda or if we do not qualify it properly. First, object-subjectivism will seem implausible if it generates a justly discredited form of ethical egoism. It would be an

---

[13] Thomas Nagel discusses the grounds for treating these two kinds of attitudes differently in his *The View from Nowhere*.

[14] Assuming it does not take him all that much work to plant olive trees, eradicate the dandelions, and so on. Otherwise, he'll strike us as simply mad (interestingly in contrast with genuinely malicious people).

uphill battle to defend object-subjectivism if it were committed to the claim that I ought not take a genuine interest in the welfare of my family members or that the object of my desire is knowing or, worse, believing that my family members are doing well rather than the welfare of my family members. However, object-subjectivism, as described so far, is not committed to the claim that the only things that could be good for me are *my* mental states; rather, the idea is that being appropriately related to aspects or properties of *someone's* mental life is required for anything to be good. Thus, as long as my family members' mental lives are appropriately related to what is being represented as good, this should not be an objection to object-subjectivism. Understood this way, object-subjectivism is compatible with various forms of commitments to objectivity in value theory, especially if objectivity is identified with something like universal validity. For instance, it is compatible with object-subjectivism that pain is an objective evil; that is, not only the person who would feel it but anyone has a reason to prevent painful states in anyone.

Secondly, it seems clear that an unqualified version of object-subjectivism is hopeless because it seems clear that sometimes the object of our desires does not include any aspect or property of our mental lives. The following can plausibly be the objects of one's desires: that there will be a beautiful sunset tomorrow; that Seurat's *A Sunday on La Grande Jatte* be preserved; that the Dallas Cowboys will not be at the next Super Bowl; and so on. None of these objects of desire explicitly mention any aspect or property of our mental lives, even as a component. Left unqualified, object-subjectivism will be faced with the Herculean task of showing that these could not be reasonable objects of desires and thus could not be good. But we can make the view more plausible by accepting a more moderate version of it. We can say that what we find valuable in these things is not independent of our mental states. It seems reasonable to suppose that our capacity for appreciating sunsets, the arts, and sports events somehow underlies the value of these objects. Thus one might want to say that although these objects do not themselves involve any aspects or properties of our mental lives, the grounds on which we take them to be desirable do involve them. So if we accept, for instance, an inference from the claim that enjoying X is valuable to the conclusion that X is valuable, there will be cases of valuable objects that are not aspects of our mental states, but their value is inferentially grounded on aspects of our mental states.

Although I think this is the correct way to qualify object-subjectivism, we must be careful here not to collapse object-subjectivism into authority-subjectivism. After all, what seems to characterize authority-subjectivism is exactly the claim that certain mental states ground all judgments of value. To avoid this problem, object-subjectivism must be characterized in such a way that the justificatory primacy in question turns out to be quite different from the role that our value-conferring attitudes play in any formulation of authority-subjectivism. We can define a qualified version of object-subjectivism as follows:

> (OS) Anything that we legitimately conceive to be good must be such that either (a) it is an aspect or property of our mental states or (b) one can justify conceiving it to be good by a piece of reasoning that makes an indispensable appeal to the fact that some aspects or properties of our mental lives are conceived to be good.

On the other hand, we can define authority-subjectivism, tentatively, as follows:[15]

> (AS) Anything that we can legitimately conceive to be good must be such that either (a) it is the object of a value-conferring attitude or (b) one can justify conceiving it to be good by showing that it bears a certain (appropriate) relation to the object of a value-conferring attitude.

It would be fallacious to move from the fact that authority-subjectivism is committed to making certain attitudes constitutive of the good to the conclusion that it must see this kind of mental state as a valuable state that underlies all other states. This would be the case only if one took this attitude toward the attitude itself.[16] But because authority-subjectivism, unlike object-subjectivism, does not place constraints on the *content* of any of our evaluations, it is possible under authority-subjectivism that one does not conceive any

---

[15] This definition will be revised when we discuss authority-subjectivism in detail in the next section.

[16] It is worth pointing this out because this illicit move seems sometimes to be at the base of certain Kantian arguments for the Formula of Humanity. See Donald H. Regan, "The Value of Rational Nature," and David Sussman, "The Authority of Humanity," on this issue.

aspects or properties of our mental lives to be good – a possibility certainly ruled out by object-subjectivism. More generally, authority-subjectivism singles out certain *attitudes* as capable of conferring value on their objects and thus as capable of justifying the acceptance of certain objects as good, whereas object-subjectivism singles out certain *objects* as capable of conferring value and thus justifying the values of other objects.

As we try to make object-subjectivism plausible, we start moving away from the idea that subjectivism is an offshoot of the popular view expressed in the saying *chacun son goût*, an idea that seems to capture the plausibility of authority-subjectivism. Rather, object-subjectivism becomes a constraint that presupposes an evaluative justificatory structure. Understood this way, object-subjectivism does not directly constrain the object of our conative attitudes; however, it does constrain the *grounds* on which we can take such attitudes. Any such constraints must be seen as anathema to, for instance, an instrumentalist position.[17]

One source of discontent with object-subjectivism comes from the thought that we rather often seem to have as ends things that seem unrelated to aspects or properties of our mental states. Although this might be compatible with the revised version of object-subjectivism I proposed earlier, it certainly speaks against its plausibility. The classical thought experiment that buttresses this claim is Robert Nozick's experience machine.[18] Nozick asks us to think about an offer to enter a machine that will provide us with any subjective experiences we might want to have (from the pleasure of eating a sandwich to providing you with the illusion that you won the Nobel Prize). Then, we are asked whether we would like to step into

[17] The instrumentalist will regard any such restrictions on the possible objects of practical reason as parochial; other beings endowed with practical rationality might desire other things. Peter Railton tries to make this charge of parochialism particularly compelling in his "Taste and Value." However, interestingly enough, in order to make the charge of parochialism stick, Railton asks us to look into beings with different *experiences*. This is some evidence of the underlying appeal of OS; what these beings experience or fail to experience should be, in the instrumentalist's view, irrelevant to the plausibility of the example.

[18] Robert Nozick, *Anarchy, State, and Utopia*, pp. 42–45. I am not claiming that Nozick takes the lessons of the thought experiment to be as I describe it here. Rather, I am characterizing those lessons in the way that is most threatening to the plausibility of object-subjectivism.

the machine. Most people answer "no" to this question, and this might be taken as evidence against object-subjectivism. Note that the argument so far seems to depend on accepting authority-subjectivism because it moves from an observation about what we care about, or what we find valuable, to a conclusion about what is actually valuable. It is of course open to the object-subjectivist to claim that the answer people give simply reflects a mistaken view about value. But this is not a particularly appealing reply; it is hard to argue that we are just massively mistaken here about what kind of life is worth having. I see no plausible way of avoiding the conclusion that life in the experience machine is, at least in many situations, worse than life outside it. Indeed, I will assume that overall there isn't much value in a life lived inside the experience machine and that if we suppose that living conditions outside the machine are fairly reasonable, then everyone should refuse to live inside it.

Although the objection seems to be targeted at any kind of object-subjectivism, it is important to note that it implicitly depends on a certain conception of mental states. The objection works only if it is true that there are no limitations on the range of mental states that can be provided by the experience machine; that is, the objection works only if it is true that any mental state that one could have outside the experience machine could be had inside it as well. However, the experience machine can only guarantee that mental states inside the machine are such that I cannot distinguish them from those I have outside the machine. But this means that they are the same mental states only if we have what can be referred to as a "narrow" conception of mental states; that is, if we think that mental states that the subject cannot tell apart are identical. The idea that mental states are "narrow" has been challenged in recent years,[19] and there is no reason for the object-subjectivist to take the "conservative" side of this debate. Indeed, the fact that the view is made implausible by accepting a narrow conception of mental states should lead one to think that the object-subjectivist should endorse a broader conception of mental states.

[19] For a defense of the view that knowledge should not be understood as (justified) belief, and some further external conditions, see Timothy Williamson, *Knowledge and Its Limits*. Similar ideas appear in John McDowell, "Singular Thought and the Extent of Inner Space."

If we take it that there is no difference in one's mental life whether one *knows* that *p* or merely believes that *p*, it is no doubt true that the experience machine can deliver the same mental states as, for instance, one would have when one *knows* that one has just successfully climbed Mt. Everest. But if knowing is a genuine mental state (rather than a hybrid of a mental state and some external condition), the experience machine cannot provide us with all the aspects or properties of our mental lives that we might have as our end. The experience machine can produce the experience of *believing* that we just climbed Mt. Everest but obviously can't produce the experience of *knowing* that we did it; indeed, stepping into the machine will only ensure that I will *not* have this experience.

It is important to note that the assumption that mental states should be conceived "narrowly" is not part of the formulation of object-subjectivism but rather is an extra and controversial philosophical assumption. Of course, it is outside the scope of this work to argue in detail for this "broad" view of mental states. Nonetheless, what I will argue is that if we do accept this view, we can come up with a plausible version of object-subjectivism; indeed, it will turn out that, understood this way, object-subjectivism is a very plausible and interesting constraint on which objects can be intelligibly pursued. This by itself will give us some reason to look with sympathy at the broader conception of mental states; after all, the fact that this way of individuating mental states allows us to make sense of important phenomena in the practical realm no doubt speaks in favor of this view.

We should start by noting that a broader view of mental states allows an object-subjectivist position to account for our understanding of the value of experiences of appreciation. This can be seen, for instance, by examining how we can try to incorporate aesthetic enjoyment into our system of values. It seems that we have one of two options. First, we can think that the value resides in the mental state that is caused by contemplating, say, a painting of a certain aesthetic merit, an experience that one might call an experience of *appreciation*. But, in this case, it is not clear why we need the painting in the equation at all. It seems that, at least in principle, the same value could be achieved as a result of, say, ingesting the right amount of drugs. Moreover, this seems to betray one important aspect of what we consider to be valuable, for it seems that we can understand the value of the experience only insofar as it is being brought about by something of aesthetic merit. When we find value in this experience, our eyes are turned to the painting itself, not to the experience.

Impressed by this fact, we might be led to the conclusion that the value resides in the painting itself, that the existence of the painting itself must be thought of as good. This in turn leads to the awkward conclusion that the mere existence of the painting is valuable and that a world in which all sentient beings have been destroyed but in which all Vermeers are left intact is in some way better than a world in which the Vermeers suffered the same fate as the sentient beings. Another way of seeing the awkwardness of this conclusion is to think of the science-fiction case in which certain machines are capable of producing great art.[20] Suppose this machine could work only at a place in the universe that was inaccessible to humans, either directly or by means of any camera or other device. Let us call this place the Artx planet. Let us also suppose that although we cannot see the machine there, we can send it to Artx, as well as regular unmanned maintenance missions to assure its proper function and its continued production of art on Artx. The view that the art should be thought of as good on its own would imply that those who appreciate art should care for the existence, maintenance, and so on of this machine on Artx. However, it seems closer to the truth that it does not make any sense to care about what goes on with the machine on Artx, at least not for the aesthetic merits that this mission enables.[21] We appear to be in a bind here: By focusing on the experience, we leave out the fact that what matters most about this experience is that it is an experience *of an object of aesthetic merit*. But by focusing on the aesthetic merit of the object, we are led to the conclusion that the object can carry its value on its own. Of course, one can try to come up with some notion of "organic unity" to account for this

---

[20] I am not sure that this is a coherent possibility; that is, that we could consider anything produced by a machine as art even if it was the case that if a physically indistinguishable object were produced by a human being, it would count as art. But I will ignore this complication.

[21] Of course, one might care for this kind of human achievement for its demonstration that human beings are capable of designing and executing a mission of this kind.

phenomenon. However, the appeal to organic unity leaves us baffled about how such a unity would come about. Here we are talking about two objects that are themselves valueless but that simply by virtue of co-occurring form a unity. Although one could insist that this is simply how it happens, it is hard to see how value could come about in this manner.

As we said earlier, the broad view of mental states is rather controversial. One might think that we should await firmer verdicts on its plausibility before we apply it as if it were a well-tested tool. However, the plausibility of this view is not completely independent of the outcome of our discussion. The fact that object-subjectivism becomes a rather plausible doctrine when conjoined with a broader notion of a mental state is itself evidence for the theoretical advantages of the broader notion. After all, our categories of mentation are not produced in a vacuum but must answer to our explanatory purposes.[22] Here we have at least one instance in which this seems to be the case: If we allow broad mental states to be considered genuine mental states, we have a rather simple explanation of an otherwise elusive form of value. Values that involve some kind of experience of appreciation under this view can be straightforwardly located in the experience – what is thought to be good is the experience of appreciation. But because the experience of appreciation is factive – it consists in part in being the perception of an object of real aesthetic merit – the experience is such that our eyes are turned to aesthetic merit itself. Moreover, no experience induced by any other means could count as the same experience of appreciation. It is hard to overstate the extent to which a factive experience seems to be what is valuable: From art to sports, from the pursuit of careers to the disinterested quest for knowledge, from puzzle solving to the pursuit of merely bodily pleasures,[23] something structurally similar to aesthetic experience seems to be at play. Moreover, the broader understanding of mental states allows us to

---

[22] Williamson makes a similar point.

[23] Elijah Millgram (*Practical Induction*, chapter 1) points out that we seem to have a similar attitude even toward our preferences for eating bread. One might not look kindly at an offer to invert one's preferences so that one forms a preference for Wonder Bread over fine Italian bread, even if it would probably be more cost-effective to have such preferences.

preserve the intuitive appeal of object-subjectivism as a constraint on possible objects of intentional pursuit. At the same time, it allows us to understand this same constraint in a way that deflects the usual criticisms against it, such as those generated by Nozick's experience machine. Of course, if the broad view of mental states is problematic on other grounds, these virtues of the conception are of no use. But if the question is whether a narrow or a broad conception of mental states has a better explanatory reach, these considerations should give some evidence in favor of the broader view.

But, of course, the success of the bootstrapping maneuver depends at least on whether there aren't further objections against object-subjectivism conceived in this manner. If object-subjectivism is true, it puts a rather substantive constraint on what we can legitimately conceive to be good. Now there might seem to be exceptions to this constraint. There arguably are cases in which something is of value but in which no aspect or property of anyone's mental life appears in the justification of its value. It is worth looking into two cases in which this seems to be true. First, one might think about the value one attaches to one's own bodily integrity. Although we might care about various aspects of our bodily integrity because of the way in which it is indispensable or contributes to the possibility of certain aspects of our mental lives, it seems that our concern about bodily integrity goes beyond its contribution to our mental lives. For instance, let us suppose that Frankie, a rather eccentric character, collects human fingertips. He is not, however, a violent person; he would never collect someone's fingertips by force. Instead, he offers to pay for them. Being wealthy, he can offer, say, $5,000 a fingertip. He also sees to it that his clients receive a prosthetic fingertip that is indistinguishable to the naked eye from the original item and also performs its functions just as well. The whole thing is done through a painless and quick procedure. Many of us would still find that there is something to be said against the proposal, despite its financial advantages. And even if we might end up accepting such a profitable proposal, we would surely experience a certain residual queasiness that indicates that we do not find parting with our fingertips to be on a par with parting with an old couch.

It is true that some people might not have any queasy feeling about it whatsoever; they might think that this is no different from selling the old couch for $5,000. But this will not help our defense of object-subjectivism because object-subjectivism rules out the possibility that *anyone should legitimately attach any value* to losing one's fingertip unless there is a justification for this attitude that appeals to the value of certain mental states. If no such justification were available, object-subjectivism would have to consider anyone who attaches any value to keeping her fingertip to be under an illusion. Of course, there are many ways in which we can try to justify this attitude in a way that is compatible with OS. We can say that one cannot but wonder what makes Frankie so attracted to fingertips or that we are afraid of a certain stigma attached to being the kind of person who sells fingertips to Frankie, for example. But I suspect that none of these answers will succeed in capturing what some might think is a reason not to let go of their fingertips. It is simply that we do not approve of one's body being used as if it were like any other marketable object.[24]

However, it is hard to see the general value of bodily integrity independently of the general value of personal (or animal) integrity – after all, we do not care much about the particular chemical composition of things such as human flesh. Thus, it is plausible to suppose that aspects or properties of our mental lives do figure in the justification of this form of value. Indeed, one might think that the fact that we are concerned about the bodily integrity of sentient beings (perhaps only of rational beings) lends support to the contention that a full account of the value of bodily integrity will rely on the value of some aspect of our mental lives, especially if our mental lives are broadly conceived.

This line of response, however, cannot be extended to apparently similar attitudes toward nonsentient forms of life and to the environment in general, and the value that some attach to them seems not to depend on features of the mental lives of sentient beings. In order to appreciate the full force of the objection, one needs to note that the objection does not depend on the view that our *obligations* to the environment can't be reduced to obligations to sentient beings or even the view that we have any obligations to the environment

---

[24] For similar ideas, see Elizabeth Anderson, *Value in Ethics and Economics*, chapters 7 and 8.

whatsoever. The objection depends solely on the possibility of legitimately taking an interest in the environment that is not justified in this manner. That is, it is enough that some people legitimately conceive of certain features of the nonsentient world as being good independently of the existence of any such justification. Must we indeed allow for this possibility? I am not sure. Think again about the planet Artx, but substitute a concern for certain features of the environment for a concern for art production. I am not sure that we can make any better sense of this concern. One might claim that concern for the environment is in general a concern for the earthly environment, but if this is true, it seems that object-subjectivism is in a good position to make sense of this concern because one plausible explanation for this restriction is the fact that the earthly environment but not others, at least as far as we know, is populated by sentient beings.

3.3 AUTHORITY-SUBJECTIVISM AND THE PROTAGOREAN APPROACH

We have closely investigated the plausibility of object-subjectivism. Boosting its case has so far only served to make authority-subjectivism look problematic. But as we look back to Mary's attitudes that seem to speak in favor of some kind of subjectivism, they speak, if anything, more strongly in favor of authority-subjectivism than of object-subjectivism. Contemporary subjectivism has taken authority-subjectivism to be *the* central requirement on the nature of value and practical reason, but there's a lot of disagreement on how contemporary subjectivists understand the nature of the requirement. First, there are two ways of understanding authority-subjectivism. Authority-subjectivism could be a claim that applies only to a subset of the proper objects of pursuit, or it could be an unrestricted claim about any putative good. Let us say that this is a matter of how *extensive* the authority of the subject would be in different versions of the view. At its most extensive, authority-subjectivism makes the unrestricted claim that what the agent judges to be good (partly) determines what is good for the agent. More restricted forms of authority-subjectivism will exempt certain kinds of good from this requirement. Most contemporary subjectivists would exempt nothing, or next to nothing, from this requirement.[25] But one might still accept that various goods fall under the scope of a constraint such as authority-subjectivism yet think that whether having friends and not having enemies is something worth pursuing or not is independent of whether the agent judges these things to be good. Also, some versions of authority-subjectivism will take the judgment of the agent to determine fully what is good for her, and others will take it to be just a necessary condition. What further conditions, if any, are necessary to make it the case that a certain object is good will determine how *unbridled* the theory considers the authority of the agent to be. The most unbridled version of authority-sub-jectivism will be the view that the agent's judgment *fully* determines what is good for her.[26] Finally, authority-subjectivism might have different views on whether what matters is how the agent actually judges or how she would judge under certain counterfactual conditions. One might think that what determines what is good for the agent is not what she actually thinks but what she would think if she were fully informed or had vivid information, for example. We can say that those are disputes regarding the *proper exercise* of the agent's authority. In its strongest, and as far as I know merely fictional, version, contemporary subjectivism would formulate the authority-subjectivism constraint in the following manner:[27]

(CS) For every X, X is good for the agent if and only if the agent judges X to be good for her.

Less extensive versions will restrict the scope of the quantifier, less unbridled versions will substitute "only if" for "if and only if" and add further conditions that determine what is good for the

[25] See, for instance, Gauthier, *Morals by Agreement*, and Donald C. Hubin, "What's Special about Humeanism." Some Kantian views seem to accept restricted versions of authority-subjectivism. Something like that seems to be underlying Korsgaard's views in her *The Sources of Normativity*.

[26] If one takes the preference level to be fundamental, there will be no way of making it merely a necessary condition. See on this issue David Sobel, "On the Subjectivity of Welfare." But this view is quite implausible, even if one thinks that, insofar as consistency is concerned, the rationality of the agent is assessed solely at the level of preferences.

[27] A version of authority-subjectivism that relies on judgments in counterfactual conditions is not, strictly speaking, a weaker version than one that relies on actual conditions.

agent, and versions that accept counterfactual conditions as determining the proper exercise of the agent's authority will substitute
"would judge" for "judges" and specify the appropriate conditions.
Because in its strongest form authority-subjectivism is incompatible
with object-subjectivism, the default position I will be discussing will
be a less unbridled and less extensive version of authority-
subjectivism that imposes some conditions of proper exercise.
However, to keep the discussion as general as possible, I will not
assume, unless otherwise noted, any specific restrictions on the
authority of the agent. At any rate, it will turn out that the best
version of the intuitions underlying authority-subjectivism is *not*
properly a version of CS. Once we do put forward a plausible version of the requirement, we can see that the scholastic view can
accommodate it quite well.

The appeal of authority-subjectivism appears most clearly when
we try to understand our general attitude toward certain optional
pursuits. Mary may put a lot of work into ensuring that she will drink
excellent coffee while reading the newspaper outdoors in the
morning. She subscribes to the paper, searches the Web for coffee
delivery services (being stuck somewhere in North America where
decent coffee cannot be bought in the streets but can be easily
ordered online), buys a top-of-the-line coffeemaker, and makes sure
that her balcony is agreeable and in working condition. In sum, the
activity can be a rather important part of her life. Of course, it would
not be as momentous for her as receiving the Nobel Prize or have
such widespread consequences for her as choosing a line of work,
but on the other hand, compared with the mundane concerns that
occupy most of our lives, it is a pretty significant project. The more
one thinks one can generalize from such cases, the less restricted the
version of authority-subjectivism one would be willing to defend.

If we are ready to think that there is nothing wrong in what Mary
is doing, we also do not think that our approval of her lifestyle
commits us to the claim that others ought to spend their mornings
the way Mary does or even to give some positive weight to adding
these goods to their lives. But, of course, this does not push us in the
direction of authority-subjectivism at all because this might merely
signal a difference in Mary's circumstances. As we said earlier, the
view that the different circumstances of a subject affect what she

should do is a view that no one would deny. Rather, what counts as evidence for authority-subjectivism is that the fact that Mary *takes it to be good for her* seems to be at least partly relevant to our considering it to be good for her. Our judgment is based on the authority of her judgment. There is no doubt that the case described is not peculiar in any way. Quite the opposite, it seems that much of importance in one's life has the characteristic that its goodness for the agent depends on the judgment that it is good.

Of course, there are many ways in which we can try to explain away this piece of evidence for authority-subjectivism. One might think, for instance, that our "forgiving" attitude toward Mary's conception of the good is just the result of our aversion to paternalism, not an endorsement of her evaluative attitudes. That is, when we say that all those things are "good for her," we are speaking imprecisely about our unwillingness to interfere with Mary's actions rather than expressing a high opinion of her reasons for action. Although it is probably true in many cases that we do say things like that, it's hard to make the case that this is true in all such cases. We can abstract from the issue of paternalism if we focus on how Mary, later in life when she no longer has these attitudes, looks back at how she conducted her life. She might think that many of the things she did were foolish, but it's hard to believe that for every case in which she no longer has the attitude, she should conclude that her pursuits were worthless. Being now only a social drinker when it comes to coffee, she might still think that it made sense to do what she did when coffee mattered so much to her and that there was nothing untoward about coffee mattering so much to her.

One might think that this is just a special case of privileged self-knowledge and that, as with perhaps many other cases of privileged self-knowledge, it can be explained by the fact that the agent has better, but not essentially different, access to the relevant pieces of information. Thus, one can say that when I say that "*X* is good for me" and my judgment carries authority, it carries merely evidentiary authority rather than constitutive authority. That is, my judging so is not the reason it *is* good for me but only the reason we can *reasonably believe* that it is good for me. No doubt, authority-subjectivism would be a constraint on the *nature* of the good rather than on our gathering knowledge about it, only if the authority in question were constitutive. One might even point out that, as we would expect if the authority were evidentiary but not constitutive, the authority is fallible. Someone might challenge my claim that, for instance, learning to appreciate classical music would be good for me or perhaps even that I enjoy a certain experience.

However, it is hard to escape the view that at least in certain cases the authority in question is constitutive. Some of these challenges are not so much challenges to my practical authority but to whether I am in a position of judging about the matter at all. The problem with the example of classical music is that what is primarily of value is not the music itself, as we pointed out, but the experience of it. Given that I have never had, or might at the moment be incapable of having, the appropriate experience, it is not clear that I am in the position to judge the matter. But, more importantly, at least in some cases, whether or not we are ready to dispute the agent's views of the matter, we still think that the good in question is good for the agent only on the condition that the agent judges it to be good. So to the extent that this view speaks against any form of authority-subjectivism, it speaks only against a version in which actual judgments are always considered to be proper exercises of the authority of the agent. For instance, suppose you insist that classical music is good for me. The scenario that we are envisaging is probably a case in which by coming to appreciate the music I form the judgment that this kind of experience is worth having. But suppose you found out that this scenario is not possible; no matter what you do to me, I will always think that there is nothing more to be said for the experience of listening to classical music than for listening to random noises. It would seem rather odd to insist that classical music is nevertheless good for me and thus that it is worthwhile for me to pursue these experiences.[28] Thus it seems more plausible to think that when one challenges the agent's authority in those cases, one is challenging whether this is a case of proper exercise of the authority or whether other conditions have been met, for example. All of this will speak against the stronger versions of authority-subjectivism but not against the weaker ones.

---

[28] No doubt, one can imagine cases in which this would be some kind of instrumental good.

Assuming thus that it is not an illusion that some goods are constitutively dependent on the exercise of the agent's judgment, how should one account for this feature of practical reason? The obvious way of doing so is to adopt what might be called a "Protagorean" approach. We can say that the constraint is the result of the fact that in the realm of values, man (in fact, each person) is the measure of all things (regarding what is good for him). The more straightforward explanation of these constraints is that there is nothing else for value to be other than what each person takes to be valuable – there is no other measure of value than the favorable (and unfavorable) attitudes we take toward some objects. I think this is the essence of most contemporary subjectivism. Of course, this kind of account will push us in the direction of a very strong form of authority-subjectivism and, as I pointed out, this might render it incompatible with object-subjectivism. However, it is not obviously[29] true that one could not impose further constraints on the conditions under which we can consider one's judgment genuine. At any rate, even if the Protagorean approach turns out to be incompatible with object-subjectivism, one might be tempted to reply "so much the worse for object-subjectivism" in view of the immense plausibility that many find in this approach. The plausibility of the approach no doubt derives from certain intuitions we have about the nature of our own authority regarding judgments of value and about what we should pursue. If the Protagorean approach is the best way of making sense of some well-founded and important intuitions, then we might think that, after all, we should reject OS in order to make room for those intuitions. But we should first investigate more closely whether the Protagorean approach is indeed the best way to accommodate these intuitions.

One way to represent the Protagorean approach is to say that each person arbitrarily picks some things to like and dislike or arbitrarily forms some preferences. The insertion of the word "arbitrarily" would probably not be welcomed by the Protagorean, and she would have to think that this signals a crude

[29] This qualifier is necessary because it is not clear that these requirements are not in the final analysis incompatible with the approach. See David Velleman, "Brandt's Definition of 'Good'," Connie Rosati, "Internalism and the Good for a Person," and the discussion that follows.

misrepresentation of her view. If we represent things as an arbitrary matter, it seems that we are saying something like "It is a matter of indifference whether one values A or B" or "It is a matter of indifference whether one prefers A over B." But it is hard not to read this as already expressing a particular evaluative stance toward A and B, namely the attitude of indifference. But even if the view that we form evaluative judgments arbitrarily does not imply a general attitude of indifference, it does seem to put the whole of practical reason in abeyance. If these attitudes are formed arbitrarily or on a whim, it is not clear why an agent should be *committed* to this attitude (that is, why the agent should pursue what she judges to be good rather than what she judges to be bad) or why the agent should guide her choices by her preference ordering than by the inverse ordering.[30] It is thus no surprise that Gauthier, for instance, talks about *considered* preferences as being the true measure of value and takes pains to reject the claim that considered preferences are formed arbitrarily:

> Subjectivism is not to be confused with the view that values are arbitrary. . . . Values are not mere labels to affix randomly or capriciously to states of affairs but rather are registers of our fully considered attitude to these states of affairs given our beliefs about them. Although the relation between belief and attitudes is not itself open to rational assessment, it is not therefore arbitrary.[31]

It is important for Gauthier, as for any other Protagorean view, to maintain that there could be no rational assessment of the evaluative attitudes we form in light of our beliefs under certain conditions. At the same time, Gauthier insists that these attitudes are not arbitrary. But how can this be so? After all, it seems that there is no rational assessment because there are no grounds for the agent's decision. If there were such grounds, we could check whether these grounds withstood scrutiny. But if there are no grounds for the decision, how could it be anything but arbitrary? The trick must be performed at least in part by the notion that they are fully considered. A fully

---

[30] This problem disappears if one accepts that preferences are fully revealed in action. But this approach also makes preferences useless for a theory of rationality. On this point, see Gauthier, *Morals by Agreement*. For a related point, see Simon Blackburn, "Practical Tortoise Raising."

[31] Gauthier, *Morals by Agreement*, p. 48.

considered preference for Gauthier is one that is "stable under experience and reflection."[32] One could say that such preferences are not just the results of whim but express what truly matters to us.[33]

It might be worth pondering briefly how these considered preferences are formed. That considered preferences or judgments, rather than any old preferences or judgments, are the measure of value is a quite reasonable constraint. It seems clear, for instance, that a judgment formed in the light of much experience and reflection should be taken more seriously than an attitude that can be read off from a rash and naïve decision. The question nonetheless is how we should make sense of this constraint in the context of a Protagorean position. In the Protagorean position, when Mary is reflecting about possibilities, what exactly is she reflecting about? Suppose she has to decide whether she would prefer to go on a vacation or save the money and skip a vacation this year. Let us look at two ways in which we can understand the point of her reflection. In the first case, we can think that she is reflecting about exactly what will happen if she decides one way or the other. She must consider carefully what else she could do with the money if she skipped the vacation. Had she made a rash decision, she might have overlooked various ways in which she could use the money to take various short trips on the long weekends and how this could make up for the lost vacation. Her lack of experience in high-season travel, on the other hand, might preclude her from realizing what it is like to be in a place when it is noisy and crowded. In short, we can think that the lack of reflection or experience ends up making some relevant information inaccessible to her. We could say that the consequences of her actions are not as clear to her as they should be. But if this is

---

[32] Gauthier, *Morals by Agreement*, p. 33. See also pp. 29–38.

[33] Gauthier might reject this characterization of the view because he often rejects the thought that we can talk about deeper "true" preferences that underlie our surface attitudes. For instance, he thinks that it makes no sense to talk about the Aztecs' "real" preferences as the ones they would have if their preferences were not formed in light of false beliefs about gods. However, I do not think that this characterization is incompatible with this point. At any rate, to the extent that this characterization is not available, it is harder to see why one should not count such preferences as merely arbitrary.

all there is to it, it can't help us explain why the decision is not arbitrary because this would just postpone the issue. After all, we said only that a less than fully considered preference would not take into account all the relevant factors, but the issue was about *how* the agent takes these considerations into account, not *which* considerations she takes into account. It might help to make this point if we think about preferences being formed by weighing various evaluative judgments. If Mary leaves the fact that she could take short trips out of the picture, she leaves something that she takes to be good out of consideration, and the preference that she forms is not a measure of what she values. If she does not know the vicissitudes of traveling in crowded places, the evaluative judgment she makes does not reflect what she values because her judgment does not have the appropriate content. But how does she make *these* judgments? Why does she give positive rather than negative weight to any vacation? Because the Protagorean is committed to thinking that these things are good because she judges them to be good, it seems that there are no grounds for this judgment and now no reason not to take it to express an arbitrary attitude. Of course, we could say that these judgments, although not rationally assessable, are not arbitrary either, if they are fully considered. But here the regress is all too obvious. One can also say that this is not an arbitrary judgment: A properly made judgment of this kind has to consider carefully whether its object is something that really matters to us. This leads us to the second way of understanding a considered preference.

We could say that what you are reflecting on when you form a preference is not (merely) what consequences you should expect from a certain course of action. Rather, you are also considering whether (and perhaps how) that course of action or its consequences really *matters* to you. This also seems quite intuitive. A rash decision might fail to express the value of a certain object for me not only because I failed to take a certain consideration into account but because I failed to give it proper weight. Suppose that during a sleepless night spent in front of the TV, I encounter a late-night ad for a uniquely designed bed that shows two people snoozing very comfortably, and the screen flashes a special price for those who call immediately. No doubt, the advertiser is trying to take advantage of the fact that at a rash moment, charmed by the view of such easy sleep, one might fail to consider properly how little one's life will be improved by a more comfortable bed (to say nothing about how likely it is that it will in fact be a more comfortable bed). If I go ahead and order the furniture, one may say that my judgment that doing so was the best course of action was not a properly considered judgment. But again this just postpones the problem. After all, whether something *matters* to me or not is itself an evaluative stance, and thus, according to the Protagorean view, it is my judgment that determines whether something matters to me or not. This might be obscured by the fact that among the things I consider is, for instance, whether it would be a pleasant experience and how pleasant it would be, to lie down comfortably in the new bed and not have to toss and turn a few times before falling asleep. Nonetheless, whether or not pleasure matters to an agent is, according to the Protagorean, a question of whether or not the agent takes the relevant evaluative stance toward it. The fact that this will be a pleasant experience is not necessarily connected to any evaluative judgment. Thus, considering whether some course of action will bring us pleasure or enjoyment is, under the Protagorean view, just like considering any other consequence of one's actions. Bringing these considerations into the account could not help the Protagorean solve the problems we encountered earlier.

One may protest that the whole discussion is misguided. It is misleading to talk about our *forming* these evaluative judgments or preferences; we just find ourselves having them. It's just part of being natural creatures of a certain kind that at certain stages of our lives we have these kinds of mental states that imply an evaluative attitude toward certain objects. No doubt, these mental states have a causal genesis, but whatever causal story we tell, what matters when one acts is that these are the attitudes one currently has.

One could say that the way we *form* preferences is irrelevant to their rationality. However, this thought cannot be endorsed by the approach in question. Whether a preference or an evaluative judgment is considered is a matter of how it is formed. Thus, we can only dispense with an examination of the process of preference formation if we are willing to give up the idea that we can distinguish between considered and nonconsidered preferences. But this will make a Protagorean approach much less attractive. On the other hand, one might think that one could distinguish considered from unconsidered preferences solely in terms of their causal genesis. One could then say that making sure that a preference or an evaluative judgment is considered is just making sure that there is no "noise" in the causal genesis of our preferences so that our preferences track what really matters to us. One might even think that this gives us exactly what we wanted: an explanation of why considered basic attitudes are not rationally assessable and yet nonarbitrary. They are just the preferences formed by the appropriate causal genesis.

However, this way of explaining the significance of considered preferences is not compatible with the Protagorean approach. The idea that some notion of "appropriate causal genesis" could underwrite the distinction between considered and unconsidered preferences would make sense only under the supposition that our preferences should "track" what really matters to us. In this picture, having the appropriate causal genesis would ensure that a preference is not the outcome of some short-circuiting in the agent's psyche but is rather the effect of the appropriate states of the agent. But, in the Protagorean view, our preferences are not supposed to be tracking anything, and consequently they are not supposed to be tracking what already matters to us. Quite the contrary, what matters to us should be a consequence of our basic preferences and evaluative judgments. In the end, this is the rub: It is hard to make sense of preference formation as anything but arbitrary if one's basic assumption is that nothing guides its formation. We fail to explain why we should care that we form preferences in a considered manner rather than in any other. If we are not trying to track anything and are not being guided by any ideal, how could it matter that we think hard about it? The same point will apply to any other constraints one tries to impose on preference formation. We can ask why we should care that we be particularly well informed in forming preferences.[34] It would be like making sure that we buy the most accurate map when our destination is "wherever we end up." We

---

[34] See, for instance, Hubin, "What's Special about Humeanism," and other works.

can also try to move from constraints in forming preferences to constraints about some features of how they are held. We can distinguish between stable preferences and preferences that are held for short periods of time. Again, it is not clear why the Protagorean would think that the longevity of a preference tracks its rational acceptability.

One may also protest that this mistakes the strategy employed by the Protagorean. The Protagorean might assert that even if the agent is the ultimate arbiter of the *content* of his preferences (or other evaluative attitudes), the agent is not the ultimate arbiter of the rationality of the *procedures* by which we determine which preferences count as *considered* preferences (or some similar evaluative attitude). Preferences formed according to such a procedure are not arbitrary exactly because they are formed according to rational procedures, or procedures that a rational agent ought to follow in forming preferences. Of course, one could claim that it makes no sense to have a rational procedure for forming preferences if one does not have an independent concept of a "correct" content – if preferences cannot be determined to be rational or irrational according to their content. But this would be to beg the question against the Protagorean. Why can't one defend the rationality of a procedure independently of its reliability in producing the right content?

It is important to see that this reply fails at different levels. First, the reply confuses two kinds of proceduralism. It is true (or at least not obviously false) that one can argue that in a certain field one "gets things right" as long as one follows the correct procedure. But here the idea is that at least part of the content of "getting things right" in this context is to follow a certain procedure. In the case of proceduralist accounts of distributive justice, the idea is that what matters in terms of distributive justice is not who ends up with different "bundles of good" but *the way in which* people end up with different bundles of good. What we should care about according to this view is fair procedures, not particular outcomes. However, there are two crucial (related) disanalogies between this kind of proceduralism and the Protagorean approach. First, although it might be true in the proceduralist view that any particular outcome is just or unjust depending on whether the procedure was or was not appropriately followed,[35] this is significantly different from the sense in which any particular preference can be rational as long as it is appropriately formed. In the case of procedural justice, the procedure actually determines the outcome; for each combination of possible applications of the relevant procedures, we get a determinate outcome (even if different combinations would result in different outcomes). However, in the case of considered preferences, it is not quite like that. The procedure does not determine anything. Different people (or the same person) could think long and hard about the same situation, examine carefully the same features, and form completely different preferences. In fact, the Protagorean approach is committed to the fact that any way one forms the preferences *after having followed* the procedure is equally rational. The analogous proceduralist view would be that a distribution would be just as long as one followed a procedure that left the outcome completely open; after following the procedure, one was still free to distribute the relevant goods in any way. There would not be much to be said for a proceduralist view of *that* kind.

This brings us to our next concern. In the proceduralist view in question, what matters is indeed the *procedure*. When justifying a system of justice of this kind, one can reasonably say that "it does not matter to us who gets what; what matters is that this outcome was arrived at by means of a fair procedure." It is easy to see the plausibility of a proceduralist position if the procedure itself is what matters to us or is at least a constitutive condition of the things that matter to us. But this is certainly not the case with preferences. If I want gumbo, then what matters for me is gumbo and not that I am choosing according to a preference formed in the appropriate way.

The Protagorean approach fails to make sense of what it seemed to be particularly well placed to explain. Because it is incapable of explaining the nature of the evaluative attitude in question, it can't a fortiori have an adequate account of its authority. This is not to say that the Protagorean approach does not have enough other advantages over other views to render this issue moot. The point of

---

[35] Although I imagine that many proceduralists would not endorse such a strong claim. It seems implausible to say that a distribution in which most people starve while a few use abundant food resources to pursue peculiar art forms could be just.

this discussion was just to show that we should not credit this approach, or subjectivism insofar as it relies on this approach, with a good account of this seemingly important feature of practical reason and value; the Protagorean approach cannot make sense of the normative authority of the agent.

3.4 IS CONSTITUTIVE AUTHORITY NECESSARY?

If the Protagorean approach fails by conceding too much for the sake of accommodating the agent's authority, other accounts of practical reason sin in the opposite direction. It is tempting to think of the agent's authority as being something less than constitutive authority. Indeed, cognitivist views of practical reason, exactly the views that are closest to the scholastic view, tend to balk at accepting any constitutive role for pro-attitudes. For instance, when dealing with the paradigmatic cases in which the agent's preferences seem to determine what is good for him, such as gastronomic preferences and preferences for light entertainment, for example, both Quinn and Scanlon argue that what matters is not what the agent desires but what he *enjoys*.[36] So, in their view, it is not my preference for beer over wine or my judgment that I would rather have beer that makes it the case that beer is better for me. It is the fact that I *enjoy* beer more than wine or, perhaps even better, that beer *tastes better* to me, that makes it the case that beer is better for me than wine. Smith has a similar proposal against the view that reasons are relativized to agents. According to Smith, that an agent has a certain preference can be a feature of his circumstances, and this feature can be relevant in determining what he has a reason to do. But, according to Smith, this does not show that there is something like a reason that is special to the agent in question or, to put it in the context of our discussion, a reason that is constituted by the normative authority of the agent.[37] If this view is correct, then when the agent forms an evaluative judgment, she is always trying to form a belief about an

---

[36] Quinn, "Putting Rationality in Its Place"; Scanlon, *What We Owe to Each Other*, p. 42.
[37] Smith, *The Moral Problem*, pp. 164ff.

authority-independent good. The agent's appetites, her likes and dislikes, might be among the relevant circumstances in determining whether something is good for her (or simply good). Because Smith has a more developed view on this issue, I'll focus on his account of the relevance of the agent's preferences. However, I think the problem is perfectly general and will also affect Quinn's and Scanlon's understanding of the apparent relevance of preferences and desires. But, at any rate, before I examine Smith's account in more detail, it is worth explaining in brief outline why I think Quinn's and Scanlon's accounts of the apparent relevance of these preferences are unsatisfactory. We can put the problem as a dilemma regarding how we understand "enjoy." On the one hand, "enjoying" is not conceptually connected to the agent's desire or evaluative judgments. In this sense, the agent can, for instance, enjoy eating ice cream without having any desire to eat it or without conceiving it to be good in any way. In this case, it seems that whether an agent has a reason to eat ice cream or whether ice cream is good for him will depend on whether or not he *wants* to eat ice cream and not on whether or not he enjoys it. On the other hand, enjoying could be such that one could not enjoy something without, at least while one enjoys it, desiring it or conceiving it to be good. In this case, the claim that what is good for me or what I have reason to do is dependent on what I enjoy is much more plausible, but it also *implies* the claim that what is good for me or what I have reason to do is dependent on my desires or evaluative attitudes.

Let us look more carefully at Smith's proposal. In his language, whether an agent has a normative reason to do something is determined by what a fully rational agent would desire in these circumstances. "What is desirable for us to do in circumstances C" (what we have normative reasons to do in C) is analyzed as "what we would desire that we do in C if we were fully rational."[38] The agent's own judgment about what she has normative reasons to do has in this view no special authority. However, the fact that, for instance, she finds the taste of beer more pleasant than the taste of wine

---

[38] Ibid., p. 152.

might be relevant in determining what a fully rational agent would
do under her circumstances:

What we have reason to do is relative to our circumstances, where our circumstances may include aspects of our own psychology. Suppose, for
example, that you and I differ in our preference for wine over beer. Preferring wine as you do, you may tell me that there is a reason to go to the local
wine bar after work for a drink, for they sell very good wine. But preferring
beer as I do, I may quite rightly reply, "That may be a reason for you to go to
the wine bar, but it is not a reason for me." ... The crucial point in this case
is that a relevant feature of your circumstances is your preference for wine,
whereas a relevant feature of my circumstances is my preference for beer.[39]

It is important to make clear what sort of thing a preference is
understood to be. If a preference is understood to be an evaluative
judgment, in Smith's language a judgment about what one has
normative reason to do, this sort of move is hopeless because evaluative judgments under Smith's views are just beliefs about what we
would desire in C if we were fully rational. Whether I actually have a
reason to drink wine in C is just, for Smith, a matter of whether I
would desire to drink wine in C. It seems hard to understand how
my perhaps false beliefs about what I would desire if I were fully
rational should affect what I would actually desire if I were indeed
fully rational. Thus, as long as one endorses my view that preferences could be nothing other than evaluative judgments, one's
actual preferences cannot be relevant in determining what one
would desire if one were fully rational. Of course, Smith himself
does not endorse this view about preferences, and I take it that he
understands the preference here as being my *motivation* in the
situation in question rather than my evaluation. Motivations or
desires are supposed to receive, according to Smith, a dispositional
analysis; they are to be understood as dispositions to act in light of
certain beliefs,[40] rather than beliefs about what one would desire if
one were fully rational. However, this analysis of preference provides a satisfactory account of the phenomenon only if we think that
the relevant circumstances can always be understood in terms of
motivation rather than evaluation. The question is how we should

[39] Ibid., p. 170.
[40] Ibid., section 4.6.

understand the agent's authority when we are trying to accom-modate our intuitions to the effect that the agent has authority over what is good for her (or, in Smith's language, what she has reason to do). If we accept for a moment this distinction between behavioral dispositions (motivational states) and evaluative beliefs, we can raise the question of whether the authority of the agent should be cashed out in terms of the contribution of her behavioral dispositions in determining what is good for her or in terms of the contribution of her evaluative beliefs in determining what is good for her. Given what was said earlier, Smith's proposal is committed to the latter being the case. It is then worth examining whether we can give a proper account of the authority of the agent solely in terms of the contribution of her behavioral dispositions toward the determina-tion of what is good for her or what she has reason to do.

It might seem at first that we can. Let us take, for instance, a case in which Larry finds himself to be more motivated to drink beer than wine, but he thinks that this shows something crass about his personality. Not wanting others to realize that he is that kind of person, he thinks that there is good reason for him to drink wine. Thinking that his crass inclinations should not be indulged, Larry thinks that there is no reason to drink beer. In order not to intro-duce further complications about Larry's motivations, we can assume that, to his chagrin, this evaluative judgment fails to muster any motivation to drink wine. He feels awful about that, but he always ends up giving in to his desire to drink beer.

I must confess I'm not sure what to say about this kind of example; it seems overall congenial to Smith's line. Our assessment of what Larry should do in this situation seems to depend solely on his motivation to drink beer and not at all on his judgment that he ought to drink wine. In fact, we probably would not give much weight to the fact that Larry thinks that there is most reason to drink wine in this situation in assessing what he actually has reason to do. We might even conclude that he is lucky that his misguided judgment does not issue in any motivation; he is fortunate enough to act as he should despite being mistaken about what he should do.[41] Of course, it is

---

[41] We would judge this to be a case of inverted *akrasia*. See Nomy Arpaly, "On Acting Rationally Against One's Best Judgment."

possible that we would come to agree with Larry on his views about beer-drinking motivation. But even if this were the case, this would not show that we take his judgment to be relevant; what it would show is that we agree in this case with the *content* of his judgment.

Moreover, Larry makes a bad judgment that is not a "purely" evaluative judgment because crass is a "thick" evaluative concept. The idea that beer drinking is a sign of a crass personality seems to have some false descriptive content, too. Thus, we have to be careful when drawing conclusions here because the false descriptive content might be what is leading us to disregard Larry's evaluative position. And, indeed, when we try to look at cases in which this aspect is absent, we can see that the solution does not generalize; there are also cases in which what matters, at least to some extent, is the judgment.

Take, for instance, Mary and Sue. They both find they are disposed to act in a certain way: Whenever they see a tall natural body, they are disposed to climb it. Mary and Sue form different opinions of the value of such actions. Mary is happy that she has such a disposition because she thinks there is something quite valuable in the activity in which she is disposed to engage. Mary thinks that mountain climbing is an enriching experience, as well as a chance to challenge oneself in the face of sublime nature. She takes up mountain climbing wholeheartedly and happily indulges her "natural" disposition to climb. Sue, on the other hand, finds the whole thing incredibly pointless, a serious waste of time. She thinks that she should try to dispose herself to act in less pointless ways than going up a pile of dirt, despite the fact that she often finds it hard to muster the motivation to engage in any other activity when she is facing the prospect of climbing up a mountain. Often, she akratically indulges in mountaineering, but she also sometimes just "gives in" and climbs up mountains for more or less the same reason an addict might give in and procure the object of his addiction: There might be no better way to deal with the craving. Now it seems to me that in this case we will want to say that Mary has a reason to climb up mountains but Sue does not,[42] or at the very least we can claim that the fact that Sue does not find this activity valuable should be

---

[42] At least not a noninstrumental reason. Climbing up the mountain might turn out to be the best means to her end of not being bothered by these impulses.

given some weight in considering the force of the reason each of them has. But even this weaker claim requires that we see Mary's evaluation as constitutive of what she has reason to do, or what is good for her. Thus, Smith's analysis does not seem to be able to capture the intuitions that lead us to find plausibility in some form of authority-subjectivism.

We can summarize the problems of accounting for authority-subjectivism as follows: If we place too much emphasis on the role of the subject in constituting value, in particular if we take the agent's judgment to be the ultimate source of value, we cannot make sense of how the agent forms this judgment. In particular, we cannot understand how the agent can take herself to be expressing what really matters to her rather than just arbitrarily settling for one thing rather than another. On the other hand, if we focus our attention on the object of choice, on the fact that the object of choice was indeed good, we can never find a proper place for the authority of the agent. Of course, one could propose a middle ground, a mixed view in which both the independent merits of the object and the authority of the subject combine to give us the proper value. No doubt, something like this must be correct. But, on the other hand, we need to do more than combine the two if we wish not just to accumulate the problems of both views. After all, if the object has independent merit, why shouldn't this settle the issue? And if the agent's endorsement is a requirement, why should there be other requirements? What we need is an account in which both sides combine into a coherent picture of a form of evaluation. This is exactly what the scholastic view can provide, or so I shall now argue.

3.5 AUTHORITY-SUBJECTIVISM AND SELF-REFERENTIAL APPEARANCES

How could the scholastic view account for the authority of the agent? The scholastic view can actually allow for two ways in which things may appear good to us, or be endorsed as such, that will introduce this kind of authority. To see how this works, let us start from a straightforward evaluative appearance (EA):

(EA) From perspective p, X appears to be good.

In order for this to become a judgment that X is good, it needs to be endorsed in an evaluative judgment. But the endorsement need not be unconditional. One way in which the goodness of X will be partly constituted by the agent's evaluative attitude is the case in which the agent's endorsement of this appearance depends on the fact that things do indeed appear to the agent in this way. In this case, the endorsement can be represented as having the following form:

(a_1) X is in fact good (or valuable) only insofar as the relevant perspective and appearance are available to the agent (insofar as one experiences X as appearing to be good).

Let us call a reflective endorsement that instantiates this form a "conditioned endorsement of X as good." A conditioned endorsement would be involved in cases in which I think that the good in question is such that it should be part of someone's general conception of the good only if she desires it and while she desires it. Realizing that I no longer desire to attend high school reunions, I might conclude that, in this case, attending them should no longer be part of my general conception of the good, while still accepting that it should have been part of my general conception of the good while I did desire to go to these reunions.

The second way in which the agent's evaluative attitudes might be partly constitutive of the goodness of an object is that the goodness of the object is conceived to be conditioned by appearance. However, in this second case, it is not only on reflection that we impose this condition, but the condition is part of how things appear to us in the first place. In this case, we would have an essentially self-referential appearance that can be represented in the following way:

(a_2) From perspective p, it appears that enjoying X is good.

"Enjoying X" is understood here to be partly constituted first by X obtaining. As our earlier discussion of OS suggests, we should not identify experiences in which I am in fact aware of X and experiences in which I am simply under an illusion of X. Second, the value of "enjoying X" is partly constituted by the fact that X appears to me to be good in this very experience. We can represent this self-referring aspect of the appearance by saying that "it appears that enjoying X is good" requires that the following be true:

> It appears that X is good only if it appears so (only if I am (one is) in the kind of mental state that I am right now in which X appears to be good).

This might seem an overintellectualized attitude, but the content simply conveys the fact that for certain things we enjoy we don't think that there would be value in pursuing a certain object even if we were not to enjoy experiencing this object. This notion of enjoyment, however, allows that our gaze is, so to speak, toward the object itself and not toward our desire for the object.[43] If I enjoy climbing mountains, I conceive the state of affairs of my climbing a mountain itself to be good, not just my enjoyment. But I think at the same time that climbing a mountain would be pointless if I did not enjoy it. And, of course, here, too, reflection could endorse or fail to endorse the content of the appearance.

What exactly is the difference between cashing out the agent's authority by means of (a_1) or (a_2)? Can either of them appropriately capture the agent's authority in the practical realm? Let us start by looking at some of the advantages, as well as problems, that both share. Because the condition, in both cases, is a condition of how it appears to the agent, the grounds on which one ultimately judges X to be good depend on a putative *judgment* rather than a mere experience. It is not an unqualified mental state that is made the condition of something having value but a mental state that already expresses an evaluative attitude toward its object. Thus these formulations make the agent's desires into constitutive conditions of the good: The agent's putative judgments are indeed the conditions of X being good. At the same time, the evaluative attitude is one in which the object appears to be good and thus one in which the agent is open to an independent putative (even if conditioned or conditional) value. Also, neither formulation is incompatible with object-subjectivism. In fact, in (a_2) what appears to be good is the enjoyment.

In both cases, it is the appearance, not the judgment, that conditions the goodness of the object. But this is as it should be. As we

---

[43] See Brewer, "The Real Problem with Internalism about Reasons."

saw when discussing the proposal based on Smith's view, we might think that one's reflective rejection of an object the value of which one is capable of appreciating is misguided. Even if one considers that aesthetic experiences are valuable (or perhaps are possible) only for those who can appreciate art (in our language, to whom art *appears* good), one need not think that someone who rejects those appearances on the basis of religious enthusiasm has no good reason to enjoy art or that enjoying art would not be good for her.

On the other hand, it seems that both (a₁) and (a₂) face the same problem as the Smith proposal when it comes to the mountain climbing example. After all, it seems that mountain climbing appears in the same way both to Mary and Sue and thus that they have the same grounds for endorsing the view. However, the situation is not quite the same. First, it does not follow from the fact that Mary and Sue share a certain behavioral disposition[44] that they share the same appearance of the good because a scholastic view is not committed to a dispositional account of desire. This reply can only take us so far because it seems that we have no reason so far to deny that, prior to reflection,[45] mountain climbing appeared to be good to both of them in exactly the same way. As we discussed in the previous chapter, forming a judgment involves moving from appearances of the good to an "all-out" judgment of what is good by means of various kinds of inferences. Let us suppose we simply infer the judgment "straight" from the appearance:

(a) From p, X appears to be good.

Thus

(b) X is good.

When assessing whether the inference is warranted, we might come to the conclusion that the inference is merely permissible but not mandatory. In this case, we do get the kind of authority-subjectivism that relates to judgment. That is, when an inference is permissible, making the appropriate judgment is necessary and

---

[44] I do not mean to deny that some sophisticated understanding of disposition might discriminate quite finely among dispositions. My point is that this issue does not even arise for the scholastic view.

[45] Of course, the idea that we can specify how mountain climbing appears to them prior to any reflection is an idealization.

sufficient to determine that the object is good. The object will be correctly included in one's general conception of the good if and only if one judges that it is good. But to say that an object is correctly included in the agent's conception of the good is no different from saying that the object is good for the agent. Thus, we get the desired result; the agent's judgment that the object is good for her is a condition of the object being in fact good for the agent. It is important to note here that the point is not that the judgment, under these conditions, is permissible, and thus an agent should not be accused of irrationality even if the judgment turns out to be in some other way defective. This might be the correct way of understanding permissible judgments in the face of ambivalent evidence in theoretical reason (assuming there is such a thing). One might think that in light of the difficulty of interpreting weather patterns, it is permissible, though not mandated, for one to believe that it will rain in the next day. Of course, this does not mean that one's judgment settles what *will* be the case, whether it will actually rain or not. Even if the agent who makes this inference is blameless and not lacking in epistemic acumen, she ends up with a false belief. However, in the case of practical reason, there is no room left for one's permissible judgment to stop short of its target. The permissibility in this case is permissibility to be *included* in one's conception of the good, and thus what one judges to be good in this case is rendered good for him or her.

But doesn't this proposal suffer from the same ills that affected Gauthier's view? After all, we argued that Gauthier leaves the agent with no grounds to prefer one thing over the other and thus has to consider any such judgment as arbitrary, as something such that it would be hard to see how it could matter to the agent. But once we introduce the possibility of merely permissible inferences, it seems that a similar problem will surface here. After all, on what grounds does the agent decide whether or not to make a permissible inference? However, this obliterates an important difference between the two pictures. Suppose that a permissive rule of inference leads one from p to q. An agent α who moves from p to q accepts q on exactly those grounds: p and the rule of inference. An agent β who accepts p but does not move to q finds these grounds insufficient. To say that the inference is permissible is to say that neither α nor β is in a

position such that proper use of the rational powers of the other
agent would guarantee that the other agent would come to accept
α's or β's position. This is to accept not that their position is
groundless but only, to use Rawls's phrase, that there is the possibility of reasonable pluralism.

However, one might protest that this presents us with a disjointed
account of what might seem to be a unified phenomenon; the
constitutive authority of the agent turns out to be expressed in two
quite independent ways in which the good may depend on one's
evaluative judgments. The constraint of authority-subjectivism is
captured by presenting first a feature of certain appearances of the
good and they accounting for those cases that escape this net by
means of considerations regarding the formation of an overall
conception of the good. But we do seem to treat different cases
differently. In the case of Larry, we found that we should not
invariably follow the agent's judgment; this was not true in the
example of Mary and Sue. Independently of how the scholastic view
accounts for such cases, it seems that *there are* two different ways in
which our evaluative attitudes can be constitutive of the good.
Moreover, to treat them as a unified phenomenon can give rise to a
rather pernicious confusion. If we look back at Smith's proposal, we
can see that he must be focusing on cases in which we have a conditional appearance and failing to take into account the cases in
which the judgment is sufficient to determine the object as good.
And we might think that part of the appeal of Protagorean views
comes from sliding from one case to another. By thinking of cases in
which we have a conditional appearance, we get the sense that the
agent's desire is necessary – there is no reason to force good wine on
someone who can't appreciate it. By thinking of cases in which an
inference is permissible, we get the sense that the judgment of the
agent is sufficient. Not marking out these distinctions might lead us
to think that there is a certain evaluative attitude of the agent that is
by itself both necessary and sufficient to determine value for her.
And this is exactly the Protagorean view.

But one may want to ask precisely what the difference is between
(a_1) and (a_2), or, better, what would be the difference between an
object being conditionally endorsed to be good and being the object
of a self-referential conditional appearance. The difference lies in

whether the condition attaches to the appreciation of the object itself or to the legitimacy of a certain way of appreciating the object. In the second case, the good in question will typically involve the good of experience. If we hearken back to our discussion of object-subjectivism, we can see that the possibility of conditional appearances, rather than being incompatible with object-subjectivism, meshes well with this constraint. We said that our version of object-subjectivism was particularly well placed to make sense of the values of experiences that involved appreciation. But it is exactly for the cases in which one could not value the object if one did not value the experience of appreciating (or "valuing") the object that it is most plausible to think that the good in question is the endorsement of a conditional appearance. If someone were indifferent to the experience of appreciating art there could not be much value in his confronting an artistic object. It is also no surprise that when we try to justify our evaluative judgments in these areas, we often appeal to features of our experiences ("It was awe-inspiring," "It hurts one's ears," "It is positively nauseating," "It is such a thrilling experience," "It feels like being a child again," etc.). This is significantly different from cases in which a good is conditionally endorsed in accordance with (a_1). These are cases in which we have what we could call "optional goods." They are cases in which the move from an appearance to the reflective endorsement depends on the fact that things appear to me in a certain way. So it may be important to me to make sure that I am in touch with all my extended family, without thinking that someone who does not desire this end should pursue it anyway or even that it would be advisable for someone who does not desire this to try to develop an interest in this kind of family activity.[46]

It might be worth asking whether authority-subjectivism, in either form, presents a constraint similar to the one presented by object-subjectivism. It is not clear how the constraint would relate to a_1. It seems simply true that our judgment is constitutive in this way in

---

[46] Some cases are more complicated. I might take the good itself not to be optional but the particular *weight* I give to it optional. So one might think of the extent of one's commitment to the project of finding the cure for cancer as optional while thinking that it is not optional for one to judge as valuable that a cure for cancer be found.

certain cases or that some inferences of this kind are permissible but not obligatory. On the other hand, it is not hard to construe a similar constraint with regard to self-referring appearances. It would read like this:

> (AS) Anything that we can legitimately conceive to be good must be such that either (a) it is the object of a self-referring appearance or (b) one can justify conceiving it to be good by showing that it bears a certain (appropriate) relation to the object of a self-referring conditional appearance.

Is this a plausible constraint? I believe it is. Note that, just as in the case of the constraint generated by object-subjectivism, there is no claim here that one needs to appeal to *one's own* evaluative attitudes in justifying that a certain object can be legitimately conceived of as good. Also, this formulation does not imply that we must appeal to how things *actually* or *currently* appear to a certain agent. One may justify a certain course of action because it would make it the case that certain things will appear good to an agent (so one may recommend that one start to go swimming even when one does not enjoy it because this way one will *learn* to appreciate swimming). We can put the intuition behind this idea in a rather coarse manner by saying that there isn't much point in living a life in such a way that one doesn't see the point of living this way. I believe that a full defense of this intuition would require a defense of a conception of autonomy that goes beyond the scope of this book. So, for our purposes, we'll just accept this constraint as a plausible, defeasible one.

4

The Objective Nature of Practical Reason

I hope to have shown that the scholastic view can accommodate "subjectivist" intuitions quite well. In the sense that it is correct to say that values or reasons are subjective, the scholastic view can endorse this conclusion. Is there any sense, however, in which practical judgments are objective? Just as in the case of "subjective," there are many things that one could mean in saying that values are objective or that one is committed to objectivity in the practical realm. The aim of this chapter is to understand how various notions of objectivity can have application in the practical realm and how these notions can be understood within the framework of the scholastic view. The chapter will not show that any particular practical judgment is (or fails to be) objective; it merely explains what it is to make claims of objectivity and correctness in the practical realm.

I start by examining how understanding the difference between beliefs and desires, and theoretical and practical attitudes more generally, in terms of the different formal ends of theoretical and practical reason can help us understand notions of objectivity in the practical realm. In particular, I want to argue that although the difference in formal ends is an important difference between practical and theoretical reason, the structural analogy between both fields allows us to use notions of theoretical objectivity to guide our understanding of what kinds of objectivity are possible in the practical realm. The following sections engage in that project.

Taking our lead from theoretical reason, we try to define various ways in which appearances of the good and evaluative judgments can be said to have objective purport.

It is worth noting that there are many distinctions to be made among various senses of "objectivity" or "correctness." I do not claim that the discussion here will be exhaustive, but by the end of the chapter we will see that the scholastic view is well equipped to explain what counts as classifying practical attitudes as objectively correct or incorrect in various important senses.

4.1　FORMAL ENDS AND OBJECTIVITY

Philosophers often try to account for what distinguishes beliefs from desires in terms of Anscombe's notion of direction of fit.[1] The idea is that whereas our beliefs are supposed to "fit" or "match" the world, the world is supposed to "fit" our desires. In the case of beliefs, if there's a mismatch between the world and our beliefs, our beliefs ought to be, or tend to be, changed. However, in the case of a mismatch between the desires and the world, the change ought to (tends to) happen to the world; we should (tend to) bring about changes in the world in accordance with our desires.[2] For our purposes, this characterization is at best incomplete; in particular, it does not tell us anything about how to assess more generally whether the practical attitudes themselves can be correct or incorrect. Moreover, there's no reason to think that a state of affairs is good or bad in any way just because it happens to satisfy or not satisfy someone's desire.

I will put forward instead the account of the difference between practical and theoretical attitudes that comes naturally from endorsing the scholastic view, namely an account in terms of the different formal ends of theoretical and practical attitudes in guiding us from appearances to an all-out conception of the truth or the good. If we understand the differences between practical attitudes in these general terms, we can understand questions of objectivity in

---

[1] See *Intention*, p. 56ff.

[2] For a recent attempt to give more precise content to the metaphor of direction of fit, see Smith, *The Moral Problem*, chapter 4. For a more normative understanding of the metaphor, see Nick Zangwill, "Direction of Fit and Normative Functionalism."

practical reason analogously to questions of objectivity in theoretical reason, and we can just ask what changes to our understanding of objectivity correspond to changes in our formal ends.[3] Of course, I do not mean to imply that questions of objectivity are clearly formulated and fully understood in the realm of theoretical reason. But there is more agreement there on what the issues are, and we can profit from trying to understand how various questions about objectivity and correctness can be raised in the realm of theoretical reason.

Let us first distinguish between an "all-out" state and a "prima facie" state in general. Belief is an "all-out" state in the theoretical realm. A belief *that p* represents one's unconditional theoretical stance toward *p*; for this reason, believing *that p* is incompatible with believing *that not p*. There is no further state of, say, "really, I mean it, believing *that p*" for which the belief *that p* provides prima facie grounds. We can contrast believing with "having it appear (to me) *that p*"; having it appear (to me) *that p* is a prima facie "version" of a belief *that p*. In the absence of countervailing evidence or any reason to think that the appearance is illusory, being in such a state will lead the subject to form the belief *that p*. Similar things can be said about desire and action (or intention) in the realm of practical reason.

The scholastic view claims that theoretical and practical inquiry should be distinguished in terms of their formal ends, the true and the good. In particular, one might want to say that, in theoretical inquiry, prima facie attitudes are (should be) taken up in all-out attitudes insofar as the agent accepts (should accept) that the content represents how things are (the truth), whereas, in practical inquiry, prima facie attitudes are (should be) taken up in all-out attitudes insofar as the agent accepts (should accept) that the content represents what he or she is to do (the good). The scholastic view can now treat the question of objectivity in practical inquiry in a way very similar to the way that we would treat it in theoretical inquiry; we would like to know how well grounded our all-out conclusions are. This will depend on how well grounded our prima

---

[3] Elsewhere I argue that notions of direction of fit collapse into the understanding of the distinction between practical and theoretical attitudes proposed here. See my "Direction of Fit and Motivational Cognitivism."

facie attitudes are and on the soundness of our inferential steps. Similarly, we can introduce a general notion of semantic adequacy that would cover both realms. In both realms, we could ask whether well-grounded attitudes must be, or are highly likely to be, semantically adequate. "Truth" marks semantic adequacy in the theoretical realm, whereas "goodness" marks semantic adequacy in the practical realm.

4.2 OBJECTIVITY IN PRIMA FACIE ATTITUDES

There are two different questions that I want to ask with regard to the commitment to objectivity. Let us start with a minimal notion of objectivity, or what I will call "minimal objective purport," regarding judgments. In the theoretical realm, questions of objectivity will be intimately related to questions of truth. However, as we have seen, the relevant notion in the practical realm is not "true" but "good." It might sound awkward to talk about the goodness of a judgment, but this is in part because we think of judgment in theoretical terms, as the endorsement of a certain content typical of a belief. So to say that an agent judges *that p*, in this sense, would imply at least that the agent believes *that p*. Talk of the "goodness" of a judgment understood this way would indeed typically be out of place.[4] We can think that this notion of a theoretical judgment is the notion of the appropriate conclusion of theoretical reason. When I arrive at a certain view of a theoretical matter, I form a judgment with a certain content, and the judgment in question is typically a belief. Extending the notion of judgment to the practical realm, a judgment would be the conclusion of practical reason. I have argued elsewhere that the conclusion of practical reason is an action,[5] and we certainly can talk about an action being good or failing to be good. The alternative view is to think that the conclusion of practical reason is an intention.[6] But even if one accepts the latter view, it is obviously unproblematic to think that what one intends can be good or fail to be good.

---

[4] "Typically" but not "always," because we can evaluate judging or believing as an activity like any other.
[5] See my "The Conclusion of Practical Reason."
[6] Robert Audi, *Practical Reasoning*, pp. 93ff.

With this generalized understanding of "judgment" in mind, we can say that a judgment is capable of being *objectively correct* (or incorrect) or of having *minimal objective purport* just in case making the judgment doesn't guarantee the adequacy of its content. Note that evaluative judgment here is the judgment that a certain content is good, a judgment manifested in one's intentional actions. This is to be distinguished from a belief that the content of practical judgment should be judged to be good[7] or the belief that one has made such an evaluative judgment. One can think that one is often unaware of one's evaluative judgment and thus capable of making mistakes in judgment about *what they are* (I might mistakenly think that my giving money to charity was done with the intention of helping others) and yet deny that there are objective evaluative judgments. We can also extend the notion of minimal objective purport so that not only judgments but also appearances can have minimal objective purport. We can say that an appearance has minimal objective purport if it is such that its endorsement in a judgment does not by itself secure the adequacy of the content of the judgment. So an appearance can have objective purport even if one rejects it or finds it illusory; indeed, there would be no reason to find it illusory if it didn't have objective purport.

This notion of minimal objective purport aims to capture the idea that a certain attitude toward a content can be correct or incorrect, or at least misleading, independent of the agent's actual attitudes toward the content. However, what we have so far is a rather trivial sense of "objective purport," and it is unclear that any appearances, theoretical or practical, could fail to have minimal objective purport. Perhaps judgments that express illocutionary acts that have no felicity conditions (assuming that there are such judgments) would fit the bill. So, if to express the judgment "I assert that I believe in Santa Claus" is enough for me to have made such an assertion, then judgments of the form "I assert *that p*" have no objective purport.[8]

---

[7] More on this distinction in chapter 7.

[8] Perhaps this is the closest case we have to my making the judgment sufficing for its truth. I am not sure that there are any felicity conditions to such a speech act that go beyond the conditions for my making a judgment. Of course, if I say the words in ignorance of their meaning, one can plausibly say that I did not make an assertion. However, it is not clear that in this case the sounds I utter express a judgment either.

However, even this very minimal notion of objective purport allows us to draw some important distinctions. First, the notion of minimal objective purport is distinct from semantic notions such as having truth-conditions, even if we generalize that notion to apply to the practical sphere (by means of a notion of, say, "good-conditions"). The judgment "I assert that I believe in Santa Claus" obviously has truth-conditions; indeed, it might be correct to say that it always comes out *true* if it occurs unembedded in a judgment of mine, but it does not have even minimal objective purport. Moreover, even if certain appearances or judgments have no minimal objective purport, it might still be true that they are subject to criticism. Even if my judging that I assert something guarantees the semantic adequacy of this judgment, there might be other questions to be raised about when it is rational to make a certain assertion. However, the notion of objective purport is clearly related to questions about the rationality of the judgment in question. Indeed, one might argue that even if judgments of the form "I assert *that p*" do not have objective purport, the fact that assertion is subject to rational criticism can be understood only by means of the relation of assertion to other attitudes that do have objective purport. Insofar as (sincere) assertion is assertion of what one believes, one can criticize assertion inasmuch as one can criticize beliefs; and beliefs, no doubt, have objective purport. And insofar as assertion is an action, one can criticize assertion if the intention embodied in the action fails to have an object that is good as its content, as long as the relevant intentions do have objective purport.

Finally, the commitment to objective purport is not obviously connected to any metaphysical commitment. One might think that some metaphysical commitments, spurious or legitimate, must accompany any commitments to objective purport. But one doesn't get this implication for free out of the notion of objective purport; one needs to do some philosophical work to show that this is the case.

At any rate, beyond these kinds of performatives, it is hard to see how anything could fail to have objective purport. Take, for instance, a theoretical judgment such as "I like ice cream" or an evaluative judgment to the effect that ice cream is good for me. Few people would like to admit much fallibility with respect to such judgments, but even fewer people should claim *no* fallibility. No matter how transparent one thinks one's mental states are, one would not want to say that *under no conditions* can one be mistaken about one's likings. No matter how much one insists that, when it comes to ice cream, one should accept that there is nothing beyond the old maxim *"chacun a son gout,"* one should not conclude that there are *no* conditions under which one judges that ice cream is good (or even just valuable) without it being so. If I am confused about what ice cream is or tastes like, if I am drunk, or if I am suffering from some kind of imaginative failure with respect to the consumption of dairy products, my pronouncements about liking it do not warrant the conclusion that ice cream is something that I actually like or something that is good or valuable for me.

However, as should be clear from our discussion of contemporary subjectivism in the previous chapter, one can accept all this and think that there is a stronger sense of "objective purport" in which there is no objective purport to these judgments. After all, at least under certain conditions, my judgment will determine whether or not I like ice cream. A stronger notion of objective purport should incorporate the fact that my judgment might fail to be authoritative for reasons that have little to do with the fact that it aims at getting things right. Something like the following would give us a more significant notion of objective purport:

> A judgment has objective purport (*sans phrase*) if and only if it can fail to be adequate even when the following conditions obtain: (a) The agent judges in conditions that are compatible with the agent nonaccidentally making a judgment whose content is adequate; and (b) the judgment is not inconsistent with other judgments the agent makes.

The rejection of contemporary subjectivism rules out the possibility of claiming that all evaluative judgments lack objective purport. But it still leaves the following questions unanswered: Do all evaluative appearances and judgments have objective purport? Are there any distinctions between ways in which various evaluative judgments (such as ethical or prudential judgments) can be considered objective? Moreover, a judgment or appearance can be objective without being universally valid. The *definiens* of "objective purport" given earlier could be satisfied by a particular agent without implying anything about how other agents should judge. We might also want to ask under what conditions, if any, an appearance or judgment would be universally valid.

These are the questions that I will try to answer in this chapter. However, it is important to keep in mind that much of the chapter is noncommittal: My main interest is to see how much conceptual space the scholastic view leaves for practical objectivity. I will thus be less concerned with the question of how much of this conceptual space is actually occupied.

4.3   OBJECTIVITY IN VALUE AND IN APPEARANCES PER SE

As we remarked before, the theoretical and the practical realms are not entirely parallel. In particular, practical reasoning involves comparison in ways that are radically different from comparison in theoretical reason. It makes sense to say that although A is valuable, B is better than A. No similar sense of "truer" is available in theoretical reason. One might think that a notion of plausibility would play a similar role, but it is important to note the differences. Suppose that I consider certain evidence e to lend some plausibility to p, but I also think that the evidence for q is better and that p and q are incompatible. Although I think that in light of e, p is plausible, I also think that in light of all available evidence, I should believe q. Now it is not true that I am also committed to the view that if the evidence favoring q were no longer available, or if it turned out to be false, then p would be *true*. I might be committed to believing that in that case it would be rational to believe p, but nothing beyond that. Moreover, I am not even committed to believing that if q weren't true, p would have been true. Suppose I have some evidence that makes it plausible to suppose that Larry murdered Jones. However, my evidence for supposing that Jones was murdered by Mary is conclusive; in light of this evidence, I form the belief that Mary murdered Jones. Suppose further that there is no further evidence that links anyone to Jones's murder. It certainly does not follow from any of this that I am committed to either of the following:

(a) Had it not been plausible to believe that Mary murdered Jones, then it would be true that Larry murdered Jones.
(b) If Mary hadn't murdered Jones, then Larry would have murdered Jones.

In the practical counterpart to this case, however, finding *A* valuable does commit one to thinking that if one were not to judge *B* to be good, one should judge *A* to be good. Given that practical reason has this nature, we can distinguish between two ways in which practical reason might have objective purport:

1. Commitments to what is valuable in one's conception of the good have objective purport.
2. Evaluative judgments have objective purport.

It's important to keep these two kinds of objectivity apart if we want to keep the effect of a common observation in perspective. Some of us bike, some of us climb mountains, some of us enjoy reading, some of us strive for routine and safety, and some of us seek novelty and adventure. Given all this colorful variety of human behavior (that one would be hard-pressed not to count as reasonable), one would expect severe limits on how far a conception of the good can aspire to objectivity. Now to some extent this is taken care of by our notion of objective purport because that notion does not rule out the possibility that there are many *permissible* ways to form a conception of the good. The notion of objective purport guarantees the possibility of error; it does not mandate that there will be only one correct conception of the good. But it is also important to note that the common observation at most imposes a limit on how objective *one's conception of the good* can be. It does not necessarily impose a limit on whether one should find certain objects *valuable* at least to some extent. This is connected with the fact that the notion of minimal objectivity allows for the possibility that objective constraints only delineate a range of permissible conceptions of the good; we can think that all these conceptions take an object that is (objectively) valuable and endorse it as good.

Similarly, we can distinguish between the notion of objectivity of an appearance we delineated earlier and a notion of objectivity of appearance qua appearance; that is, a notion that something ought to appear some way to someone. I will refer to this notion of objectivity of an appearance as objectivity of an appearance per se, and we can talk about an appearance having objective purport per se insofar as we can distinguish in a nontrivial way between how things actually appear to someone and how they ought to appear.[9] It might sound absurd to think that appearances can have objective purport per se. However, such a notion is applicable even to the theoretical case. J. L. Austin famously complained that the philosopher's claim that things looked small from afar was incorrect – they just looked like normally sized objects seen from afar. However, whatever one's stance on this issue, there would be something wrong with someone for whom things looked from afar just as they look when they were right in front of her – or worse, if they looked bigger from afar than when they were nearby. Moreover, something is wrong with someone's visual perspective if she does not fall for certain well-constructed illusions – if lights flickering in a certain way don't look to her to be a moving object. It seems correct to say that things ought to look a certain way to someone under certain circumstances, even in the cases in which the appearance does not correspond to reality. It is part of having a well-functioning visual perspective that things ought to appear in certain ways. As long as we can identify the appropriate functioning of a visual perspective, and as long as it is legitimate to ask whether things appear to a perceiver as they ought, we can say that visual appearances have objective purport per se.

Accepting that visual appearances can have objective purport per se does not commit us to denying that someone could have distortions in her visual perspective and yet learn to make the correct perceptual judgments. Someone could learn that distant objects look bigger to her and adjust her theoretical judgments accordingly. However, this person's judgments would not just be an endorsement of the visual perspective; they would be judgments involving compensatory inferences from how things appear *incorrectly* to her.[10]

---

[9] This clause is intended to rule out understanding how things ought to appear to one in accordance with the equivalence "It ought to appear to X that p if and only if p."

[10] Gareth Evans makes a similar point with regard to "quasi-memories" when he argues that the concept cannot be understood independently of the concept of memory. See his *The Varieties of Reference*, chapter 8.

When we move outside the realm of the perceptual perspective, it is unclear whether it makes sense to talk about objective appearances per se, at least for cases in which appearance and reality conflict.[11] But even if the possibility of objective appearances per se does not go beyond the case of perceptual appearances in the theoretical realm, there is no reason to rule them out from the practical realm without further argument.

It is also important to note that a relativized or conditional notion of objectivity applies to theoretical perspectives that are non-perceptual because an appearance might be correct relative to an illusory perspective. If I find narrative perspectives tempting, it should appear to me that someone who is boasting about her good luck will pick the short stick (rather than having it appear to me that this will happen to her next-door neighbor). For the superstitious, it might be important to keep track of those things, but objective appearances per se put an agent under normative requirements only if they are not relative to illusory perspectives. Thus, in the case of theoretical reason, a notion of the objectivity of an appearance relative to a perspective is of very limited interest. But this is not so with respect to practical reason, especially in cases of permissible perspectives.

Etiquette is certainly a plausible candidate for a practical perspective; various things appear to be good from the point of view of a polite person. From the "etiquette perspective," it appears that one should put the fork in a certain position in order to have a proper dinner, for example. It now seems plausible to suppose that

---

[11] However, I am not convinced that there are no other cases about which we can say that appearances have independent objective purport per se. For instance, it would be strange, to say the least, if the following inference did not appear invalid to those uninitiated in logical theory:

$$p \mathrel{\&} \sim p$$
Therefore, q

One can say here that this inference appears invalid *at first* or that it appears invalid from the perspective of "naïve logic." No doubt, one could be forced to accept the inference with the resources of what I've been calling "naïve logic." One can imagine saying, in Socratic manner, "But isn't it true that if one knows that p is true, one also knows that p or q is true? And isn't it true that if one knows that p or q and $\sim p$ is true, one knows that q must be true?" But, arguably, without the aid of logical theory, this reasoning carries an air of paradox.

there are certain appearances that are objective per se relative to this perspective, whether or not one thinks that this is a perspective one ought to have. And if we think that etiquette is a permissible (but not mandatory) perspective, then we will take it to be the case that whether the content of these appearances is indeed good or valuable will depend on whether or not one endorses this perspective in one's conception of the good. Nonetheless, the question of the objectivity of the appearance relative to the perspective can be settled independently of whether one endorses the perspective, and, indeed, one's commitment to the perspective will probably depend on the judgments one makes about what the perspective commands.

Now this kind of objectivity might not seem to go beyond anything that a sophisticated Humean is happily to allow for; a sophisticated Humean grants the possibility that one could be subjectively committed to the rules of etiquette.[12] However, it is important to notice that even this fairly weak notion of objectivity does not sit well with a Humean or an instrumentalist picture.

It will be clearer why this is so if we first note that the Humean thinks that there is nothing genuinely practical in the objectivity in question. Hume famously stated that there are ways in which we can speak, in an improper manner, of a passion's being unreasonable. Hume acknowledges, for instance, that when we fear an imaginary object, or set out to get a peach that, unbeknownst to us, is sour, we can be said to have, in an improper sense, unreasonable passions.[13] And the reason that this is an improper manner of speaking rests on the fact that it is the judgment that effects the passion (such as "There is a goblin under my bed" or "This peach will taste like the one I had last week") that is unreasonable, not the passion itself. In other words, properly speaking, we can make mistakes only in the employment of theoretical reason. Thus, acting on a commitment to etiquette, in the Humean view, can be improper or incorrect only insofar as the action in question embodies a theoretical mistake. One might, for instance, mistake a fork for a knife and thus set the table in a manner contrary to one's commitment to etiquette.

---

[12] Needless to say, the example of etiquette is explicitly discussed as something that one can be subjectively committed to by Philippa Foot in "Morality as a System of Hypothetical Imperatives."

[13] David Hume, *Treatise of Human Nature*, Book II, Part 3, section 3.

Of course, the Humean can allow for different kinds of mistakes without granting that there is anything genuinely practical in these mistakes. One might think of rules of etiquette as an axiomatic system whose rules of application are provided by first-order logic. Or one might think that there are certain conventions that set out what is required by etiquette. For instance, perhaps there is an etiquette arbiter whose word is final. A polite person, in this view, would be someone committed to an axiomatic system or to a set of conventions, or to act in accordance with the statements of the etiquette arbitrator; the polite person could then be mistaken either about what any of these "sources" says or in applying a rule to a particular case. All these mistakes, however, are clearly within the province of theoretical reason.

However, this understanding of the polite person is at odds with how polite people typically reason. Participants in the practice of etiquette engage in reasoning without appearing to rely on any explicit axiomatic system or any clear arbiter or authoritative text.[14] One might think that with a bit of ingenuity we could come up with such an axiomatic system, but it's hard to see any independent reason to be optimistic about the prospect of finding such a system, and even harder to see a reason to think that this is what a polite person takes herself to be committed to. But more importantly, there is a feature of this reasoning that makes it hard to conceive of it as a self-contained axiomatic system. Because of its practical nature, reasoning about etiquette takes it for granted that polite behavior aims at the good. That is to say that what counts as polite behavior depends on what one can expect from someone who has reasonable practical aims. Etiquette cannot recommend (in the normal course of events) one's starvation, financial ruin, betrayal of one's political principles, and so on. Except for extreme cases (such as being shipwrecked), the rules of etiquette cannot even give you *a* reason to starve that is then overridden by reasons from other perspectives. Advising someone not to leave the table before everyone is finished eating when a poisonous snake is moving in her

---

[14] Of course, there are characters such as Miss Manners in many newspapers that dispense etiquette advice. But they are taking the role of experts; their authority is not supposed to be what *makes* their answer correct.

direction is not just insane; it is also bad etiquette advice. Less dramatically, etiquette advice must depend on what can be expected to insult or offend a reasonable person or make her sad or distraught, and this itself depends on what it is sensible to care about (and to what extent). As Philippa Foot correctly points out, the rules of etiquette are categorical; they must tell how a polite person *would* behave in those circumstances, not what the polite person has *some* reason to do in certain circumstances. But we cannot tell how a polite person would behave in abstraction from the fact that the polite person aims to act well in general.[15] Unless one has an axiomatic system on how to live in general, one cannot specify what the rules of etiquette command in every particular case.

We can say that etiquette has a *practical orientation* and thus that what it dictates depends partly on the importance one can reasonably attach to the concerns of etiquette and the role that one's concern for etiquette should play in one's life more generally. As a result of its practical orientation, etiquette exhibits this kind of practical objectivity in a way that is irreducible to any form of theoretical objectivity. Judgments about what counts as polite behavior can be correct or incorrect independent of one's judgments of correctness (and even of one's judgments of correctness under suitable conditions) in a way that cannot be explained in terms of the objectivity of the theoretical judgments on which judgments of etiquette depend. However, from what we've said so far, the objectivity of etiquette might be wholly internal to its perspective and thus merely relative. That is, the correctness of the judgments of etiquette does not give us any reason to act in any way, unless the perspective of etiquette is legitimate. Thus, the judgments that can be said to be objectively correct (in the sense of "objective" in question) should be prefaced by a clause such as "insofar as the perspective of etiquette is legitimate." Indeed, this is the safer conclusion that can be drawn from Foot's discussion of the nature of reasons for etiquette. Foot defines an internal sense of "categorical" according to which the commands of etiquette are categorical. When Miss Manners claims that one ought to put the fork on the left side

---

[15] See my "Ethical Internalism and Glaucon's Question" for a similar difficulty of ethical externalism.

of the plate, the validity of the command is not supposed to depend on how much, or even whether, one cares about the commands of etiquette. Thus, the commands of etiquette are not hypothetical in the way that advice such as "Take the 3 P.M. train; otherwise you won't be in London before 5 P.M." is. This latter piece of advice, unlike the advice given by those who dispense advice on manners, is typically predicated on the presumption that the person has some kind of interest that will be served by heeding the advice in question (in our case, presumably the wish to be in London before 5 P.M.).

Foot claims, no doubt correctly, that the fact that the rules of etiquette are categorical in this sense does not guarantee that there are reasons to do what etiquette commands; a person may happily concede that etiquette recommends that she attend a ceremony and yet think that the rules of etiquette are balderdash. Foot goes on to argue that whether one has a reason to obey the commands of etiquette depends on whether one cares about its commands. But this last step represents a leap. This only warrants that we conclude that whether one has reason to pay heed to the rules of etiquette depends on whether the *perspective itself is* legitimate. Foot's early views commit her to the claim that the perspective of etiquette is legitimate for a certain person if and only if she finds herself caring for this perspective, but this is not a particularly plausible assumption.[16] The rules of etiquette are complex and demand that one perform various actions that do not seem to be either immediately pleasant or instrumental in the satisfaction of any obvious need of the agent. A general commitment to its rules based on a brute desire to do what etiquette commands is bound to strike us as a fetish, or simply as the effect of the imaginary pressures of an illusory ideal. Indeed, one may suspect that "fetish" and "illusory ideal" are apt words to describe those slavishly under the spell of the commands of etiquette.[17] However, this issue should not be settled by one's general theory of practical reason; philosophy should leave room for the possibility that there is nothing untoward about those who take these rules seriously. This is especially true once one notices that the

---

[16] Foot herself has changed her view on this issue since her "Morality as a System of Hypothetical Imperatives." See her *Natural Goodness*.

[17] This point is similar, and obviously related, to Smith's criticism of Foot's externalism about moral motivation. See Smith, *The Moral Problem*, pp. 77–85.

same consideration applies to any kind of perspective that involves a commitment to complex rules and institutions. The trustworthy person, the law-abiding citizen, even perhaps the sports fan, just as much as the polite person, will be rendered under the grip of illusions and fetishes.[18]

The possibility of appearances being objective per se in the theoretical realm is of limited interest. After all, if the appearance does not deliver knowledge, it is unclear why we would be interested in coming to the conclusion that things appear to the knower as they ought. No doubt, a resourceful epistemologist might find some use for such a notion, but, at first, it does not seem that we learn anything about the world if we learn that things appear to the knower in the way that they ought to appear from that perspective, and we seem to learn even less by means of the relativized notion. But as should be clear from the discussion of etiquette, the same is not true in the case of practical reason. First, the possibility of permissible perspectives requires that an agent appeal to the relativized notion in assessing another agent's actions. The object of someone else's action need not be something that I judge to be good, or that I would judge to be good if placed in the same circumstances given my conception of the good. Yet if what my fellow agent brings about in her actions is grounded on perspectives I consider to be permissible, I have, other things being equal, no reason to find fault in her actions. But I can only come to the conclusion that her actions are properly grounded if I can come to the conclusion that the object of her action is warranted relative to the relevant perspective. Moreover, even abstracting from my interests in assessing the actions of others, questions about the correctness of appearances per se, relativized or not, are important insofar as they are involved in determining what is valuable. Answers to questions about what is valuable are important not only for purely contemplative reflection about what one should have done in various counterfactual situations but because foregoing valuable things calls for certain appropriate emotions (regret, sadness, moderation in one's joyfulness,

---

[18] Arguably, a similar misconception might be the basis of the claim that certain deontological theories are committed to some kind of rule-fetishism. More on this issue in chapter 5.

etc.) and might even determine what would be good to bring about in other actions (it might require *expressing* regret, apologies, etc.).

4.4 OBJECTIVITY IN ALL-OUT ATTITUDES

The envious person sees good in various actions that the virtuous person is committed to thinking cannot be good. The problem here is not that the envious person might be wrong about what envy requires. The problem, it seems, is that there is something wrong with the practical orientation provided by the perspective of the envious person; there is no reason to think of the objects of envious desires as good on these grounds. The perspective of the envious person can be contrasted with two perspectives. First, it should be contrasted with the perspective of the trustworthy person, which seems to be such that one *ought* to have it; failing to find good in the object of the desires of the trustworthy person is itself a failure. But it should also be contrasted with the perspective of the person who finds pleasure in vacationing on sunny beaches, a perspective that seems permissible but not obligatory.

My aim here is not to argue that envy is a vice and trustworthiness a virtue, and that finding pleasure in wallowing on sunny beaches is neither a virtue nor a vice. It might turn out that all these claims are incorrect. My question is not whether these are indeed objectively correct or incorrect perspectives, but how to understand claims to objectivity in light of the scholastic view and what could, in principle, justify such claims.

The first step is simple. To say that a perspective is objectively required for an agent is to say that an agent ought to have the perspective and that practical reason commands the agent to cultivate that perspective if he doesn't have it or has it in an imperfect manner. Objects that appear to be good from this perspective are in fact good, or at least valuable. To say that a perspective is objectively impermissible for an agent is to say at least that the agent must not incorporate the appearances from this perspective into his general conception of the good or into his actions (his unqualified judgments of the good), although it might also imply that the agent ought not to have this perspective. To say that a perspective is neither impermissible nor required is to say that, on the one hand, other things being equal, there is no reason for the agent to have or give up the perspective; under certain conditions, that objects appear to be good from such a perspective would be necessary and sufficient for them to be good, or at least valuable. On the other hand, it also means that it is not true that one ought to have such a perspective. However, as soon as one puts things in this way, questions arise. In particular, one wants to know the upshot for how one ought to form one's conception of the good and how the objectivity of perspectives could make all-out practical judgments objectively correct. This is what we will investigate in this section.

Let us start with questions about justification. We will continue to take our lead from theoretical reason. Because we are now trying to understand how *all-out* attitudes can be justified in the practical realm, we should start by considering a few ways in which a belief can (arguably) be justified:

(a) *Empirical Support.* A belief might be supported by empirical evidence of some kind.
(b) *A priori Justification.* A belief might be justified by being intuitively obvious or by being inferred (by means of a priori rules of reasoning) from other justified beliefs.
(c) *Overall Coherence.* A belief might be justified because adding it to one's system of beliefs adds to the overall coherence of the system.[19]

Taking this list as a working basis from which to pursue the question, a priori justification is the one that sounds most promising for the scholastic approach to practical inquiry. Many of those who think, for instance, that morality issues objectively practical injunctions take our knowledge of these injunctions to be justified a priori.[20] Of course, one can be a skeptic about whether any of this alleged a priori knowledge counts as knowledge, but this form of

---

[19] Arguably (c) is a particular case of (b), but it does not matter for our purposes if the items are not exclusive.

[20] Of course, many ethical externalists think that moral claims are capable of being true and false and that they are empirically known. But for these ethical externalists, morality is not, strictly speaking, a realm of practical inquiry because morality does not, on its own, motivate or give reasons for actions. See, for instance, Peter Railton, "Moral Realism."

skepticism tends to be a general skepticism about practical reason, not a particular qualm about whether a priori justification is fit to provide knowledge when the good, rather than the true, is the formal end of the inquiry in question. The same is not true, however, when it comes to empirical justification in the practical realm. Our empirical knowledge of the world, one often complains, cannot tell us what we ought to do or not do beyond telling us that this is an opportunity to apply a certain practical principle.

Although I think that this view is implicitly held by many philosophers, G. A. Cohen comes closest to providing an explicit formulation and defense of the claim that there can be no genuinely empirical practical knowledge. In comparing how we might learn from experience in the normative realm with how a child might learn simple arithmetical truths with the help of experience, Cohen says that

> It is typically in and through experience that people form and adjust their principles, but facts of experience are nevertheless immaterial to their ultimate principles.... But, if ... [someone] is (perhaps unusually) reflective, she will realize that she has come to believe ... principle[s] whose authority for her is independent of any facts of experience that she or others might have learned.[21]

What Cohen actually argues for is the claim that all normative principles presuppose what he calls "fact-insensitive" principles; that is, the claim that there must be normative principles that are both independent of matters of fact and that ultimately justify all normative principles. Cohen argues that for every case in which we would think that a fact F justifies a certain normative principle P, we can ask what explains why F grounds P, and, according to Cohen, the appropriate explanation would ultimately uncover a fact-insensitive normative principle. Because the fact-insensitive principles that Cohen has in mind seem to be all a priori, one could try to extend this argument to rule out the possibility of empirical practical knowledge. For any piece of practical knowledge that is apparently justified empirically, one must be able to show how it is a

---

[21] G. A. Cohen, "Facts and Principles," p. 232.

consequence of applying certain a priori normative principles to empirically known factual conditions.[22]

In this view, we would know a priori that we should pursue aesthetic enjoyment and use this knowledge, together with our empirical knowledge, to come to the conclusion that on those grounds we have at least some reason to travel to New York.

However, this argument against empirical practical knowledge is either confused or begs the question. To some extent, it relies on a version of the naturalistic fallacy. The general idea is that one cannot infer what one ought to do from empirically known truths about the world. Knowledge about what to do thus cannot have a merely empirical source. However, even if we grant that the naturalistic fallacy is a fallacy, it simply tells us not to infer practical conclusions from theoretical ones. It's completely neutral about the *sources* of practical knowledge. In particular, it might be true that our empirical knowledge *of the world* could at most tell us how to apply practical principles, but accepting this point tells us nothing about whether there can be empirically based practical knowledge. The claim that we have empirical practical knowledge is not necessarily the claim that we can legitimately use empirically grounded[23] all-out theoretical attitudes in the formation of all-out practical attitudes without the mediation of practical principles. It could be the case that legitimate prima facie practical attitudes are themselves empirically grounded. In other words, the claim that we have empirical practical knowledge is the claim that legitimate appearances of the good are empirically grounded. This is no doubt much more plausible than a commitment to move from "ought" to "is." However, one might object that this attempt to escape the naturalistic fallacy quickly dead-ends. After all, empirical knowledge is knowledge based on information received by means of our sense organs. And the senses give us information about the world, not

---

[22] Cohen explicitly says that his view implies that all norms are ultimately grounded on a priori norms ("Facts and Principles," p. 234, n. 28). To be fair, Cohen actually restricts the claim there to moral norms, but there is nothing in the argument that depends on these being moral norms in particular, as opposed to any kind of practical norms.

[23] For a very interesting attempt to show that something like theoretical induction is at work in most of the ways in which we gain knowledge in the practical realm, see Elijah Millgram, *Practical Induction*.

about the good, and thus, so the argument goes, we have yet to find any room for empirically grounded practical knowledge.

But this objection is a version of the same confusion. One could insist that we count as empirical sources of knowledge only the direct contribution of the five senses (however one spells this out). But this would beg the question in favor of the view that all our empirical access to knowledge is theoretical. Traditionally, empiricists took the "internal senses" to be also part of what constitutes our experience, so that emotions and feelings would have counted as constituents of experience just as much as the deliverances of the five senses. If we do not foreclose the possibility that we can gain practical knowledge through emotions and feeling, we can say that just as our senses constitute our receptivity to empirical data, we also have an analogous "practical receptivity." After all, our feelings and emotions seem not to be under the full, direct control of our rational capacities; they do not seem to be simply the effect of how we reflectively recognize that we ought to behave in, or react to, a particular situation. And yet they do seem to play an important role in presenting objects to us as good; they are the sources of most of our perspectives on the good. Just to cite an obvious example, it would be hard to say that one's sensitivity to gastronomic goods was arrived at by means of the unaided employment of our rational faculties. And it is equally implausible to think that the goods of friendship and love, both in their general desirability and their desirability in particular instances, are the conclusion of pure practical reason.

Now the claim that there is empirical practical knowledge is just the claim that we're justified in accepting these perspectives as legitimate even if our finding them legitimate depends on our having certain feelings or emotions. This claim I find undeniable; denying it would make us into complete revisionists about ordinary conceptions of the good. It might be worth emphasizing here that this claim does not depend on a particularly controversial view about the nature of emotions or feelings. One might think that only a cognitivist about emotions would endorse such a claim. But I am making no claim about the nature of emotions; in particular, I am not saying that to have an emotion is to judge or believe that something has a certain evaluative property. I am making the much more modest epistemological claim that there are certain things that we are justified in finding good and valuable that we would not be justified in taking so had we not experienced certain feelings and emotions. It is important to be clear on the nature of this counter-factual. I am not saying, though I tend to think that this is correct, that it would be impossible for a being devoid of these emotions and feelings to appreciate these goods. I am only saying that, in many cases, the appreciation of these goods is epistemically dependent on experiencing certain feelings and emotions.

It might also be worth noting that it need not be the case that when our emotions and feelings are grounds for incorporating objects into one's conception of the good, our practical knowledge is purely empirical. To the extent that accepting something into one's conception of the good is justified, our inferential capacities must be exercised to some extent.[24] But this is no different from the way in which the contributions of the senses are incorporated into knowledge in the theoretical realm.[25]

When one thinks that practical knowledge is always ultimately justified by certain a priori principles or truths, one is probably thinking of quite general principles, and more specifically of moral principles. One the other hand, the clearest examples of what I have been considering to be empirical practical knowledge are cases on which we know that things like canoeing, biking, reading novels, and so forth are valuable. But one could press the case against empirical practical knowledge even for cases in which we know we have reasons to canoe, bike, and read novels. One could argue that even in these cases there's an underlying a priori normative principle such as "One should engage in activities that one enjoys or appreciates" that is simply applied to certain factual conditions. But it is important to note that this strategy cannot account for the kind of knowledge possessed by someone who knows that he has reasons to pursue these activities. One must first note that there are difficulties in spelling out the principle "One should engage in activities that one enjoys or appreciates" in a non–question-begging way.

---

[24] This does not mean that we deliberated or that anything of psychological significance must happen. An exercise of an inferential capacity can be expressed just in the way that one would choose without "thinking."

[25] See, on this issue, Jennifer Nagel, "The Empiricist Conception of Experience."

That is, it is not clear that there is any version of the principle that is both acceptable and such that the relevant notion of "enjoying" or "appreciation" does not already imply that there is reason to engage in the activity in question. But independently of this problem, knowledge of this principle cannot substitute for fundamental empirical practical knowledge. "One should engage in activities that one appreciates" is not, properly speaking, a normative principle, at least not a basic one. The more basic explanation of why I have reason to bike is not that I should engage in activities that I enjoy or appreciate, but that biking is a valuable activity. But I can only directly[26] know that biking is a valuable activity if I have the appropriate practical sensibility.

This discussion might strike some as trivial. After all, most arguments against empirical knowledge in the practical realm are intended to rule out moral knowledge, not practical knowledge in general. However, a number of these arguments take the practical nature of ethics as the key premise.[27] If this is the form the argument takes, there should be no distinction between moral knowledge and practical knowledge, and some practical knowledge is doubtless empirical. Kant himself took the impossibility of deriving morality from empirical principles to follow not from its practical nature but from its claim to universality and necessity. This argument is immune from the criticisms stated earlier, but it is a much more modest argument than some of the Kantian arguments in contemporary ethics.[28]

Are there any grounds for overall coherence in the practical realm? Michael Smith has argued that, insofar as one is rational, one strives to have a set of desires that are maximally coherent. This might strike us as odd; from the fact that I desire to practice some dangerous sport, such as mountain climbing or car racing, it does

---

[26] "Directly" is an important qualification here because biking might be in my conception of the good not because I ever biked but simply because I realize that so many people enjoy it.

[27] Of course, most notable of all is Korsgaard's argument in chapter 1 of *The Sources of Normativity*. The argument there rules out empiricist accounts of practical reason on the basis of their incapacity to yield reflective endorsement.

[28] "Modest" in the sense that it does not claim that reflection on the structure of practical reason as such already commits us to the a priori nature and ground of moral claims.

not follow that I should also desire to practice other dangerous
sports, and certainly it does not follow that I should pursue or desire
other dangerous activities, even if, arguably, these further desires
would add coherence to my conception of the good.[29] But a demand
of coherence is certainly a constraint on practical knowledge. There
is something odd, to say the least, about someone who likes reading,
but not on Tuesdays, or someone who likes oranges, but not if they
have been wrapped in paper.[30] Coherence can be understood as a
demand similar to the demand (discussed in chapter 1) that all
desires are desires from a certain perspective. The demand can be
put, as a first approximation, as the demand that a desire is legitimate only if it is a desire from a legitimate perspective on the good.
So if my desire for hearing jokes on this Sunday morning is legitimate, so is the perspective from which hearing jokes appears good.
Because the perspective makes hearing jokes on this Sunday
morning appear good in a way that probably does not depend on
their being told on Sunday, ceteris paribus, the perspective should
make hearing jokes appear good on any day of the week. Because
the legitimacy of the desire requires the legitimacy of the perspective, one can demand that someone who desires to hear jokes this
Sunday must find hearing jokes to be valuable on other occasions as
well.

The requirement so stated, however, is just an approximation. It
does not take into account, for instance, the fact that a legitimate
perspective can be an optional one for which there is no legitimate
requirement that one cultivate it, or endorse it, or even find any of
the things that would appear good from this perspective prima facie
good. In order to accommodate the possibility of such perspectives,
one would need to tinker with the formulation of the coherence

---

[29] Geoffrey Sayre-McCord raises a similar problem in "The Metaethical Problem."
See Michael Smith's reply in "In Defense of *The Moral Problem: A Reply to Brink,
Copp, and Sayre-McCord*."

[30] Of course, there's nothing wrong with someone who *decides* not to read on Tuesday
(because, say, Tuesday is sports day), or who consistently *chooses* not to eat oranges
that are so wrapped (for, say, aesthetic or environmental reasons). But these are
cases of overriding conflicting desires. What does seem to fall short of the ideal is to
see the attraction of reading on other days of the week but not see the attraction of
reading on Tuesday for no further reason other than "But this is Tuesday
reading!"

requirement we provided. However, I do not want to pursue a more precise version of the requirement here. My aim is just to establish that improving overall coherence can be a way of expanding our practical knowledge and arriving at well-grounded prima facie or all-out attitudes in the practical realm. And this will turn out to be true independently of the particular formulation of the requirement of coherence we favor in the end.

So far, we have seen that as long as we keep in mind the different formal ends of theoretical and practical reason, similar methods of inquiry will be available in both realms, at least at a high level of abstraction. Because whether some action is in fact good or not will depend in part on what is true, sceptical problems in the theoretical realm will spill over to the practical realm. If I'm a brain in a vat and I try to save a vat child from the vat crocodile pool at great (real) pain to myself, what my action accomplished is probably not all that good.[31] On the other hand, it's not clear that there are similar brain-in-a-vat scenarios that are sui generis practical. Could it be the case that our empirical epistemic access to the good was distorted in similar ways by evil geniuses? Could mad scientists turn our sensibility around so that things appear to be good to us that are in no way good?

Let us think about this possible scenario. Start with a mad scientist who wants Boris to appreciate a well-worn example of a pointless pursuit. Boris is made into a grass blade counter. Let us start with a relatively modest endeavor on the scientist's part. The scientist just wants to make Boris into a dilettante grass blade counter, someone who enjoys counting blades of grass. He doesn't want to make Boris into a grass blade counting junkie, someone who will kill and steal in order to satisfy his craving for grass blade counting, or into a fanatical grass blade counter, someone whose life's meaning depends on counting blades of grass. When the scientist finishes his work, Boris will simply be someone who, given the

---

[31] However, under certain Kantian premises, the choice could still be regarded as correctly choosing the greatest good available. If virtuous activity is a condition of anything counting as good, and if a virtuous agent would certainly try to save the vat child, then a case in which no pain occurs as a result of my viciously ignoring the plight of the vat child would be worse (rather than a case in which I accidentally choose the best). We will discuss this Kantian view further in the next chapter.

opportunity, will count blades of grass unless something he considers more important can be pursued on that occasion. He regularly engages in the activity, but the activity is not at the center of his life and does not make more demands on him than stamp collecting makes on the amateur, nonobsessive stamp collector. How should we think of this relatively mild intervention of the mad scientist? I think it depends to some extent on how Boris sees his craving for counting blades of grass. Let us look at two broad categories. Suppose Boris experiences grass blade counting as a painful craving to engage in some pointless activity. In this case, in our view, the mad scientist fails to implant something that counts, properly speaking, as a "desire,"[32] except for the desire to rid himself of a bothersome craving. But, of course, *that* desire is a quite reasonable one with a perfectly intelligible object. Note that the analysis of this case does not depend on the mildness of the urge. Had the scientist implanted an irresistible craving that would frequently recur and force Boris into a life of nothing but counting blades of grass, he would have made Boris's life rather unfortunate, but he would have made no headway in implanting a desire for counting blades of grass, and thus he would not have put Boris under any kind of illusion.[33]

However, the scientist might have implanted an urge such that Boris seems to think of its object as worth pursuing. He engages from time to time in the activity, but now when asked about counting blades of grass, he gives the same kinds of answers he would give when asked about the point of other activities we recognize as valuable. "It's just so much fun to do it; we never know what kind of number will turn up," "It is the Zen of knowing that blades of grass are in some sense under your control; you know *exactly* how many of them there are," or even, perhaps more realistically, "It's hard to explain; you need to get into it to see how great it is." In this case, there is no doubt that the mad scientist has succeeded in implanting

---

[32] See chapter 1.

[33] See, on a similar point, Elijah Millgram's discussion of the question of whether it is possible to desire "at pill" (i.e., whether one can implant a desire on oneself just by taking a pill). Millgram points out that this purported possibility is plagued with difficulties similar to those of the purported possibility of believing at will. See his *Practical Induction*, chapter 2.

the desire in Boris's psyche. However, what is far from clear is whether he succeeded in putting Boris under an illusion. After all, another tempting line would be to say that Boris *appreciates* counting blades of grass and thus that it is, after all, a valuable activity. It's true that Boris might be incapable of persuading others to engage in the activity, but this does not speak against its making a legitimate claim on Boris's conception of the good. Short of resorting to quite radical brain surgery, no one can or could persuade me to engage in fishing or golfing, but this does not mean that fishing or golfing cannot be a legitimate part of anyone's conception of the good. Especially if we take away the oddity of our mad scientist, this is generally how we relate to pursuits that others value but that *we* see as pointless. As long as they are well circumscribed and do not take on an inordinate importance in the agent's life, we tend to think that they offer something valuable but that we fail to appreciate the value (a failure that is not an instance of a practical mistake). We rarely suspect that the agent is under an illusion and wasting away these parts of her life.[34] Of course, we might doubt that there's any real appreciation going on. If Boris stops counting the blades whenever we snap our fingers, or if he engages in grass counting only when he's completely drunk, we might think that this case is not one of genuine appreciation. Less dramatically, this is often how we relate to the transgressions of adolescents and their pursuit of ends that we find pointless. We might find that these transgressions are done in the pursuit of status and recognition, and in this case we withdraw our ascription of any kind of appreciation for the activities themselves. That is, we think that this is not a basic state of appreciation of the object (as opposed to a state of finding derivative value in the object as a means of pursuing status and recognition).

Finally, it is important for our example that what the mad scientist implanted in Boris was a desire for something that we previously found merely *pointless*, not for something that we previously would have found objectionable. Had the mad scientist made Boris into someone who yearns to hear cries of pain from fellow human beings, we might have had reason to think the objects in question

---

[34] No doubt, we might think that the agent could be doing something *better* at this time, but this does not show that the activity is not valuable.

could *not* be correctly judged to be good. In this case, in light of certain legitimate evaluate perspectives, we would have reason to think that the mad scientist implanted in Boris an *illusory perspective*. But the reason for thinking that the mad scientist left Boris in the grip of an illusion in this case is its conflict with a well-grounded perspective, not, so to speak, the intrinsic groundlessness of the evaluative perspective implanted by the mad scientist.

But in the absence of these reasons to suspect that we're not in the presence of genuine appreciation, it seems plausible to suppose that the activity has *some* value, at least in the sense that a good deliberator who was capable of appreciating this kind of activity would make it part of her conception of the good. A rational grass blade counter would prefer counting blades of grass over howling to the moon. This is enough to establish that in this case counting blades of grass is a valuable activity. Thus the mad scientist succeeds in implanting the desire in this case but fails to make it a desire for something that is not valuable. Thus we have the following principle, which I'll call the "No Appreciation without Value Principle." The principle states that if an agent genuinely appreciates an activity or an object (and no perspective that the agent ought to have gives the agent a reason to consider this appreciation to be an illusory perspective on the good), then the activity or the object is valuable to some extent.

Now the caveats about cases in which it would be wrong to attribute appreciation to an agent may raise the suspicion that there's a catch here. "Appreciation" has a factive ring to it, and thus it is no surprise that if we can say that a mental state is one of appreciation, then there must be value to the object in question. It would be no different from thinking that one has made a great discovery about the mind-dependent nature of the world by noticing that whenever one attributes knowledge *that p* to an agent, *p* must be true. In this case, of course, one has only noticed the factive nature of knowledge attribution. But note that with regard to knowledge there is a corresponding nonfactive state of belief. In particular, we can say that knowledge attributions and belief attributions stand in the following relation: If I attribute knowledge *that p* to an agent and then find out *that p* is not true, I must withdraw my knowledge attribution and attribute instead (merely) a belief *that p*. I revise these attributions *solely* on the grounds of my theoretical inquiry into *p*, independently of what else I might have learned about the agent in question. My point is that there's no corresponding possible move in the realm of genuine appreciation. If I attribute to an agent appreciation of *A*, I cannot revise this attribution by the result of my practical inquiries into *A* but only by learning something new about the agent in question.

One might also think that the difference between attributing knowledge and attributing appreciation to an agent lies in the fact that we are comparing attribution of an all-out attitude with attribution of a prima facie one. It is claims about plausibility rather than about truth that need to be compared with claims about value. If it appears to me *that p* then *p* is to some extent plausible. Now I'll leave aside reasonable concerns about the truth of this last sentence. Let us also grant that if it appears to me *that p* from some perspective, and I have no general reason to suspect that this perspective is illusory, and it does not appear to me *that not p* from any other perspective, then I should believe *that p*. However, it does not follow from this claim, and it would be insane to assert, that if those conditions obtain, *p* must actually be *true*. However, the corresponding claim is correct in the realm of practical reason. If an agent appreciates *A* and nothing valuable competes at the moment with the pursuit of *A*, then *A is* good.

This leads us to another caveat. We mentioned cases in which we could not count the agent's enthrallment in such activity as genuine appreciation: If the agent was drunk, drowsy, or otherwise impaired, it would not count as genuine appreciation. However, this makes it sound like the only constraints on mad scientist type cases of genuine appreciation are procedural. This is not correct because the appearance in question will be illusory if a reflective practical judgment correctly renders it so in light of another appearance of the good. So if the mad scientist, for instance, implants a desire to engage in senseless episodes of torturing, the "appreciation" in question might be completely illusory. But it is important to note again that what renders the appearance illusory here is its conflict with a different perspective, for instance a perspective that mandates that one never takes causing pain in others to be noninstrumentally good. If one endorses this perspective, one must deem appearances to the contrary to be illusory. However, for the mad scientist to succeed in putting the agent under an illusion, there must be another perspective that rules out the possibility of this being a genuine appreciation of value; the illusion cannot be established simply from the fact that the agent had no *further* grounding for the judgments in question.

Let us now look into the significance and consequences of the "No Appreciation without Value" principle. First, it is important to note that the principle does not imply the kind of existentialism that is supposed to accompany a number of conceptions of practical reason that give some kind of constitutive role to the agent.[35] By "existentialist" I mean a view according to which the agent confers value on an object by means of a choice that is not (fully) grounded in any recognition of value or any principle of choice. There are a number of objections against such views, and, to my mind, they are decisive.[36] In particular, it is unclear how such a groundless act of the will is possible, and even if it were possible, why we would think that such a groundless act could confer value. However, appreciation is a prima facie attitude, not a judgment, and it is thus not an act of the will, even under a very modest understanding of what counts as "activity." Appreciation is no more an activity than perception; even if one thinks that theoretical *judgment* is an activity, one would be hard-pressed to find reasons to think that *perceiving* is an activity, an exercise of the will for which one can be responsible.[37] If the agent then goes on to incorporate the object of the appearance into his conception of the good, he would do so on the basis of the object appearing good to him, not by means of groundless acts of the will.

However, the truth of the "No Appreciation without Value" principle does speak against a thoroughgoing Platonism about values. Given that the good is not fully independent of what we happen to appreciate, it seems correct to conclude that the realm of

---

[35] Korsgaard is supposed to be a prime example of such an existentialist view. See her *Sources of Normativity*, especially chapter 3.

[36] For some of these objections, see Donald Regan, "The Value of Rational Nature." For a response, see David Sussman, "The Authority of Humanity."

[37] John McDowell suggests that spontaneity has a role to play in perception. However, he wants to maintain this claim while accepting that experience (including perception) is passive. See his *Mind and World*.

value is not wholly independent of our sensibilities. Our sensibilities are partly constitutive of it. This might lead one to think that the "No Appreciation without Value" principle allows that basically anything could correctly be judged to be good, and this in turn leaves the scholastic view without its initial motivation and without any room for genuine objectivity. Let us take these charges in turn.

First, it might be thought that the principle is incompatible with the Anscombean view that not just any object of desire is an intelligible object; in fact, anything could turn out to be good if there is someone who appreciates it. If this is true, it seems that rather than trying to stretch our notion of the good to accommodate the intuition that choice can be rendered rational simply by the fact that one desires the object of the choice, one should accept that, at least in some cases, desires do not aim at the good. Sometimes we are simply motivated by what we happen to desire without any view of the good, and we have reason to pursue the objects of these desires simply because we desire them rather than by the fact that we conceive them to be good. If this line of reasoning is correct, it would constitute a major blow to the scholastic conception.[38]

However, it does not follow from the fact that appreciation guarantees value that desires, understood in the nonscholastic way, can also guarantee value. In order to see this, we can contrast the mad scientist who succeeds in implanting the desire with the one who does not. Both succeed in implanting a disposition to behave in a certain way; however, only in one case do we have a genuine case of conceiving something to be good. It is only in this case that the desire suffices to guarantee value. It's also important to contrast this scenario with the more ambitious mad scientist who either (a) makes Boris into a grass blade counter junkie or fanatic or (b) adds similar desires (such as rearranging dishes in the kitchen, going up and down stairs, hopping on one foot, howling to the moon, etc.) that

---

[38] Quinn and Scanlon seem to be eager to resist any suggestion that our desires could have such an important role to play in determining what is good or what we have reason to pursue. See "Putting Rationality in Its Place" and *What We Owe to Each Other*, respectively. No doubt, their reluctance to accept any principle like "No Appreciation without Value" is grounded on an assumption that acceptance of such a constitutive role for our desires would threaten the view that reasons or the good are not determined by the fact of desiring.

jointly dominate the agent's practical life. The "No Appreciation without Value" principle does not imply that these are real possibilities or that the mad scientist in these cases would not just be ending the practical life of the agent. All that the principle implies is that our earlier suggestion about how to understand the constraint of intelligibility is correct: No isolated activity always violates it.

This also answers the second concern. To say that appreciation suffices for value does not imply that pursuit of this value is good in a certain context or even in any context. So whatever threat to objectivity it represents, it certainly does not present a threat to the objectivity of judgments of the good. Moreover, it does not even prevent the appearances from being illusory, as we said earlier. The only thing it does allow is that appearances need no further grounding to reveal value; at least provided that there are no legitimate conflicting perspectives, the mere fact that the agent can appreciate a certain activity suffices to ensure that the activity is valuable. It is worth emphasizing the importance of this proviso. Let us assume that some evaluative perspective that prevents us from judging that enjoying the suffering of others is good; that is, a perspective one ought to have. Let us also assume that good reflection will always conclude that the appearances from this perspective ought to be endorsed. In this case, any perspective that seems to provide an agent with "appreciation" of any kind of sadistic enjoyment is one that ought to be rejected as illusory on reflection. Consequently, any purported appreciation of sadistic enjoyment would have to be judged to be illusory, and in this case nothing that the mad scientist could do to an agent could render enjoying the pain of others in any way valuable.

Of course, even with these caveats, whether one thinks that the principle "No Appreciation without Value" does damage to our conception of practical objectivity will depend on what one was expecting practical objectivity to be. However, it certainly does not prevent us from distinguishing between correct and incorrect practical judgments.

4.5   THE GOOD VERSUS THE TRUE

So far, I have been trying to show that we can conceive of objectivity in practical reason, on a parallel with theoretical reason as long as we keep in mind that the formal ends of theoretical and practical reason are different. However, the difference in formal ends might generate important differences in the claims of objectivity that can be made in each realm. Indeed, we can see some of these differences by looking at two completely implausible views about what makes for a correct judgment in theoretical reason.

The Personal World View

For at least some judgments that do not contain any demonstratives or indexicals, the question whether p is true or false will vary from utterer to utterer due to the fact that certain propositions can be true of an agent's personal world without being true of another agent's personal world.

The Multiworld View

For at least some contradictory judgments p and *not* p, both are true in an actual world due to the fact that there are multiple legitimate actual worlds. So p might be true of W_1 and *not* p be true of W_2 where W_1 and W_2 are equally real and actual.

The proponent of any such views would be raising a challenge to the objectivity of theoretical judgments. If different people have different worlds, or if there is more than one actual world in which our statements can be true or false, the idea that our judgments are made true by the facts of a mind-independent world seem to be challenged. However, similar principles seem to be true in the realm of practical reason. Let us take a look at the following principles.

The Personal Good View

For at least some judgments that do not contain any demonstratives or indexicals, the question of whether p is good will vary from utterer to utterer due to the fact that certain things that ought to be part of an agent's conception of the good ought not to be part of another agent's conception of the good.

The Plurality of Goods View

At least for some contradictory contents p and *not* p, either p or *not* p could be a legitimate part of some agent's conception of the good due to the fact that there are multiple legitimate conceptions of the good for an agent. So p might be part of a conception of the good G_1 and *not p* be part of G_2, whereas G_1 and G_2 are equally flawless conceptions of the good.

Now at first these principles seem true. One might think that we only need to think of two persons with different inclinations regarding fishing to see the plausibility of the first principle and to substitute p for "The third box of laundry detergent to the left is placed in the shopping cart" to see the plausibility of the second principle.

However, the case for these principles is not as obvious as it might seem at first. Cases of picking rather than choosing, such as picking a laundry detergent box among many indistinguishable ones, do not show that there is a different conception of the good that is correct containing each of these actions. There is only one correct conception of the good: one that recommends that one act with the intention of grabbing *a* laundry detergent box. Moreover, the case of fishing does not show that the Personal Good View is correct. Suppose Larry likes fishing but Mary doesn't. It is true that the sentence "I go fishing at t," where t is a time that would be appropriate for Larry to go fishing would be in Larry's conception of the good but not in Mary's. However, the sentence does have an indexical, so it does not suffice to establish the truth of the principle. On closer examination, the case for either view does not seem as strong as it seemed at first, so it is worth examining in more detail whether a case can indeed be made. I'll focus on the Personal Good View and try to show that it is indeed correct, and I hope at the end it will be clear enough that similar arguments can be made in favor of the Plurality of Goods View.

Let us go back to our fishing case. As we said earlier, the fact that "I will go fishing at t" might be in Larry's but not in Mary's conception of the good does not suffice to establish the truth of the Personal Good View. Can we make further progress by examining whether each conception of the good includes "Larry goes fishing at t"? Now it might seem at first that this sentence appears in Larry's conception of the good but not in Mary's. After all, only Larry should care about his going fishing, not Mary. But even this point is more contentious than it might seem at first. What would it mean to say that "Larry goes fishing at t" should not appear in Mary's conception of the good? Recall that a conception of the good does not include simply what the agent will set herself to do but also various backup plans. To simplify matters, let us ignore the causal consequences of Larry's going fishing; that is, we leave aside the reasons that Mary has to choose to bring about that Larry goes fishing not because of the value of his going fishing but because his going fishing brings about something that is good or bad. In this case, to say that "Larry goes fishing at t" does not figure in one's conception of the good is to say that either Mary ought to prefer that Larry does not go fishing at t or that she ought to be indifferent between Larry going or not going fishing at t. The second might seem the more natural suggestion; after all, why should she care one way or another? However, there is an even more natural answer to this question, which is "because Larry cares." If we are assuming that going fishing at t is a legitimate element in Larry's flawless conception of the good, it is far from obvious that this, by itself, does not give Mary *some* reason to prefer, other things being equal, that Larry goes fishing. Hume points out that we all naturally do small kindnesses to strangers when we can do so at no cost to ourselves, and we all prefer walking on the pavement over stepping on someone's gouty toes.[39] So if Larry is too short to move the latch that opens the gate to the fishing pond but Mary is right there and she's tall enough, she would probably perform the small kindness of extending her arm to let Larry in, in this way bringing about that Larry goes fishing. Of course, Hume makes a descriptive claim, whereas we are interested in a normative claim, the claim that Mary ought to find it valuable that Larry goes fishing. However, a plausible explanation of the truth of the descriptive claim is the truth of the normative claim; that is, people perform those small kindnesses because they recognize that they ought to do this – they recognize that their conception of the good must include small kindnesses. At the very least, as we stand now, it seems that the truth of the Personal Good View depends on the claim that, despite appearances, there is no rational demand that we find some value in legitimate members of flawless conceptions of the good of other agents.

However, denying that others' conceptions of the good make demands on ours is not the only route to establishing the Personal Good View. Even if we accept that Mary has some reason to bring

---

[39] David Hume, *An Enquiry Concerning the Principle of Morals*, chapter V, part II.

about that Larry goes fishing, she and Larry seem to be in different
positions regarding the project. Bringing about that Larry goes
fishing plays a much larger role in Larry's conception of the good
than in Mary's. And one can argue that this difference must appear as
a difference in what counts as a flawless conception of the good for
Larry and Mary. The best conception of the good for Larry would
give much more importance to bringing about that Larry goes fishing
than would Mary's best conception of the good. Of course, one could
adopt a radical impersonal view according to which to the extent that
there is reason to bring about that Larry goes fishing, the reason must
recommend that Mary and Larry weigh the importance of this state of
affairs in the same way and that any difference of investment required
for either of them to bring about this state of affairs must be
accounted for with reference to the distinct contributions that their
actions could make to bringing about that Larry goes fishing; Larry
can easily see to it that it happens, whereas Mary can barely affect its
likelihood. However, this kind of radically impersonal view is quite
implausible,[40] and I will just leave it aside. Nonetheless, one can
accommodate the fact that Larry and Mary should weigh the
importance of Larry going fishing differently without giving in to the
Personal Good View. Thomas Nagel's discussion of the distinction
between agent-relative and agent-neutral reasons can help us here.[41]
One can take the differences in the demands to be the result not of
different personal good but of different implications of shared elements of the best conceptions of the good for Larry and Mary. After
all, there can be demands of self-reliance or similar demands
requiring that one pay less attention to the pursuit of the goods
enjoyed by others; one might think that it is valuable not only that
Larry goes fishing but also that he can achieve this goal without
having to rely (much) on the help of others. In this case, Mary and
Larry could have identical conceptions of the good, but this

[40] Bernard Williams famously argues against the plausibility of such a view. According
to Williams, any view that requires that the agent weigh the projects of others in the
same way he weighs his own will recommend assaults on the agent's integrity. The
objection first appeared in his famous exchange with J. J. C. Smart in Smart and
Williams's *Utilitarianism: For and Against.* For a better statement of the argument,
see his "The Point of View of the Universe: Sidgwick and the Ambitions of Ethics."
[41] See Thomas Nagel, *The Possibility of Altruism.*

conception of the good will make quite distinct demands on each of them with respect to the pursuit of goals such as Larry's going fishing. However, this attempt to avoid the Personal Good View involves a strained account of why Mary ought to give less weight to Larry's fishing in her deliberations. According to this view, Mary's reasoning, if made perfectly transparent, should be something like the following: "Larry's going fishing is valuable, and I consider it just as valuable as Larry himself does. However, because Larry's fishing is something that *Larry* would enjoy, I should refrain from investing in the pursuit of this goal as much as I otherwise would to give Larry an opportunity to pursue this goal on his own." This seems highly implausible. The more intuitive reason that Mary is not, and should not be, willing to invest many resources on Larry's fishing is that she does not, and has no reason to, care very much about whether Larry fishes or not. But only the Personal Good View can deliver this result. Moreover, it only becomes more difficult to reject the Personal Good View if we want to allow for things like positional goods. If it is a legitimate part of Larry's conception of the good that Larry is the best fisherman in the world, and it is also a legitimate part of Mary's conception of the good that Mary is the best fisherman in the world, then it is difficult to reject the Personal Good View.

The contrast between the personal and impersonal is often thought to go hand in hand with the contrast between objective and subjective. But the relation between these two distinctions is more nuanced than it might appear at first. It is worth examining how different positions regarding personal goods allow, or disallow, the possibility of different kinds of objective judgments in the practical realm. But first we need to make a more precise distinction between personal goods and impersonal goods.

Let us first define an *idealized agent* as someone whose conception of the good cannot be improved. Now several things follow from the idea of the idealized agent. First, the agent's conception of the good never recommends an action that is not in fact good. The idealized agent must also have a set of perspectives on the good whose appearances ground the conception of the good. An idealized agent's appearances are never illusory, and acquiring or losing perspectives on the good could not improve her conception of the good. That is, if the idealized agent were to acquire new perspectives on the good and form a new conception of the good based on appearances from those perspectives, the agent's new conception of the good would not be an improvement over the old one. Moreover, the idealized agent's conception of the good is well grounded on those appearances, and no conception of the good could be better grounded on those appearances. Finally, the idealized agent is not ignorant or mistaken about any of the relevant facts. Let us call the sum of the agent's perspectives on the good, appearances of the good, and the agent's conception of the good, as well as the various justificatory relations among them, *the epistemic practical state of the agent.* Keeping the epistemic practical state of the agent fixed, we can say that X is an impersonal or objective good in a certain circumstance C (that does not include the epistemic practical state of the agent) if all idealized agents in circumstance C would judge that X is good. Something is a personal good for an idealized agent α in circumstance C if α would judge that X is good and X is not an impersonal good.

We haven't yet defined how the notion of a personal good would extend to nonidealized agents. However, for our purposes, all that we need is to provide the general structure for such an extension. The most straightforward way to extend the notion would be to say that X is a personal good for agent α in circumstance C if α would have judged it to be good if α were an idealized agent. But this proposal encounters two related problems. The first is the threat of the conditional fallacy; it might be the case that the closest possible world in which the agent becomes an ideal agent is one, say, in which the agent has come to appreciate mountain climbing. This would be no argument in favor of the claim that climbing up mountains in certain circumstances is a personal good for α. Second, certain things might be personal goods for the agent in virtue of the fact that the agent finds himself in less than ideal circumstances. An acceptable extension of the notion of personal goods would revise the straightforward proposal given earlier to accommodate these problems, but, for our purposes, the details of such a revision are irrelevant.

These partial definitions allow us to distinguish four views about the relation between impersonal and personal goods:

(a) *The Exclusivity of the Impersonal.* All legitimate members of a conception of the good are impersonal goods.

(b) *The Primacy of the Personal.* All legitimate members of conceptions of the good of particular agents are ultimately grounded on members of conceptions of the good that are personal goods.

(c) *The Exclusivity of the Personal.* There are no impersonal goods.

(d) *The No Primacy View.* Some legitimate members of one's conception of the good are impersonal goods that are not grounded on personal goods, and some are personal goods that are not grounded on impersonal goods.

We are now ready to develop a notion of practical objectivity and see how these various views relate to the two different kinds of objectivity in the practical realm. But before we go on, it might be worth distinguishing this notion of impersonal and personal goods from similar notions in the literature and make it clearer what counts as a personal or an impersonal good according to the scholastic view. Some philosophers think of X being good for an agent as implying no more (or less) than that X is a good that is part of the agent's life. In this view, my happiness is good for me insofar as it is part of my life, and Joe's happiness is good for him insofar as it is part of his life.[42] Such a view has no necessary implications about whether Joe or I should pursue different things or whether we ought to bring about the same things, so to say that something is good for me in this understanding of "good for me" does not imply that it is a personal good in the scholastic sense. Similar things can be said about the notion of well-being discussed by many contemporary philosophers because it is compatible with these views that we all have the same kind of reason to pursue anyone's well-being.[43] Classical hedonism, on the other hand, is a view that postulates the existence of personal good: My pleasure is something that I ought to judge to be good, whereas no one for whom my pleasure is not instrumental to their pleasure has a reason to judge it to be good. But, of course, the scholastic notion of personal good does not in any way require that all personal goods will be pleasures or even any

---

[42] For a recent advocate of this view, see Don Regan, "Why Am I My Brother's Keeper?"

[43] See, for instance, James Griffin, *Well-Being*; and L. W. Sumner, *Welfare, Happiness, and Ethics*.

subset of one's own mental states. The idea of a personal good is not the idea that this is some good that is somehow especially good for the agent either because it's part of his life or because it's what contributes to his happiness or well-being in a special way. Rather, the idea is of a good that makes a special *demand* on the agent: an object that a particular agent (but not all agents) ought to judge to be good. Perhaps the notion closest to our notion of personal goods would be, for correlative reasons, Thomas Nagel's notion of agent-relative reasons. However, the extent to which for each agent-relative reason there is a correlative personal good depends on how one makes room for these reason in the general framework of a teleological conception of practical reason. One way is to make them correspond to agent-relative (and time-relative) goods.[44] This kind of strategy for handling certain moral rules would generate personal goods of a rather strange kind; that is, time-sensitive personal goods. However, if we understand these same moral rules as deontic constraints on the pursuit of agent-neutral goods, then agent-relative reasons would not generate personal good. Introducing deontic constraints in this manner might be difficult to reconcile with the scholastic view, but, for our purposes at the moment, unless we rule out the conceptual possibility of this kind of understanding of constraints within the framework of the scholastic view, we cannot say that for each agent-relative reason there is a correlated personal good.[45]

4.6 TWO KINDS OF OBJECTIVITY

We can distinguish two dimensions of objectivity. The first, discussed earlier, can be called *the possibility of error dimension*. To claim that judgments of the good are objective in this sense is to say that there is a possibility of substantive, nonprocedural error in one's judgments of the good. Note that all the views we have discussed are compatible with the claim that judgments of the good are objective in the possibility of error dimension. Even the exclusivity of the

---

[44] See, for instance, James Dreier, "The Structure of Normative Theories."

[45] As will become clear in the next chapter, I think that the best way for the scholastic view to understand certain rules is different from either of these views.

personal view does not obviously rule out the view that an agent can make nonprocedural errors in her or his evaluative judgments. The second dimension of objectivity we can call *the nonaccidental inter-subjective agreement dimension* of objectivity. To claim that judgments of the good are objective in this sense is to say that agents placed in the same circumstances (not including under these circumstances their practically epistemic states)[46] ought to arrive at the same judgment when the content of the judgment is specified without indexicals. So, for instance, one might think that no agent should judge that torturing small children for fun is good, that *any* person who judges that torturing small children for fun is good is manifesting some kind of cognitive failure.

We cannot draw a similar distinction between two dimensions of objectivity in the realm of theoretical reason. We can perhaps conceive of a successor to the Protagorean view that says that each man has his own truth (or his own world) and yet claim at the same time that a man does not have infallible insight into what is true for him. However, it is hard to avoid the conclusion that this view is essentially a form of skepticism about objective knowledge. In theoretical reason, it is hard to imagine a view of "getting things right" that would not connect getting things right to our capacity to gain information about a world that is (in some sense) mind-independent. However, the idea of getting things right in the realm of practical reason is *not* connected in the same way to the idea of tracking an independent world. If anything, the question of whether one gets things right in practical reason is the question of whether one is living a good life or acting well. But because there are as many lives as there are subjects, we cannot rule out in advance the possibility that what is objectively good for one person will not be objectively good for another. Thus, in the realm of practical reason, we can distinguish these two dimensions of objectivity, which correspond to different demands on what would count as getting things right. We can put this point in terms of our distinction between formal ends.

---

[46] The reason for excluding epistemic states for the circumstances is to prevent requirements of consistency from interfering with our judgment of what is good for the agent. One might think, for instance, that an agent who erroneously thinks that it is always better to give a job to a relative ought to judge that offering the job to her brother is good.

We can say that truth, the formal end of theoretical reason, requires that the truth be the same across subjects – that if a conception of the true is adequate for one subject, it must be so for all subjects. But the formal end of practical reason makes no similar demands. It does not seem to be a requirement of the formal end of practical reason that a conception of the good can be adequate for one person only if it is adequate for everyone.

However, there is a dimension of objectivity that seems to be missing here. When thinking about theoretical reason, we tend to think of objectivity in terms of mind-independence. So, for instance, we might think that judgments about secondary qualities lack objectivity in some important way because of the mind-dependent nature of secondary qualities.[47] But, of course, the notion of mind-independence has some of the same ambiguities as the notion of objectivity. It is worth noting that, according to the scholastic view, no further mind-independence is possible in the practical realm other than that provided by the notions of objectivity we have stated. We should note that if practical judgments are objective in either of the two dimensions noted, they also satisfy some weaker notions of mind-independence. A relatively weak notion of mind-independence is already present in the dimension of possibility of error; whether a judgment that is objective in this sense is or fails to be semantically adequate is not fully determined by one's views on the matter. In theoretical reason, a similarly weak notion of mind-independence might require that the truth of a certain proposition be independent of what anyone happens to think about the matter. Moreover, as should be clear from what we said earlier, in the realm of theoretical reason, any notion of mind-independence will come coupled with a requirement of "subject-invariance," a requirement that what is true does not change from subject to subject. But a similar requirement is met by any judgment that is objective along the intersubjective dimension.

Now one can certainly think of more demanding notions of mind-independence in the theoretical realm. One such notion can

---

[47] In fact, John McDowell distinguishes between two kinds of objectivity, one that pertains to primary qualities and the other to primary and secondary qualities alike. See his "Values and Secondary Qualities."

be vaguely put as follows: "A judgment is objective only if its truth is independent of the existence of any human beings." However, this is not a particularly compelling requirement for objectivity in the practical realm. In fact, the scholastic view rules out the possibility of meeting this requirement because OS is incompatible with it. A perhaps more significant notion of mind-independence in the theoretical realm would be a strong notion of verification trans-cendence that could be put roughly as follows: "A judgment is objective only if its truth is independent of whether any human being could ever be capable of knowing its truth." Of course, the strength of this requirement depends on the strength of the "could." However, under most common readings of the require-ment, the constraint of authority-subjectivism would rule out the possibility of any corresponding requirement in the practical realm. After all, AS is at bottom a demand of accessibility, a demand that whether something is good or not must depend on the possibility of someone being able to appreciate it. Insofar as we accept AS, this kind of objectivity is beyond our reach.[48]

Rejection of contemporary subjectivism as a theory of practical reason commits us at least to the claim that practical judgments are objective in the possibility of error dimension. However, this dimension is compatible with all the views about the relation between personal and impersonal goods noted earlier, including the view that there are no impersonal goods. One might think that only contemporary subjectivism would lead us to accept the Exclu-sivity of the Personal View. But one could arrive at it by accepting views about the nature of the good that are obviously incompatible with a subjectivist position; one could, for instance, arrive at it by thinking that each human being has a different divinely

---

[48] Of course, if someone thinks that the corresponding requirement is one that cannot be met in the realm of theoretical reason either, then the fact that no similar requirement can be met in the realm of practical reason is of very little significance. For views that seem to rule out the possibility of some kind of corresponding requirement in the realm of theoretical reason, see Cheryl Misak, *Truth and the End of Inquiry*; McDowell, *Mind and World*; and, more radically, Michael Dummett, "What Is a Theory of Meaning (II)."

ordained vocation and that this vocation determines what is good for her.[49]

However, accepting that some practical judgments are objective in the intersubjective dimension *does* seem to rule out the Exclusivity of the Personal View. But it is important to note that the Primacy of the Personal View is not ruled out by this position; after all, the requirement that different subjects agree on what counts as good says nothing, on its own, about the nature of the grounds of these judgments. We will see in the next chapter how a promising account of impersonal goods would be in line with the Primacy of the Personal View.

Are these two notions of objectivity related? To some extent, the answer to this question will depend on the grounds on which the objectivity of these different claims is established. One possibility, which I take to be the most plausible one, is to think of the first dimension as a dimension of practical reason's *permissions and conditional demands* and the second dimension as a dimension of practical reason's *absolute demands*. Consider a permissible perspective on the good: taking elements of one's conception of the good to be grounded on their being good from that perspective does not, on its own, constitute a mistake of practical reasoning. Insofar as one has that perspective, some demands might now follow. Let us say, for instance, that Joe is someone who does desire to watch movies, so that what we may call "the cinephile perspective" is one available to him. On certain occasions, the availability of this perspective will make demands on Joe that would not be made on those who do not have the perspective available. Moreover, the kinds of demands it makes on Joe will depend on what other perspectives he has available to him. If he regards food as nothing more than a means to keep body and soul together, then going to a slow-serving, expensive restaurant will rarely compete for resources against the things that are valuable from the cinephile perspective. Furthermore, one can think that the *importance* of a perspective varies from agent to

---

[49] One could think that in this case the impersonal good is "following one's vocation," but this will be determined by the shape of the theory. It might be a feature of the theory that following one's vocation is not what is considered to be good but rather that if your vocation is to do X, then doing X is good for you. (Similarly, one could think that "the satisfaction of desire" is not good, but if one desires X, then bringing about X is good for that person.)

agent. This can be captured in terms of various permissible ways to move from certain appearances of the good to their place in the agent's overall conception of the good. So for one person good practical reasoning might require checking the movie listings every Thursday before making definite plans for evening entertainment, whereas in other cases it might allow one to leave movies out of consideration for a while. Moreover, beyond the question of whether a perspective is merely permissible, there might also be room for permissible disagreement *within* a perspective. One might have two different attitudes toward eating popcorn while watching a movie: One might think that the crunching noise destroys, or at least distracts from, one's appreciation of the experience of watching a movie, or one might think that eating popcorn is part of the experience. There might be no general correct answer as to which view is preferable inside the cinephile perspective.

However, these various realms of permissibility do not foreclose the possibility of conditional demands. As we said earlier, for certain movie lovers, failing to look at the movie listings on Thursday might be a practical mistake, whether they recognize it or not. Moreover, it would not be too bold to assert that one needs to be in the grips of a certain illusion to think that one can find cinematic value in watching Andy Warhol's *Empire*.[50] Whether or not we're in a position to be confident in other cases, it seems hard to deny that many other demands follow from endorsing a permissible perspective or considering it to be important. Although the demands are conditional demands, these should not be seen as demands of consistency. First, the question of whether certain perspectives are permissible or not and whether a particular perspective leaves room for reasonable disagreement is not up to each subject. It is a question about the nature of the perspective itself and a question about how, in fact, a certain perspective should or can be incorporated into a subject's conception of the good. Moreover, the conditional demands in question, in this picture, are genuine, detachable demands.[51] The demands on the movie lover are not well captured

---

[50] The movie is a still 24-hour-long shot of the Empire State Building.

[51] In contrast with the undetachable demands made by consistency principles such as the Instrumental Principle. See, on this issue, John Broome, "Normative

if one says that she ought to either bring about that she no longer
has the perspective or read the weekend section of the paper on
Thursday. She *ought* to read the weekend section of the paper; the
availability of the perspective and its proper incorporation into the
agent's conception of the good *demands* that she read the paper on
Thursday.

On the other hand, the second dimension of objectivity cannot
make demands that are dependent on the availability of certain
perspectives, otherwise its demands would not be necessarily
intersubjective. Of course, there could be a perspective that is
shared by all subjects as a matter of contingent fact, and a recom-
mendation from that perspective might be one with which all
rational agents are required to comply. So, one could hold that
there is no rational requirement to treat animals well but that all
agents *in fact* take a special interest in animal welfare. It would be
true under this view, at least if the view takes the perspective of the
animal lover to be permissible, that the demands of animal loving
are demands made on all of our conceptions of the good. However,
it is still possible under this view that there is an ideal practically
rational agent for whom animal loving appears nowhere in her
conception of the good. Of course, to say that the second dimension
of objectivity does not depend on the availability of a perspective
does not mean that in order to claim that something is objective in
the second dimension one is committed to the claim that a certain
perspective is *in fact* available to all agents. The claim might simply
be that this is a perspective available to all ideal agents and that
insofar as one lacks it one fails to be a practically ideal agent to that
extent. To say thus that generosity is objectively good is to say
that agents for whom acts of generosity do not appear in their
conception of the good fall short of being practically ideal. Possibly,
for such an agent the right demand to make is that he not only act
generously but that he endeavor to cultivate the perspective of
generosity.

It is important to note that there are certain demands of
objectivity in the second dimension that are compatible with the

Requirements"; and Patricia Greenspan, "Conditional Oughts and Hypothetical
Imperatives."

exclusivity of the personal and thus do not translate into the recognition of any impersonal goods. One might defend some kind of perfectionist view according to which one's conception of the good needs to have elements from various perspectives without demanding that any particular perspective be part of the conception of the good for any particular agent. Or one might think that it is a demand of practical rationality that one try to appreciate as many goods as possible, and thus that one try to cultivate many perspectives without thereby accepting that any particular perspective ought to be cultivated. If one's acceptance of the objective demands of practical reason extends only to demands that are "formal" in this way, one could accept that there are objective constraints on one's conception of the good that are valid for all practically rational agents without thereby accepting the existence of any impersonal good. These demands are not simply undetachable consistency demands,[52] but they still fall short of producing a conception of impersonal goods.

4.7 IMPERSONAL AND PERSONAL GOODS

If there were no impersonal goods, practical reason would find itself in a kind of Hobbesian state of nature; there would be things that had to be in X's or Y's conception of the good but nothing that had to be in everyone's conception of the good. All shared ends would be so only contingently, determined by the fact that our ends happen to coincide at this point. There would be no ends shared on the grounds of being the kind of thing that is worthy of pursuit as such rather than worthy of pursuit conditional on the availability of a certain perspective for the agent. This seems to me a deeply unsatisfying position in which to end up, and I hope that most of us would accept that this conclusion would be unsettling to our self-conception as practical agents. What I want to focus on are two ways in which one might postulate impersonal goods. I will call them "built-up" and "basic" views of the nature of the impersonal good.

---

[52] Not all accept that all consistency demands are undetachable. See Niko Kolodny, "Why Be Rational?"; and Mark Schroeder, "The Scope of Instrumental Reason."

In very rough terms, a built-up view is one that takes impersonal goods to be constructed out of personal goods. A basic view takes impersonal goods to be independent of personal goods.

The most straightforward version of the basic view of impersonal goods is the claim that it is part of the nature of certain things that they be intrinsically valuable and that the fact that certain objects have the property of being intrinsically valuable is not reducible to, or explicated by appeal to, anything else. Many find such views metaphysically problematic[53] or a form of "dogmatism,"[54] but these objections depend on rather thin conceptions of reality and of our rational faculties that I certainly have no intention of defending.[55] However, these appeals to intrinsic value do not sit easily with the scholastic view. If AS and OS are correct, it is hard to see the grounds on which one could put forward a claim that a certain object has intrinsically valuable properties that are independent of the subject. The easiest way would probably be to appeal to some notion akin to Moore's organic goods, in which the demands of AS and OS are incorporated in the description of the state of affairs that is supposed to be valuable. So, if one thinks that what is intrinsically valuable is neither beautiful objects themselves nor just the feeling that is typically elicited by a beautiful object but a combination of the two (perhaps with further conditions), one would be able to accommodate AS and OS within this view. But it is hard to avoid the feeling that there must be some explanation for the fact that two things that are valueless can combine in such a way that although no new nonevaluative property is produced, an evaluative property does come into existence. And if we allow for some kind of explanation of the emergence of impersonal value, the most natural place to look for it would be the personal value that is already around us. It seems that what would most recommend the basic view is the absence of an alternative, so it's worth investigating what a built-up view would look like.

---

[53] Classically, J. L. Mackie makes this claim in *Ethics: Inventing Right and Wrong.* However, it's possible that expressivist views allow for similar views without the supposed metaphysically problematic claims. But then expressivism has its own share of problems.

[54] Korsgaard, *Sources of Normativity*, chapter 1.

[55] I also find them groundless; see my "Realists without a Cause: Deflationary Theories of Truth and Ethical Realism."

This issue will occupy much of the next chapter, but before we move on, it is worth distinguishing between two ways in which we could understand the Primacy of the Personal View that depend on how we understand the claim that impersonal values and the impersonal good are grounded on personal values and the personal good. First, it could be that the *content* of impersonal goods, or how we determine what *counts* as an impersonal good, is grounded on the content of personal goods. Second, one could think that the *justification* for accepting something as an impersonal good and incorporating it into one's conception of the good on those grounds is based on one's justification for incorporating personal goods into one's conception of the good. That is, one might think that the reason agents have to pursue impersonal goods is ultimately grounded on the reasons they have to pursue personal goods. Utilitarian positions in ethics, though not generally presented in these terms, can be used to clarify this alternative. Almost any utilitarian is committed to the view that the content of impersonal goods depends on the content of personal goods. According to a common understanding of utilitarianism, anything that an agent's conception of the good deems valuable is also impersonally valuable, or anything that is good for the agent is also impersonally good. And at least in a plausible understanding of utilitarianism, the personal good is primary: The impersonal value brought about by a possible action is measured by adding up the various personal values of what one brings about in a certain action. Few utilitarians would think that we determine what is good for me by first figuring out what is impersonally good and then finding which part of the impersonal good bears a certain relation to me (such as, for instance, being part of my life); what is impersonally good in such a case would be the action that brings about the greatest amount of impersonal value. However this kind of utilitarianism does not obviously imply any answer to the question why we ought to pursue the impersonal good; it is silent on the issue of the justification of incorporating impersonal goods into one's conception of the good.

Arguably, Mill's attempt at a proof of the principle of utility is an attempt to show that the grounds for pursuing impersonal goods are derived from the grounds for pursuing personal ones. Various Hobbesian views might fit this description, too, insofar as they try to

show that the pursuit of one's own good gives one reason to coop-
erate with others in the pursuit of shared ends. Finally, Korsgaard
seems to endorse a similar view when she argues that the grounds
for accepting that humanity in general is an end in itself rests on our
taking our own humanity to be an end in itself.[56] What I said about
the plausibility of the Primacy of the Personal View speaks only for
the view about the *content* of the impersonal good.

The next chapter will try to show how a scholastic view can
accommodate a conception of the impersonal good in these terms.
It will do this, however, within a more general framework of what I
will call "deontological goods." So far, the scholastic view seems to
privilege teleological accounts of practical correctness and rationality. The next chapter will try to show how the view can maintain
that, at least in certain contexts, the right is prior to the good. I will
understand the claim "The right is prior to the good" to imply at
least that the justification of claim of the form "X is right" does not
depend on the justification of claims of the form "X is good." In
particular, I will argue that, at least in certain cases, the justification
of certain practical rules or prescriptions does not depend on the
goodness of the states of affairs that they bring about. In some cases,
the goodness (or value) of certain states of affairs cannot be
grounded on anything other than the validity of certain rules. The
class of such states of affairs is what I designate by the label
"deontological goods." One plausible way to understand impartial
goods in line with the Primacy of the Personal View is to understand
them as a particular kind of deontological good. Given the seemingly teleological character of the scholastic view, one might have
expected the view to sit well only with teleological conceptions of
ethics. It is a consequence of the argument in the next chapter that
the scholastic view can be congenial to deontological theories in
ethics.

[56] See Korsgaard, "Kant's Formula of Humanity."

5

Deontological Goods

So far, we have understood practical reasoning as governed by the ideal of forming a legitimate general conception of the good. Most of the reasoning described so far seems completely teleological in character: A certain object appears to be good; we reflect on the adequacy of this appearance; we infer from the fact that this object appears to be good that other objects also appear to be good; and so on. Moreover, the good in question is an object of pursuit, the kind of thing that could be brought about in an action. For non-consequentialists, this will seem like a serious strike against the theory; there seems to be no room in it, for instance, for deonto-logical constraints. Concerns of this kind have made non-consequentialist authors wary of the notion of good, and certainly of the notion of the good as something to be promoted or brought about. Scanlon, for instance, gives primacy to the notion of a reason and defends a "buck-passing" account of the good according to which "being good, or valuable, is not a property that itself provides a reason to respond to a thing in certain ways. Rather, to be good or valuable is to have other properties that constitute such reasons."[1] Moreover, Scanlon claims that various things we have reason to do, such as being good friends, cannot be understood as cases in which we have a reason to promote a certain good.

---

[1] Scanlon, *What We Owe to Each Other*, p. 97.

Insistence on the primacy of reasons is itself problematic, however, because it might leave us baffled about why we have those reasons, about the *point* of acting from these reasons.[2] Moreover, deontological constraints are difficult to account for; they seem to clash with some basic intuitions about the nature of rationality.[3]

In this chapter, I will show how the scholastic view can accommodate the possibility of what I will call "deontological goods." Deontological goods are goods that are made possible by certain rules and that cannot be intelligibly promoted unless one abides by these rules. Deontological goods thus explain the possibility of deontological constraints. It will turn out that not only are deontological constraints compatible with the scholastic view but that this way of understanding deontological constraints is independently plausible. Perhaps the most serious consequentialist objection to deontological views is that deontological constraints sometimes require us to refrain from pursuing the greatest good. The conception I defend does not commit us to the idea that deontological constraints sometimes require that we refrain from pursuing the greatest good. Because most of the cases in which deontological constraints seem plausible come from the ethical realm, I will focus on this case. In particular, I will focus on whether a conception of deontological constraints as constitutive conditions of deontological goods is plausible. This will also allow us to see how a notion of an impersonal good can be constituted in keeping with the Primacy of the Personal View. Although a great deal of the chapter will be spent putting forward a broadly Kantian conception of ethics, the aim of the chapter is not to provide a conclusive defense of Kantian ethics or anything near it. The aim is to show that the scholastic view can make room for deontological constraints and to show how these same resources can be used to construct a notion of an impersonal good. More generally, I do not aim to convince consequentialists of the truth of deontology here; this would certainly lie beyond the scope of this book. The scholastic view does not have any apparent

---

[2] See Robert Adams's "Scanlon's Contractualism: Critical Notice of T. M. Scanlon, *What We Owe to Each Other*" for a version of this objection to Scanlon. See also Barbara Herman, "Leaving Deontology Behind."

[3] See Samuel Scheffler, *The Rejection of Consequentialism: A Philosophical Investigation of the Considerations Underlying Rival Moral Conceptions*, 2nd edition, Appendix.

difficulty in accommodating consequentialist views of ethics, or, for that matter, of any subfield of ethics. What I aim to show is that to the extent that one is sympathetic to deontological views, one will not only be able to express these views in the framework of the scholastic view but also use this framework to help answer difficult problems that deontological theories often face.

5.1 CONSEQUENTIALISM AND DEONTOLOGY

Consequentialist theories come in various flavors. I will be most concerned with what can be called "maximizing" versions of consequentialism because they present the starkest contrast with deontological theories. Consequentialism, as I understand it, can be quite liberal about what can be counted among the consequences of an action; any state of affairs, including the performance of the action itself, can count as a consequence. I will start by considering one version of this kind of consequentialism, which I will call "narrow consequentialism." According to narrow consequentialism, the sole principle of morality is that we should always maximize the general good, where the good in question, insofar as it is something we all have reason to promote, is an impersonal good.

Narrow consequentialism often seems to run afoul of our moral intuitions. For instance, it seems that narrow consequentialism would require us to kill an aging patient with healthy organs if those organs could be used to provide a long and healthy existence for four other persons. Of course, most consequentialists would probably reject this implication of the theory, but that rejection takes some work. Deontology, on the other hand, seems to be in a much better position to endorse these intuitions. Deontological theories tell us that we should abide by moral rules (like the rule against murder) that are justified independently of their capacity to bring about the greatest good. Here it seems that deontological theories have an important advantage over consequentialist theories, or at least over narrow consequentialism: A great deal of the appeal of deontological theories is their apparent congruence with our ordinary views.

On the other hand, this way of describing the contrast also shows the advantage that consequentialism has over deontology. After all, this seems to imply that deontological theories will often forbid us from pursuing the greatest possible good because doing so would violate a moral rule. The requirement to conform with a certain rule might force us to settle for a worse state of affairs when a better one could have been promoted. This is what is often called the paradox of deontology.[4] On the whole, it appears that deontological theories face an uphill battle to explain why we are bound by the rules they prescribe, whereas consequentialism, by enjoining us to pursue the greatest good, seems to wear its theoretical plausibility on its sleeve. The theoretical advantage of consequentialist theories seems to be independent of any particular substantive view about what the impersonal good might be.[5]

So it seems that we face a trade-off between "intuitive" and "theoretical" considerations. One might simply think that one kind of consideration overrides the other and try to settle the issue in this manner.[6] However, if one does not want to make these trade-offs, one might try to show either that consequentialism does not conflict with our ordinary judgments or that there is a defensible theoretical view that can give moral rules the role that the deontologist wants to give them. Typically, deontologists have met this challenge in one of the following ways. First, one can try to provide some theoretically acceptable rationale for various constraints on the pursuit of the greatest good.[7] Second, one can challenge the consequentialist assumption that the notion of promoting the good has what might be called "unrestricted application." One may, for instance, deny the claim that in all situations in which the moral agent finds herself there is something that can be described as the "greatest good"[8] or

---

[4] For a detailed exposition of the paradox (and an attempted solution), see Christopher MacMahon, "The Paradox of Deontology."

[5] Shelley Kagan, for instance, tries to provide a defense of consequentialism without relying on any particular theory of the good. See his *The Limits of Morality*, especially p. 7. Samuel Scheffler has also famously argued that deontological constraints are paradoxical under any conception of the good. See his *The Rejection of Consequentialism*, especially chapter 4.

[6] Although they might not like to put it this way, one can think that Singer and Kagan represent one side of this strategy and Williams (and some particularists) the other.

[7] For some such attempts, see Thomas Nagel, *The View from Nowhere*, especially pp. 175–188; and Frances Kamm, "Toward the Essence of Nonconsequentialism."

[8] See Philippa Foot, "Utilitarianism and the Virtues." Foot also argues in this paper that if we accept that other ethical views enjoin us to pursue a lesser good, they will

the state of affairs that is most valuable, impartially conceived. In this view, cases in which nonconsequentialist theories seem to be enjoining us to pursue the lesser good, there is in fact nothing that could possibly count as a greater good, impartially conceived. Finally, one can restrict the application of the notion of promoting the good by arguing that "promoting" is not the only appropriate attitude that one can have toward a value, so that cases in which we seem to be required to promote a lesser good are better conceived of as cases in which the relevant attitude to the value is not "promoting" but, for instance, "respecting."[9] None of these ways of defending deontology is obviously compatible with what we have seen of the scholastic view so far. The idea of a constraint on the pursuit of the good seems problematic for the scholastic view; it is hard to escape the conclusion that any such constraint would itself have to be conceived of as good. One could propose that the constraints function as rules of inference in deriving one's conception of the good, but, viewed this way, they wouldn't be constraints on *the pursuit* of the good but rather constraints on what *counts* as being good; after all, rules of inference should determine when we can or cannot conclude that a certain object is good.[10]

Multiplying the number of attitudes that one has toward the good does not sit easily with the scholastic view. Concluding that something is good is, according to the scholastic view, to pursue it, or at least to form the intention to pursue it. It is not clear what role other attitudes could play in this conception.

However, these considerations do not make it impossible for the scholastic view to accommodate deontological moral theories, or so I will argue. Deontological theories can be understood as accepting that the morally good agent, when acting in accordance with the

seem implausible in comparison with the straightforward consequentialist commitment to always promote the best.

[9] For the idea that "promoting" is not the only appropriate attitude toward a value, see Christine Swanton, "Profiles of the Virtues"; and Thomas Scanlon, *What We Owe to Each Other*, especially chapter 2. For a somewhat similar division of nonconsequentialist views (but that does not raise the possibility of the kind of view I will be pursuing in this chapter), see Philip Pettit, "Consequentialism and Respect for Person," especially pp. 119–120.

[10] Our final proposal will be similar in certain ways to a view that considers the rules of deontology to be rules of inference. See the discussion that follows.

rules proposed by these theories, always acts to promote the greatest
general good or the most value. In fact, deontological theories can
be thought of as proposing a theory of how to determine the
impersonal good in a way that is compatible with the Primacy of the
Personal View. I hope to show that conceiving them in this way is not
just an ad hoc move to make such ethical theories compatible
with the scholastic view; it is a compelling way to conceive of
deontological theories insofar as it can do away with the paradox of
deontology.

The rest of the chapter proceeds as follows. I first introduce the
general notion of a deontological good. Section 5.2 explains the
notion of a deontological good and gives two examples of them –
the ideal of polite behavior and what I will call the "maximizable"
good in general (as conceived by classical decision theory). Section
5.3 asks whether we must conceive of deontology as placing constraints on the pursuit of the greatest good. I argue there that the
possibility of deontological goods shows that it is possible to accept
that certain moral rules are "prior" to the pursuit of the good
without accepting that they can come into conflict with, and thus
forbid, the pursuit of the greatest impersonal good. Section 5.3
sketches how one can plausibly construct a conception of an
impersonal good using the example of the Kantian understanding
of the relation between virtue and the highest good.

5.2　DEONTOLOGICAL GOODS

Suppose we think that a certain instance of swimming is good. We
might ask what makes it the case that swimming in this particular
case is good. Suppose that the answer is that swimming is good in
part because it is a form of exercise. Now this might not imply that
all forms of exercise are good or that it would have been equally
good at this point to engage in any kind of exercise. It might be that
this particular kind of exercise is particularly good. Moreover, it
does not mean that as long as I had exercised by swimming, what I
would have done was good. It might be that had I swum in certain
clumsy ways I might have exercised even more but that this would
not be a case in which it would have been good that I swam. Being a
form of exercise thus is a necessary (but not sufficient) condition for

swimming to be good, and the fact that swimming is a form of exercise is essential (or at least so we are assuming) to the justification of the view that swimming is good. I will say that in this case being a form of exercise is a *constitutive condition* of the goodness of swimming. Given the assumption that the fact that swimming is a form of exercise is essential to the justification of my conception of swimming as good, there would have been no point in my actions had I tried to swim in such a way that swimming would not be a form of exercise (if I could do it, for instance, by effortlessly floating in the water). I will say that a good is a "deontological good" if its being an instance of a certain rule is a constitutive condition of its being something of value.[11]

Is it plausible to think that there are deontological goods? In this section, I will argue that it is. I'll look at two rather different cases of deontological goods. First I will show that the good of polite behavior is of this kind. Then I will show that a decision-theoretic understanding of what I will call "a maximizable good" is one in which the subjective good is a deontological kind of good. Both these cases will pave the way to the view that moral rules are constitutive conditions of anything that purports to be an impersonal good.

Let us start with rules of etiquette. Rules of etiquette are at times just arbitrary rules, and compliance with them seems at times to result in nothing of much importance, and at times they can be instrumental in achieving ends that we can identify independently of the existence of these rules: Avoiding fistfights, for instance, would be one of them. But some rules of etiquette seem to be constitutive conditions of an ideal of politeness that would not be available independently of these rules. It is plausible to say that the full-fledged concepts of rude and polite behavior do not make sense apart from certain rules of etiquette that determine what in different places and on different occasions counts as rudeness or politeness. I am rude to my neighbor when I fail to greet him in the street, but I can be rude in such a way only if there are certain rules that determine what

---

[11] Sometimes I will speak loosely of the rule itself being a constitutive condition.

counts as greeting, when and whom it is appropriate to greet, and so forth.[12]

To say that a rule is a constitutive condition of a certain good does not mean that following the rule suffices to secure the good in question. It is important to notice that this is true for at least some of the goods that have as their constitutive conditions the rules of etiquette. Indeed, insofar as the rules of etiquette can provide for more than an arbitrary ritual, they help constitute an ideal pattern of human action that it seems reasonable to suppose is an important good. We can characterize this ideal as a mode of interaction that falls in between mere indifference and intimacy. Because we do not want to ignore the existence of our neighbors but also do not want to be friends with the whole world, we want to be able to find a form of sociability that falls short of intimacy.[13] The rules of etiquette determine this form of sociability. Following the rules of etiquette, of course, does not guarantee that we will succeed in achieving this form of sociability. The rules of etiquette might mask indifference, they might be misinterpreted by our neighbor, or our efforts in accordance with those rules might be sabotaged by stepmotherly nature, if, for instance, bad lighting makes my innocent waving look like an obscene gesture. Nevertheless, the rules of etiquette not only help promote this end but also make the end intelligible, and because of this latter point they are constitutive conditions of the value of polite behavior. If one were to live in a society that predates

---

[12] Elizabeth Anderson also points out that the rules of etiquette are constitutive of their ends in such a way that it would be hard to make sense of an injunction to maximize the pursuit of these ends by violating these rules. See her *Value in Ethics and Economics*, pp. 75–76. Anderson's conception of this relation is somewhat different from mine, and she does not try to show that a similar relation might hold between moral rules and a conception of an impartial good. Rather, her case against consequentialism depends on rejecting the claim that "values of states of affairs can be globally compared" (*Value in Ethics and Economics*, p. 47). This is no doubt a possible way of trying to reject the intuitive appeal of consequentialism but also notoriously problematic. For some criticisms of Anderson's views on incommensurability, see Ruth Chang, "Introduction."

[13] Of course, this is not to say that the value of other ends could not override the value of the ends of etiquette. Also, I am oversimplifying the issue somewhat because the institution of polite behavior is more complex than what is generally regarded as the "rules of etiquette." The institution involves complex and difficult norms that will probably allow for exceptions to the rules that are commonly regarded to be the rules of etiquette.

any rules of etiquette, one might have a vague yearning for some sort of social interaction other than friendship but not the specific aim of living in polite interaction with one's fellow human beings.

It is important to note that to say that etiquette rules function as constitutive conditions of the value of polite behavior is *not* to imply that the end prescribed by etiquette is to avoid rule violation or that the comparative value of actions from the perspective of etiquette is assessed by counting the number of violations. The end of etiquette is polite behavior, and it is not even clear that etiquette recommends that we minimize violations of the rule even in cases in which we are faced with a choice between more or fewer violations of the same rule. Consider the following cases in which there are different numbers of violations of the rule of punctuality depending on what I do. Suppose that I am supposed to be at a meeting at noon, another at 1 P.M., and a third at 2 P.M. Each meeting takes fifty minutes, and it takes ten minutes to go from one meeting to another. However, the meeting at noon conducts business for only thirty-five minutes. The last fifteen minutes are mostly spent bantering, but if the meeting were running late, people would skip the bantering and the meeting would end at 12:50. The same is not true of the meeting at 1. There are fifty minutes worth of business that will be conducted to the bitter end even if this means staying past 1:50. Let us assume that it is considered extremely impolite, immeasurably more impolite than arriving late at the meeting, to leave the meeting before its official ending even if not much business is being conducted at that point, or to announce at the beginning of the meeting that there should be no bantering at the end of the meeting because one is running late or to try to rush the meeting in any other way. As I am leaving to go to the first meeting, I realize that I must run an errand by 1 P.M. and that it will take me ten minutes to run it. If I do it now, I will be ten minutes late for the noon meeting and on time for the two others, but if I do it after the first meeting, I will be late for both later meetings. What should I do now? One possible solution to this problem is that we minimize rule violations, and thus I run my errand before my first meeting, arrive there late, but then arrive on time for my two other meetings. But it is far from obvious that this *has* to be the conclusion that the polite person must draw. In order to see this, we should consider how the polite person will apologize to the people in the first meeting. Suppose she just reproduces the reasoning just given. This might evince the following (hopefully muted) reaction: "Oh so that's how much she cares about our meetings. She probably thinks that our bantering is a waste of her precious time." One might come to the conclusion that the polite person would approach the situation differently; she would arrive punctually at the first meeting because there is still time to run her errand after her meeting, and she should proceed properly and hope for a miracle and allow herself to come late for a meeting only when time has run out even for God to perform a miracle. (After all, the first meeting might find, for the very first time, that there was no business to be conducted, or the other participants might have turned into a surly bunch overnight.) This might allow her to say truthfully that she was hoping to arrive punctually but her late arrival turned out to be unavoidable. At any rate, minimizing violations in this case is just one rationale, and not a very compelling one, for extending the rules of etiquette to this case.

What this example also shows is that there may be no obvious solution to the problem of how to pursue a deontological good in light of rule conflicts. Of course, insofar as these rules are constitutive conditions of the good in question, we have to think of the reasoning by which we settle what to do in the pursuit of this good as reasoning by which we *refine* (or revise) the constitutive rules; we try to improve our understanding of what are and are not permissible exceptions to the punctuality rule. But conceiving of those goods as deontological goods allows us to think that the reasoning will be such that one might appeal both to the constitutive rule and to the constituted good. One can try to see which revision would be more in keeping with one's conception of the good in question, or one might try to understand better how one should apply a more general rule to the case in question.[14] At any rate, it is important to note

---

[14] It is worth comparing the plight of the polite person in this situation with the plight of judge Hercules as described by R. M. Dworkin. See "Hard Cases" in his *Taking Rights Seriously*. It would certainly be unhelpful to give to judge Hercules, as a piece of general advice, the following directive: You should always make decisions that minimize violations of legal rights. This would still be bad advice if it were limited to cases in which the legal rights in question were similar enough.

that accepting that a certain good is a deontological good does not commit one to any particular way of solving problems in which rule violations seem unavoidable.

If rules of etiquette are indeed constitutive conditions, this gives us some hope that moral rules might be conceived also as constitutive conditions of some kind of good. After all, the ends of etiquette are in many ways similar to the ends of morality, and some argue that they are even *part* of morality.[15] If this is the case, deontology is the correct view for at least a subset of the moral goods, albeit not a particularly significant subset. But perhaps more akin to the role one might envisage for moral rules in the constitution of a conception of an impersonal good is the role of rules of consistency in the constitution of a conception of the comparative value of various options under conditions of uncertainty in a way that allows for maximization of value (or utility) as proposed by classical decision theory (CDT). A conception of the good that conforms to CDT in the way it compares value can be called "a conception of a maximizable good." One could think that it is a demand of rationality that one's conception of the good be the conception of a maximizable good, but I will set this issue aside. The question here is how to understand the rules of CDT if we *assume* that this demand is indeed a demand of rationality. It is worth noting, however, that the argument does not depend on the particular consistency conditions of CDT being correct; the argument will go through with any decision theory that postulates *any* consistency conditions. It is also worth pointing out that although I am interpreting CDT as making normative demands compatible with the scholastic view, much of what I'll have to say here would apply also to other interpretations of CDT.[16]

Classical decision theory seems to be a typical consequentialist theory with regard to its realm. It seems to tell you that one ought to maximize utility, no matter how, and that there are no rules by which one must (nearly) always abide. This is to some extent correct. As long as one is maximizing expected utility, one cannot be doing

---

[15] See Sarah Buss, "Appearing Respectful: The Moral Significance of Manners."

[16] But, of course, not all such interpretations. Nothing I say here applies to purely descriptive interpretations of CDT.

anything wrong according to CDT. But there is also something clearly incorrect about this characterization. After all, there are inviolable rules that, according to CDT, an agent must follow: These are the rules that specify the consistency conditions. Classical decision theory is also often identified with subjectivist theories of practical reason, but as long as we understand CDT as presenting only a *necessary* condition on any theory of the individual good, one might accept CDT and impose further constraints on the rationality of preference or comparative valuing. However one interprets CDT, it does contend that an agent does best by maximizing expected utility.[17] Note that the correct sort of utility function cannot be ascribed to an agent who does not satisfy the consistency conditions at some level,[18] and thus nothing will count as doing well (maximizing utility) or badly for the agent in question. It is also important to note that CDT does not recommend minimizing violations in situations where one might violate the axioms of consistency more than once. If CDT is correct, it is *never* worth violating the axiom of transitivity as a shortcut to maximizing utility because violating the axiom of transitivity guarantees that one fails to satisfy one of the conditions of having a utility function to begin with. However, this is not to say that CDT imposes rules that cannot be overridden by the maximization of utility or that CDT says that sometimes we need to forego the pursuit of our greatest maximizable good for the sake of the transitivity rule. If CDT is correct, something could only count as maximizing the good (utility) if the agent's choices obey the rule of transitivity.[19] This, of course, does not mean that the

---

[17] This is imprecise. Because CDT is a theory of decision *under risk*, there is no guarantee that the agent who follows its dictate will always do better than the agent who doesn't. The only thing that the theory can guarantee is that an agent can *expect* to do better by following it than by not following it. I will ignore this complication for now but it will turn out to be important later.

[18] This qualification is to make room for the less extreme versions of the CDT hypothesis. These versions are not committed to the claim that the actual behavior of the agent satisfies the consistency conditions but that a rational preference ordering can be ascribed to the agent that satisfies these conditions.

[19] One might think that matters are complicated by the fact that we must find a way of speaking of the preferences of agents who fail to comply with the consistency conditions imposed by CDT. After all, *none of us* fully comply with these conditions. However, as long as we think of CDT (or any other such theory) as the correct normative theory, this is not really a problem because CDT still represents an ideal for which we ought to strive, and according to this ideal, we ought never to violate the rules of consistency for the sake of greater value.

rules of consistency exhaust the good, even if we set aside any further demands of practical reason. The rules of consistency only guarantee that my conception of the good is of a maximizable good. Moreover, it would be incorrect to say that my end is to maximize instances of my following the consistency conditions; my aim is to pursue the good (or maximize utility).

Now one can accept the demands of CDT and not think that they are constitutive conditions of the maximizable good because a constitutive condition also requires that being an instance of the rule is essential to the justification of the goodness of the thing. But one might think that the fact that ideal conceptions of the good satisfy the axioms of CDT is simply a consequence of the substantive demands that one makes on a conception of the good. So, for instance, one might think that everyone ought to maximize pleasure. Because choices that are guided by the demand to maximize pleasure are a fortiori choices that conform to the axioms of CDT, one satisfies the axioms of CDT simply by following no principle other than the demand to maximize pleasure. One can then accept that ideal conceptions of the good ought to conform to the axioms of utility theory without thereby being committed to their being constitutive conditions of the good.

However, to the extent that one accepts authority-subjectivism, it will be hard to avoid the conclusion that something like the axioms of rational choice are constitutive conditions of a maximizable good. It might be easier to see this point if we take a detour through a speculative history of subjectivism's commitment to the thought that the axioms of CDT (or at least of some alternative rational-choice theory) are constitutive conditions of each person's good. From our characterization of contemporary subjectivist theories in chapter 3, we can say that they are committed to the following two claims:

(a) Under certain appropriate conditions, certain attitudes (or judgments) of the agent will *fully* determine what counts as the agent's good. I will call these attitudes (or judgments) *good-determining attitudes*. (Desires and preferences, for instance, are commonly regarded as good-determining attitudes.)

(b) There are no objects that will necessarily be good for all agents.

It might be worth thinking of subjectivism in this context as growing out of dissatisfaction with hedonist normative theories of the individual good.[20] One possible source of dissatisfaction is the following. Suppose someone desires something that gives her no pleasure whatsoever, and when her desire is satisfied, she still maintains that she got what she wanted despite the fact that the object of her desire afforded her no pleasure. Let us also assume that no amount of further information or new experiences would change her mind about this issue. What would hedonist theories have to say to such a person? There might be ways in which the hedonist can avoid this conclusion, but the most straightforward hedonist response would be to say that such an agent is simply irrational or wrong; she desires something other than pleasure. This response makes the hedonist position a nonsubjectivist view by denying that the agent has normative authority. But the problem of hedonism can be generalized: If we want to maintain the normative authority of the agent, we cannot think that any object, even an internal state of the agent, is intrinsically desirable; for any such object, it is possible that the agent, even under ideal conditions, will fail to have the relevant "good-determining attitude" toward this object.[21] So what is needed is not a new independent thing, the maximization of which is the goal of practical reason. What is needed is to sort out the conditions under which an attitude could count as good-determining and the conditions, if there are any, under which that attitude would misfire. So, for instance, given that the individual good must guide action, we might think that the attitude cannot be one that recommends conflicting choices or that the attitude cannot be such that we could, under normal conditions, regret having achieved its object, and so forth. These considerations might lead us to think that preference rather than desire, or that considered preference rather than "raw" preference, is the paramount good-determining attitude.

So it is of the very nature of the move to subjectivism that we should expect that subjectivist theories would not be consequentialist

---

[20] This is a purely expository device. I make no claims here of historical accuracy.
[21] Although, as we saw in the last chapter, this position generates serious problems for the subjectivist.

theories in the sense that there is a good to be pursued that is independent of certain rules. This is because subjectivism *starts* from the point of view that the individual good is not *given* prior to the exercise of the agent's normative authority but is constituted by the exercise of that authority, so that there is nothing to be maximized by the agent before the basic conditions of constituting the good have been satisfied.[22] But any subjectivist theory that goes beyond recommending whatever the agent chooses to do or feels like doing will have to impose some such conditions as constitutive elements of the individual good. So it is no surprise that under subjectivist theories of the good, certain rules make a conception of the individual good possible. Note that this point holds for any position that assigns a certain kind of normative authority to the agent, whether it is subjectivist or not; that is, for any position that accepts (a) whether or not it also accepts (b). The point follows from accepting a commitment to some version of authority-subjectivism, not from endorsing a contemporary subjectivist theory of practical reason.

We can now see the close connection between deontology with regard to the maximizable good and a conception of the impersonal good as a deontological good, at least if we think that in moral theory, too, there is no independent good that one is supposed to maximally promote (such as happiness). If we think that the content of the impersonal good should be based on the content of personal goods constrained by authority-subjectivism, we will need to understand how we get from these personal goods to a general conception of impersonal good. Just as we needed to specify the basic conditions constituting a maximizable good that was valid for an agent considered in isolation, we must now specify the basic conditions constituting the impersonal good because there are no quanta that make up the various individual goods that we can straightforwardly maximize or add.

No doubt, even if one agrees that there must be such constitutive rules with respect to the impersonal good, there is no guarantee that

---

[22] It is worth emphasizing again that I am not saying that the agent will always satisfy these conditions, only that the good will be determined by these (possibly counterfactual) circumstances in which the agent satisfies these conditions.

these rules will turn out to be the moral rules that deontological theories tend to uphold; they might look more like consistency rules than prohibitions on murder. In the next sections, I will try to motivate the view that the constitutive rules in question can indeed be rules we recognize as moral rules. But before we move to this task, it might be worth taking a quick look at a seemingly more straightforward way to move from a view that accepts authority-subjectivism to a conception of the impersonal good. It might seem that all we need to do is to accept the possibility of interpersonal comparisons of personal goods, or as it is better known in the literature, the possibility of interpersonal comparisons of utility. If interpersonal comparisons of utility are relatively unproblematic, it would seem that the most plausible understanding of the impartial good would be a straightforward function from individual utilities to the general utility. The simplest picture would be to add the personal utilities, but even if one needs to allow for somewhat more complex functions, it would still seem that such a function would be a more plausible way to come up with a conception of the impersonal good than anything as substantive as Kantian ethics.

In fact, it might seem that the possibility of interpersonal comparisons of utility is quite intuitive; we seem to engage in such interpersonal comparisons all the time. So it might seem that this strategy of coming up with a conception of the impersonal good is on firm ground and thus a significantly more plausible view than an alternative that would appeal to the basic principles of something like Kant's ethics. However, one must note that insofar as one is committed to authority-subjectivism, an appeal to interpersonal comparisons of utility is very far from being unproblematic. John Harsanyi seems to provide exactly such an account of general utility that is based on what seems to be only innocent modifications of CDT to accommodate interpersonal comparisons of utility. However, it is important to note that the apparent innocent modifications of CDT to allow for interpersonal comparisons might throw us back into a hedonist conception of the individual good. Such interpersonal comparisons require that we postulate a fixed unit of utility and determine a zero point. However, at least one natural interpretation of these moves is to think of utility as a measure of something independent of our judgments of preference.

For instance, let us think that there was a state (let us call it "satisfaction") such that the end of all humans beings ought to be the maximization of satisfaction. Then we could talk about a zero point (the absence of "satisfaction") or a fixed-unit point (a certain quantity of "satisfaction"). This understanding, however, conflicts with the normative authority of the agent because it postulates something that the agent must pursue independently of whether or not she or he judges, or would judge under the appropriate conditions, that this is worth pursuing.[23]

Of course, this is not the only possible interpretation one can give to zero points and units of utility. However, given that this understanding is incompatible with the normative authority of the agent, insofar as one wants to uphold this normative authority, one must provide an alternative understanding of these modifications of CDT. Indeed, as one would expect, Harsanyi does not try to base his understanding of interpersonal comparisons of utility in terms of a measure of something that we must accept to be desirable. I cannot enter here into a detailed discussion of Harsanyi's defense of a measure of interpersonal comparisons of utility.[24] However, one important element of his defense is his view that these comparisons are unavoidable: We engage in such comparisons all the time, and we ought to engage in them if social choice is at all possible.[25] It is certainly true that "when we have only one nut left at the end of a trip, we may have to decide which particular member of our family is

---

[23] Note that if we substitute "pleasure" for "satisfaction" we are back to a hedonist position. It is worth noting that Harsanyi also accepts the "principle of consumers' sovereignty," which he defines as saying that "the interests of each individual must be defined fundamentally in terms of his *own* personal preferences and not in terms of what somebody else thinks is 'good for him'" (*Rational Behavior and Bargaining Equilibrium in Games and Social Situations*, p. 52). He also defends the principle that he calls "the principle of preference autonomy," according to which "in deciding what is good and what is bad for a given individual, the ultimate criterion can only be his own wants and his own preferences." See his "Morality and the Theory of Rational Behavior," in Amartya Sen and Bernard Williams (eds.), *Utilitarianism and Beyond*.

[24] For some important criticisms, see Daniel Hausman, "The Impossibility of Interpersonal Utility Comparisons;" and James Griffin, "Against the Taste Model." The criticisms that both Hausman and Griffin raise are quite congenial to the points that I am making here.

[25] See Harsanyi, "Morality and the Theory of Rational Behavior," section 5.

in greatest need of a little extra food."[26] However, all that this
implies is that we need to be capable of making claims about
"greater and lesser good"; it does not imply that this notion is
grounded on interpersonal comparisons of utility. The idea that we
check who "needs it most" might seem to imply otherwise, but this is
not true. The most obvious interpretation of "who needs it most" is
who is the hungriest, not anything that would require an attempt to
assert the absolute position of "eating when hungry" in each child's
preference ordering. Under ordinary circumstances, the stoic
character of one of the children is largely irrelevant in answering the
question of "who needs the food most." We are so far left with no
reason to think that we even have available to us a notion of interpersonal comparison of utility. Of course, this is only one way to
move from personal goods to an impersonal good by means of a
straightforward function that accepts authority-subjectivism. But I
confess to know of no other, and for our purposes, showing that the
success of this proposal cannot be taken for granted is all that we
need.

5.3 THE UNRESTRAINED PURSUIT OF THE IMPERSONAL GOOD

The possibility of deontological goods opens up the possibility that a
scholastic view will be compatible with a deontological ethical theory. All that would need to be shown is that our conception of the
impersonal good is the conception of a deontological good that has
ordinary moral rules as its constitutive conditions. If this is the case,
we can say that we pursue the greatest good by following moral
rules; one can push "absolutism" as far as one wants without thereby
committing oneself to the claim that one's moral theory requires
that one pursue the "lesser good." In the following sections, I want
to explore the possibility that this is a very plausible way of understanding deontology; if this is true, it will turn out that rather than
being hostile to deontology, the scholastic view can provide us with a
particularly compelling version of deontology. Part of the plausibility of this conception of deontology lies in the very fact that,

[26] Harsanyi, "Morality and the Theory of Rational Behavior," p. 49.

conceived this way, moral rules are not *in tension* with the ideal of pursuing the greatest value but are the rules that make this ideal possible. This conception of deontology thus has the advantage of escaping the paradox of deontology.

It is often taken for granted that any moral view that starts from a conception of a moral action as action that falls under a certain rule will place constraints on the pursuit of the greatest impersonal good. But it should be clear by now that this relies on the assumption that a notion of an impersonal good is unlike the ideals of behavior that we looked into in the last section in that it can be understood independently of constitutive rules, or, in other words, that a conception of an impersonal good can itself be formed without an appeal to any moral rules. But it is not clear why this must be true. It is at least conceivable that the notion of an impersonal good depends on the acceptance of independently justified moral rules.

On the other hand, even if one were to accept that this is conceivable, it might seem implausible to say that typical moral rules can be constitutive of the impersonal good in this way. We seem to be confident about at least *some* of our judgments about which states of affairs (or outcomes of actions) are better or worse, and one might try to build on these intuitions to make a case that following moral rules can be incompatible with the pursuit of the greatest impersonal value. It seems intuitive to say that states of affairs that contain earthquakes are, ceteris paribus, worse than states of affairs that do not contain them. Similarly, the loss of four lives seems to be, ceteris paribus, a greater evil (lesser good) than the loss of one life, and deontologists are famous for denying that we can always opt for the loss of one life over the loss of four lives. These are judgments of impersonal value that are uncontroversial.[27] But these uncontroversial cases also seem to be cases in which either (in the first case) no moral rule plays any role whatsoever or (in the second case) moral rules might forbid us from pursuing the greatest value.

---

[27] The strategy doesn't even require that there be a definite set of such comparative judgments on which everyone agrees, as long as for any such set on which reasonable people may agree we can find instances of comparative judgments such that, at least in certain situations, the deontologist calls for the pursuit of the lesser good.

Let us start with the second case. First, note that even if it is uncontroversially true that, ceteris paribus, the loss of one life is a lesser evil than the loss of four lives, it is not uncontroversial that cases involving intentional killing do not violate the ceteris paribus clause. Because the deontologist does not consult an independently given value in his defense of a moral rule, it might seem unavoidable that there will be cases in which the rule will prevent us from pursuing the greatest value. But again, this seems an unavoidable conclusion only if we assume that our judgments about impersonal value are not determined, or even informed, by moral rules. However, it is not merely *conceivable* that moral rules play this role; they often seem to be doing just that. If I won the lottery, for instance, I might decide to distribute some of the money among my family members. When I decide how my winnings will be distributed, I might choose to fund my niece's education but not to fund my cousin's purchase of a lifetime season ticket to the Dallas Cowboys games. I might think that I am doing this because the former is of greater impersonal value, but my opinion about the impersonal value of each option seems to be informed by certain moral principles about what can count as a legitimate claim that a family member can make on my resources. Pleasure, for instance, might seem like a clear example of something that makes a positive contribution to the impersonal value of a state of affairs independently of the rules of morality. But even in this case, it turns out that this appearance is illusory. As Kant points out, the pleasures of a vicious person, such as the pleasures of a sadist, do not seem to make a positive contribution to the impersonal value of a certain state of affairs.[28] In all of these cases, when I decide what can and cannot make a positive contribution to an impersonal good, I am certainly relying on my views about which pleasures are worthy of being pursued and supported, views that do not seem to be independent of prior moral conceptions.

It might be a platitude that we make judgments about the impersonal good without further ado and that these judgments seem

---

[28] Kant, *The Metaphysics of Morals*, p. 264. Kant talks about happiness, but he clearly thinks that the same holds for pleasure. Of course, Kant is not the only one to make this claim. For a more contemporary example, see Jonathan Dancy, *Moral Reasons*, p. 61.

indispensable to moral judgments. Ethical decisions will often involve comparative judgments about the welfare of different people in different scenarios. It seems natural to describe these judgments as judgments about which courses of action will promote the greater or lesser general good. But it does not follow from this platitude that we can make judgments about which actions promote the greater value that do not depend on the application of the moral rules identified by the deontologist. It is the more controversial claim that allows for the possibility that the pursuit of the greater value as determined by these intuitive comparative judgments would conflict with the actions prescribed by the deontologist. This claim, but not the platitude, requires the further assumption that we can make judgments about the greater value that are not determined by moral principles.

Of course, nothing prevents the consequentialist from rolling up her sleeves and going to work to defend this further assumption by showing that the underlying conception of the good in these comparative judgments does not depend on any moral principles. But because it is hardly imaginable how this can be done without relying on a specific theory of value, these remarks should suffice to establish that one cannot just take for granted that traditional deontological theories will *constrain* our pursuit of the greatest impersonal value. At any rate, we cannot rule out in advance the possibility that the correct view is that constraining our actions by these moral rules is what makes possible the pursuit of the greatest good.

Before examining how a theory of the impersonal good can conceive of moral rules as constitutive conditions, we must try to deflect a preemptive strike. One might argue that whether or not our intuitive judgments about impersonal good can deliver a challenge to deontology, deontological theories will invariably require us to pursue what the *theory itself* must consider to be the lesser value. Scheffler, for instance, can be seen as arguing that this is an unavoidable consequence of theories that set an absolute prohibition on certain actions.[29] Let us consider for instance an absolute prohibition on intentional killing.[30] If someone has a choice between killing

[29] See Scheffler, *The Rejection of Consequentialism*. I come back to his view in the last section of this chapter.

[30] Of course, I am talking in terms of absolute prohibitions to simplify matters. It is rather implausible that there are any such absolute prohibitions.

a person or letting two die, and if the deontologist does not want to say that this is a case in which we are required to pursue a lesser good, then he must consider letting two people die the greater value in this situation. But what if he is confronted now with the choice of committing a murder himself or letting two people be murdered (if a terrorist says she will kill two innocent people unless the deontologist kills one)? It seems that the deontologist must say that murdering one person is the lesser evil. Even if we accept that killing is worse than letting die, why shouldn't two killings be worse than one?

This objection would be devastating to the deontologist if he were simply to identify instances of obedience to a moral rule with units of good, so that in cases of conflict between various instances of the same rule, the greatest value would necessarily coincide with the greatest number of instances of obedience (or the least number of violations). We can already note that the deontologist might want to deny this assumption; she can simply insist that a violation of a moral rule never promotes the greatest value. If the rule is indeed a constitutive condition of the impersonal good, one could not bring about the impersonal good by violating the rule. However, there are further problems with conceiving violations of the rule for the sake of preventing further violations as failures to promote the impersonal good. In particular, it might seem hard to accept this point and still think that the good in question is really impersonal. I'll come back to this point momentarily. But first I want to pursue a different objection.

One might think that if we insist that the end is not to minimize violations of the rule, we are committed to an even less satisfactory view because now it seems that there is no further end to my following moral rules; we follow them simply for their own sake, with no end in view.[31] We can put this objection as follows. One could say that there is an end other than just following the rule that is promoted by following the rules of morality. But if we can identify an end that these moral rules promote, wouldn't it be possible to find "shortcuts" to these ends? Could the rule then be anything other

---

[31] This is reminiscent of the accusation that deontology amounts to "rule-worship" made by J.J.C. Smart in *Utilitarianism: For and Against*.

than a reliable, although certainly fallible, route to the end? How can we be sure that any rule other than "promote this end to the greatest possible extent" will always be the best way to promote an end? This is not to deny that a consequentialist can accept a form of rule-consequentialism if it turns out that following certain rules and accepting certain institutions is the best way to promote the greatest good.[32] But even in this case, these rules are the consequences of a more basic demand that we pursue a certain end to the greatest extent. The justification of the rule in this case depends on the justification of the end. What is hard to envisage is that a plausible account of morality will show that it is the justification of the end that depends on the justification of the rule, as would be required in the case of a deontological good.

One could, on the other hand, say that following the rules correctly is ipso facto promoting the good. This way we could avoid the consequentialist characterization of certain moral rules as constraints on the pursuit of the greater value. This certainly would allow the deontologist to say that by not murdering one to prevent the murder of five, I would be promoting the greater value. But this view seems to be rather implausible because the deontologist seems to be saying that our end now is to follow rules for their own sake, thus leaving us with no explanation of why we should care for such rules; at best, the move seems to be just a "gimmick," an artificial way of presenting the deontological view that seems to be motivated by nothing other than an attempt to hide the paradoxical nature of deontology.[33] Moreover, this seems to misrepresent drastically the

---

[32] See John Rawls, "Two Concepts of Rules." For an attempt to extend Rawls's account of rules in a way that could provide a theoretical framework for Kantian ethics, see Tamar Schapiro, "Three Conceptions of Action in Moral Theory."

[33] A number of philosophers have tried to replace deontological views with consequentialist views that use agent-relative, time-relative notions of the good (see, for instance, James Dreier, "The Structure of Normative Theories"). Although pursuing the plausibility of these views would take us too far astray, I must say that I am skeptical that this move could do much to solve the problem of the paradox of deontology. I think that the most plausible accounts of these agent-relative (and time-relative) values analyze them in terms of agent-relative (and time-relative) reasons. But this just seems to me to restate the paradox, namely why someone would have a reason to pursue something other than the greatest (impersonal) good. For an interesting discussion and criticism of such views, see Mark Schroeder, "Teleology, Agent-Relative Value, and 'Good.'"

way in which a virtuous agent represents her end, for it leaves no room for the fact that among the ends of the virtuous agents, there must be ends that can be brought about and prevented from happening by causes other than human agency. It seems rather obvious that nature can support and sabotage the ends of the moral agent. It is certainly plausible to say, for instance, that earthquakes, disease outbreaks, and less radical forms of bad luck thwart the ends of virtuous agents; it seems that any plausible theory of the impersonal good should accommodate the fact that the absence of disease outbreaks is better than their presence. However, if the extent to which a certain course of action promotes the good is determined by how well or how poorly we follow certain rules, it would seem that as long as I have followed certain rules, I have achieved the end of morality to the fullest extent. Stepmotherly nature, to use Kant's expression, *could* not stand in my way. So it seems that the deontologist faces the following dilemma: Either she must require us sometimes not to pursue the greatest good or she must end up with the rather implausible view that the sole and complete good is to follow rules for their own sake.

However, the notion of deontological goods allows us to carve some space here for an acceptable notion of the impersonal good that can make moral rules as absolute as one would like. The rules of etiquette are constitutive conditions of the ideal of polite behavior, but the ideal is not achieved simply by following the rules; the same goes for the relation between the consistency conditions of CDT and the maximizable good. The question is whether it is plausible that the same relation will hold between moral rules and the impersonal good. In the next section, I try to suggest that it is.

5.4 KANTIAN DEONTOLOGY AND THE IMPERSONAL GOOD

I will argue in this section that thinking about Kantian moral theory as conceiving of moral rules as constitutive conditions of an impersonal good yields a particularly plausible view of the priority of moral rules. I will not argue in detail that this is the correct moral view, or even the best interpretation of Kant.[34] Rather, I want to

---

[34] See Herman, "Leaving Deontology Behind," for a similar conception of Kant's theory as a conception of value. However, the way she conceives of the "Kantian good" is somewhat different from the way I conceive of it here.

show that deontological theories can be well accommodated within a scholastic view. For the same reason, I hope it will be clear that similar moves can be made with different deontological theories.

Kant's conception of the highest good gives us a natural way of thinking of moral rules as constitutive conditions of the impersonal good without thereby committing us to the view that the good is just acting in accordance with moral rules. The highest good for Kant is not merely happiness but happiness conditioned by virtue or happiness ensuing from virtuous behavior. There is no sense in talking about whether we might break the moral law in order to pursue the highest good more directly; the end that the highest good envisages is an end that is made possible by virtuous willing – that is, by following the moral law. But virtuous behavior does not by itself exhaust the highest good. Far from it: Kant thinks that morality requires that we assume the existence of a powerful being who properly allocates happiness to the virtuous exactly because virtuous willing is not guaranteed to achieve its ends.[35]

Of course, this can only take us so far. Without further articulation, one might think that Kant's views on the highest good just make it obvious why deontology is so implausible because it seems that the highest good is an artificially concocted end. Instead of mere rule worship, Kant gives us rule worship topped with an afterthought that there might be something else worth having. If we haven't previously understood the point of following the rule for its own sake, the afterthought can't help us much.

But before I can make this thought more plausible, it is important to clarify the nature of the relationship between rules and ends that I have in mind here. There is a sense in which, for instance, the rules of baseball make certain ends possible. But the rules of a game do not stand in the right kind of intelligible relation with its ends; they might be necessary for the advancement of a certain end, but they are not part of its justification. The point of playing baseball is not given by its rules; ultimately, we do not pitch and bat because the rules of baseball command us to do so but because we find that baseball is fun and this kind of fun can be had only if we follow those rules. Following the rules of baseball is perhaps a condition of

---

[35] Kant, *Critique of Practical Reason*, pp. 92–100.

possibility of our enjoying a certain kind of pleasure. It might be the case that I couldn't experience this enjoyment without playing baseball and would thus be unable to see its point or pursue it until I first follow the rules of baseball. However, the rules of baseball do not provide us with a justification to pursue this kind of pleasure. If asked why I keep on playing baseball, my ultimate reason is not "because the game is over only after nine innings, and this is only the seventh inning."[36]

By contrast, in the view I envisage, the *justification* of the end is itself made possible by the *justification* of the rule. It provides the reasons to take a certain end to be worthy of pursuit, and thus it is an ultimate reason. Of course, some rules are derivative and thus depend on other rules. Perhaps deontology will make only one rule, such as Kant's Categorical Imperative, fundamental. In this case, all other rules would depend on the categorical imperative for their justifications. Still, that a certain end stands in violation of the Categorical Imperative is the ultimate reason for refraining from adopting it. In general, we can say that according to a deontological conception of the impersonal good, we are justified in accepting a certain conception of the impersonal good at least in part because we are justified in accepting certain moral rules.

Let us now return to our Kantian theory of the impersonal good. We can ask first how we come to this conception of the highest good. A Kantian theory of the impersonal good can be conceived of as the result of reflection on the conditions in which my ends could be objectively good in the second dimension of objectivity discussed in the previous chapter. We start from a point of view according to which all our ends are personal; everyone pursues and ought only pursue his or her personal good, without giving any special weight to the fact that other people pursue other things. In this view, the fact that Joe ought to judge something to be good, by itself, ought to play no role in anyone else's conception of the good. Each person's conception of the good is what we can call "purely personal."

---

[36] Of course, in certain contexts, I might give exactly this answer, but only because it is part of the background of a conversation in which my ultimate reasons are taken for granted.

Now suppose that we start from these personal goods but want to inquire into the possibility of forming a conception of impersonal goods that will satisfy the demands of the second dimension of objectivity. Can we construct a "higher ideal" of objectivity out of these personal goods? If this higher ideal were possible, then one's ends would be such that all rational beings can find them worthy of being pursued. However, we cannot just form this ideal by demanding that all agents pursue anything that would have been judged to be good by some agent on the basis of her purely personal conception of the good; there is no guarantee that all these things can be pursued at the same time. Thus, not just anything that figures in a purely personal conception of the good can become an impersonal good. We can think of moral rules as the conditions under which I can take an end that I set for myself, an element in my conception of good, to be an impersonal good.

One suggestion is that anything that can count as an impersonal good must be such that all rational beings can or ought to adopt it. (Otherwise it would not be something that ought to be judged good by all agents.) According to this suggestion, the constraints that I accept on my willing so that I can conceive of the object of my will as being good are the rules that constitute an impersonal good. The Categorical Imperative is exactly such a rule; when I will in such a way that I can also will that the principle of my actions governs the will of rational beings, the object of my will is good. Note that abiding by a moral rule in this case just guarantees that what I set as my end is impersonally good; it cannot guarantee that I actually achieve my end. But also my end can't be good if I do not abide by the Categorical Imperative because abiding by it is the condition under which I can conceive of the end I set as good. Of course, one might complain here that this at best gives us a conception under which *my ends* are good, but it does not give us a conception of an impersonal, *general* good. However, insofar as abiding by the Categorical Imperative is what determines that the object of my will is good, then the object of the will of every agent who abides by the Categorical Imperative will be good. This will indeed generate something like Kant's conception of the highest good: happiness conditioned by virtue. Note also that in this view, ceteris paribus, things will be better if more people abide by the Categorical

Imperative. But this does not mean that I should try to minimize violations of it at all costs, for if I fail to abide by the Categorical Imperative, I cannot see the ends of my actions as being impersonally good, and so I cannot see them as having a *greater* value than if I did abide by the Categorical Imperative. What I set myself to bring about, the object of my will, can only be correctly judged to be good if it is set in conformity with the Categorical Imperative. Note that it does not follow from this view that states of affairs that are not actual objects of the will, states of affairs that I do not bring about, or even states of affairs that I could not bring about cannot be considered as good. I can still consider them as *possible* objects of the will; that is, I can consider whether I would bring them about or prevent them if they were in my power. So this view allows us to think of states of affairs that have no relation to our agency to be better or worse. At the same time, we can rest assured that the pursuit of the greatest good and our commitment to the Categorical Imperative will never part company.

Kant is committed to the view that I cannot bring about someone else's virtue, and this turns out to be quite fortunate. This commitment prevents Kant from being plagued by questions about how his position handles cases in which in order to bring about someone else's virtuous willing I must violate the Categorical Imperative. In particular, he need not be concerned with the possibility that what an agent must judge to be more valuable (his virtuous willing rather than bringing about the virtuous willing of five others) other agents must judge to be less valuable. But it's hard to see how Kant's fortune might extend more generally to deontologists who are not committed to his particular conception of the impersonal good or to his views about the possibility of bringing about someone else's virtuous willing. It might thus be worth looking again at Scheffler's general objection against deontological theories. Scheffler argues that any ethical theory that accepts a certain restriction S such that sometimes we are not allowed to violate S in order to prevent further violations of S will prevent us from pursuing the greatest good, however construed. According to Scheffler, for any such theory, "there exists no non–agent-relative principle for ranking overall states of affairs from the best to worst such that it will always be permissible to produce the best state of affairs so characterized."[37] If this is correct, deontological goods cannot be impersonal goods because there will be no evaluative judgment (free of demonstratives or indexicals) that is valid for all agents. But let us see whether a conception of deontological goods cannot be fully impersonal.

To simplify matters somewhat, let us assume that our ethical theory imposes an absolute prohibition on intentional killing. Consider our terrorist case from the point of view of the person who has to make the choice (let us call her Arabella). She will consider that the correct action is to let the terrorist kill the two people. Now what about the perspective of a third person (let us call him Jude) observing the events? For Jude it will look like the choice of two killings over one, and Jude will probably have to say that the latter is the better state of affairs. In general, at least, one would think that, ceteris paribus, two killings are worse than one. Thus, what seems better from Arabella's point of view is worse from Jude's point of view, and we have here no possibility of an impersonal good. But if we think that the states of affairs that are being evaluated are possible objects of the will, we will see that the evaluations are only different if the evaluated states of affairs are different. For Arabella, the choice is between bringing about a death or choosing to let the terrorist be undeterred in bringing about the death of two people. In order to mark the fact that Arabella must represent the deterred and the undeterred terrorist as possible objects of her will, I will describe the latter possible choice as "bringing about that the (bringing about of the) death of two persons goes undeterred." If Jude looks at the same choice, he should be putting himself in Arabella's position and he should come up with exactly the same conclusion (he would do the same in that situation); if one has to choose between bringing about a death and bringing about that the (bringing about of the) death of two persons goes undeterred, one should choose the latter.

The sense in which he is judging that one murder is better than two must be that he sees the following as the object of his will: He could either bring about that the bringing about of two deaths goes undeterred or that the bringing about of one death goes

[37] Scheffler, *The Rejection of Consequentialism*, p. 80.

undeterred. In this case, Arabella might agree with Jude: She might think that the state of affairs in which one death is brought about is better. However, this cannot be the object of her will. What she would bring about is not that bringing about the death of one person goes undeterred; she would bring about the death itself. Note that the agent does not bring about that she brings about the death of an agent. By killing, an agent brings about death itself.[38] Of course, one can always build bizarre scenarios in which what she would be doing is bringing about that she brings about the death of an agent. We may imagine, for instance, that God descends from heaven and says something like: "You must press a button. If you press the red button, you will one day kill one person, but if you press the green button instead someone else will one day kill four persons." It might be plausible to say that if she presses the red button, the object of her will is not someone's death but that her bringing about someone's death will go undeterred. On the other hand, this kind of setup does seem to change our "intuitions" in the matter; it is not clear that in this case she should not press the red button.

The preceding discussion has an important consequence: If Kantian ethics involves, for instance, a prohibition against intentional killing,[39] it will be a restriction on having the death of a person as an object of my will. But this says nothing so far about how I should evaluate someone's bringing about a death as a possible object of my will. So there is so far no reason to see these events as any different from events in which someone's death is brought about by other causes. This is no doubt a happy consequence because there is something ludicrous about the idea that in general killings are worse than natural deaths.[40] Think about the superhero who fights the evil, conniving character. The evil character runs away with an innocent child he intends to kill. The evil character contrives to have his escape route pass through a pond in which he knows that two children are drowning (though through no fault of his own) in

---

[38] Of course, one can deny the legitimacy of this distinction. More on this point follows.

[39] Of course, Kantian ethics will (hopefully) not imply an absolute prohibition on intentional killing.

[40] Thomas Nagel makes a similar point in *The View from Nowhere*, p. 178.

the hope that he will shake loose the superhero as she tries to save the children. It seems a strange kind of hero who would say to the drowning children, "Sorry kids, killing is worse than death brought about by other means." In my book, if the superhero is virtuous, the evil plan will succeed because she will stop to save the children from the pond. If I am correct, she can do this and still be a superhero for the deontologist.

Now some caveats are in order. First, given what I said here, the option that the virtuous agent discards is not good (but certainly valuable), and this might give us trouble explaining the appropriateness of regret or the existence of residual obligations in cases in which one is forced to bring about one of two evils. A full defense of the plausibility of this account would need to address these issues, but I don't see any reason in principle that this cannot be done within the framework proposed here. More generally, this view of the impersonal good does not allow for a clear way in which the value of the state of affairs is a function of the value of various elements of the state of affairs. There's no sense in which in determining the overall value of the state of affairs one is adding the disvalue of a death or the disvalue of bringing about some death. But this is a consequence of the top-down nature of the Kantian approach, in which the value of the action is determined by a principle that issues an evaluation of the situation of a whole without first evaluating its parts. This again will raise questions about how the Kantian approach can underwrite various judgments of value that one wants to make about various elements of the discarded (or accepted) options. And again a full defense of the approach would require giving an account of these issues, but for our purposes we can rest content with showing the plausibility of the general approach.

Of course, one may argue that the Categorical Imperative cannot ultimately provide a good rationale for discriminating between intentional killing and allowing deaths to happen or be brought about by other agents (or bringing about that deaths go undeterred). This is closely connected to the worry about whether any theory can show that there is a morally relevant difference between doing and allowing in the relevant cases in a way that will allow us to explain why it is better (in the relevant cases) to allow something to happen rather than to intentionally do it. Given, however, that intentional killing and allowing death involve two different attitudes toward the will of others, I think the Categorical Imperative is in a particularly good position to deliver this result. However, pursuing this line of inquiry is also beyond the scope of this chapter.[41] The proper place for such a dispute is in trying to settle which theory provides a better conception of the impersonal good. At any rate, the aim of this chapter was not to establish the truth of a particular deontological theory but rather to show that the scholastic view does not put them in a particularly difficult spot. Indeed, conceiving deontology in a way that is compatible with the scholastic view is not only possible but also serves to disarm a major objection against deontological ethical theories.

---

[41] Indeed, I think the kind of rationale that Warren Quinn finds for the doctrine of doing and allowing and for the doctrine of double effect would be (as he himself notes) quite congenial to a Kantian perspective. See his "Actions, Intentions, and Consequences: The Doctrine of Doing and Allowing" and "Actions, Intentions, and Consequences: The Doctrine of Double Effect."

6

Motivation without Evaluation?

Unintelligible Ends, Animal Behavior, and Diabolical Wills

We can think of an apparent continuum of behavior and actions that starts from the most fully deliberated actions of human beings in one extreme and ends at the other extreme at the movement of the "dumb" animals. The scholastic view seems to be at its best in dealing with one end of the spectrum: fully deliberated actions performed by reasonable agents at their most reflective moments. I hope to show, however, that it can also account for a wide range of human behavior that includes merely intentional and merely voluntary actions. However, as we approach the other end of the spectrum, the scholastic view might seem to be in a poor position; in fact, it may seem that it is completely inadequate to explain the actions of the perverse, the odd or mentally ill, children, and other mammals. And one could argue that a view that tries to understand human action in a way that cannot accommodate these instances of human and nonhuman action cannot claim success. After all, the fact that there is such a continuum seems to speak in favor of a unified explanation for the whole spectrum of animal behavior.

The last three chapters try to show how the scholastic view can reach far into this spectrum and, perhaps, to the very end of it. At first, it might seem that the troubles for the scholastic view start much before the end of the spectrum. So the last three chapters need to examine first the charge that the scholastic view has to regard fairly reasonable adult human action as sui generis and, if so, whether this is a liability of the theory. The scholastic view equates motivation (desiring) with a form of evaluation (conceiving to be good), and one may reasonably think that the theory cannot account for cases in which those things seem to come apart. There are three possible ways in which motivation and evaluation can come apart. First, we can have cases in which a being is motivated in some way but there is no corresponding evaluation; the agent seems to desire something that is in no way conceived to be good. This will be the subject of chapter 6. The second possibility is that the agent's motivation and evaluation are out of tune: What the agent judges to be best is not what the agent is most motivated to do. These are cases of *akrasia*, and they will be the subject of chapter 7. Finally, there might be cases in which it seems that the agent makes an evaluation and conceives or judges something to be good but is not at all motivated accordingly. These are cases generally described under the heading of *accidie*, and they will be the subject of the last chapter.

According to the scholastic view, intentional explanations aim to place the agent's behavior within a certain "normative sphere," a sphere within which human actions are susceptible to normative expectations and rational criticism. It is true that some human movements are not within this sphere, and movements that are beyond our control and therefore outside of this normative sphere are outside the purview of the scholastic view. The movement of sleepwalkers, of people under the influence of particularly unsettling drugs, and of those in the depths of insanity might be like that. No doubt, if behavior exhibited in this condition is similar to more typical human behavior, we might find it appealing to make use of the categories of intentional explanation in our attempts to understand the behavior in question. The fact that the categories of intentional explanation will appear in ordinary explanations of those cases is not in itself a refutation of the scholastic view; we find that the vocabulary of wants, beliefs, and so forth even figures in folk explanation of the functioning (and malfunctioning) of certain artifacts. It would be wrong to infer directly from this fact that the appearance of this vocabulary there should be understood literally, rather than metaphorically, in what one could call "as-if explanations." On the other hand, the theory would lose plausibility if too many of the explanations that seem seamlessly continuous with the more typical intentional explanation get pushed into the category of as-if explanations. So it is important to try to see how far the scholastic view can accommodate anomalous behavior.

This chapter in particular will also look into types of behavior that seem quite far out on a spectrum that takes its central cases to be fully deliberated actions. We start with actions that manifest obsessive or compulsive behavior. The worst forms of this behavior are those manifested by patients who suffer from obsessive–compulsive disorders (OCDs). The intent, of course, is not to provide anything like a scientific overview of obsessive–compulsive disorders but rather to look into an example of behavior that seems to have as its object of pursuit an end that is not much different from counting blades of grass, taking hold of saucers of mud, and other similar pursuits. In these cases, we know that agents exhibit complex behavior in pursuit of seemingly unintelligible ends. The question I raise in the first section of this chapter is whether this possibility raises problems for the scholastic view. Because the main threat is that an unintelligible end can be desired in just the same way as an intelligible one, I will often simply assume that various forms of obsessive behavior do not pursue any intelligibly good object. It is worth noting that this kind of behavior cannot be assimilated to cases of merely intentional actions or cases in which (like those we discussed in chapter 4) we can assume that the agent is capable of appreciating certain values that most of us cannot. First, unlike either of those cases, compulsive behavior is often behavior that the agent would rather not engage in and that the agent recognizes as irrational or unreasonable. Moreover, compulsive behavior often causes disruptions in the pursuit of important ends. For an obsessive agent, the object of her obsession is not something that is secondary to her execution of other projects or a hobby that she engages in sporadically.[1]

Higher mammals and infants also seem to engage in complex behavior in the pursuit of ends. In these cases, the ends in question are quite similar to the ones we pursue and find perfectly intelligible. However, given their cognitive abilities, it is hard to say that

---

[1] It is worth noting that most of us exhibit symptoms similar to those exhibited by OCD patients. However, one is only diagnosed with OCD if such symptoms result in significant disruption in one's life. See the definition of OCD from DSM-IV in note 10, this chapter.

higher mammals and infants conceive of the objects of their pursuit as good. And if it is plausible to say that the object of the obsession is not something the agent wants in the case of obsessive disorders, disallowing the possibility that animals and infants want things that they do not conceive to be good would amount to denying that it is possible for these creatures to have desires. It is surely contrary to common sense to deny that infants have desires. Section 6.2 tries to examine more precisely what the scholastic view has to say about the complex behavior of those whose cognitive capacities do not quite match those of adult human beings.

Unintelligible, infant, and animal behaviors pose a common threat to the scholastic view: They seem to suggest that desire explains behavior in a way unconnected to the intelligibility of the content of the desire. A somewhat different threat is posed by behavior that seems to be motivated by the wrong kind of evalua-tion; in particular, a negative evaluation. The scholastic view also seems to disallow the possibility that agents will engage in certain behavior *because* it is bad. But ruling out this possibility seems to fly in the face of the phenomena: Human beings can be quite perverse and often desire and do things simply because they are bad.[2] Even if one were unreasonably kind to human nature and came to the conclusion that human beings never desire something simply because it is bad, it seems at least coherent to think that there could be a satanic agent who desires the bad under the guise of its being bad. The last section of this chapter examines whether there is any case to be made that this is a genuine possibility left out by the scholastic view.

6.1   THE SCHOLASTIC VIEW AND UNINTELLIGIBLE ENDS

If an agent walks toward a newsstand, hands some money to the vendor, and comes back with a newspaper, we generally have no problem coming up with a preliminary explanation of the agent's behavior. Most likely, she wanted to read the paper and knew that she could do it by buying a paper at this location. One could also check this preliminary understanding with the agent herself by

---

[2] See, for instance, Augustine's famous description of stealing pears in *Confessions*.

asking her why she performed these actions. Of course, appearances might be illusory: The agent might have wanted simply to give some money to the store owner in a way that wouldn't be embarrassing to him, the agent might lie or be unaware of her motivations, or there could be some other reason. There might also be further explanations of the behavior, especially if an action is fully deliberated: We might want to know why the agent is interested in buying a newspaper and why in this particular location, for example. And in the case of merely voluntary actions, the primary explanation will be simply a report that the actions were *not* done for a reason. For many, if not most, human actions, a preliminary explanation is readily available. Obsessive behavior, however, is not like this, and it is hard to agree on any kind of preliminary explanation of these actions. For instance, suppose that we observe that an agent keeps coming back to his home to check if his stove is still on, a common instance of OCD. What would be a cogent preliminary explanation of this behavior? One possibility is to describe it as a failure of theoretical reason: We can ascribe a normal desire to prevent fires caused by negligent handling of the oven to the agent but see him as failing to revise his beliefs in an appropriate manner, taking him to be someone who does not revise the subjective probability of having left the oven on after having already checked that all the knobs were in the "off" position. If every case where we have a seemingly unintelligible object of pursuit can be explained in this manner, the desires that give rise to this kind of behavior are no different from the desires that give rise to the behavior of typical intentional explanations. A second possibility is that compulsive behavior is an extreme case of *akrasia*. One can think that the agent in the preceding example has a weak but normal desire to be in possession of even more reliable evidence that he did not leave the oven on, but although he thinks that, on reflection, it is more important to pursue other interests than to satisfy this desire, he akratically chooses to satisfy the less important desire. Again, if this preliminary explanation is correct, compulsive behavior is no different from akratic behavior.

A more interesting case for our purposes would be a Freudian explanation of compulsive behavior. Freudian explanations are far from being typical intentional explanations of behavior, but they do

seem to make compulsions at least minimally intelligible.[3] Let us
take a case in which Freud tries to explain obsessive behavior. This
is an (abridged) example of such an *explanandum*:

An eleven-year-old boy had instituted the following obsessive ceremonial
before going to bed. He did not sleep until he told his mother in the
minutest detail all the events of the day; ... the bed must be pushed right
up to the wall; three chairs must stand by it.... In order to get to sleep he
must kick out a certain number of times with both legs.

The early Freud explains these obsessive actions in the following way:

Years before a servant-girl who had to put the handsome boy to bed took
the opportunity of lying upon him and abusing him sexually. Later on
when this memory was awakened by a recent experience, it manifested
itself in consciousness in the form of a compulsion to perform the ceremonial described. *Its meaning was easily guessed* ... the chairs by the bed-
side and pushing the bed against the wall – so that no one could later come
near the bed; ... kicking the legs – pushing away the person lying on
him; ... the circumstantial confession to his mother – because he had
concealed from her this and other sexual experiences in obedience to his
seductress.[4]

The kind of intelligibility in question is, admittedly, not typical.
Nonetheless, it is true that the agent is less enigmatic to us, and not
in the sense that we can write off those events from the history of the
agent (as would be the case with physiological explanations). The
Freudian explanation does allow us to see how these actions took up
some meaning even if they are just at the borderline of making the
agent intelligible. Indeed, this sense of understanding comes forth
in Freud's confidence that this is all obvious, that the significance of
these events can "be easily guessed," and that the reader will not
need more than the sentence-long explanation of the symptoms to
be well disposed toward the psychoanalytical account of the obsession.[5] Although one might imagine at first that the desires in this

---

[3] For the view that psychoanalytical explanations of actions are an extension of
ordinary explanations, see Richard Wollheim, "Desire, Belief and Professor
Grünbaum's Freud."

[4] Sigmund Freud, "Further Remarks on the Defence Neuro-Psychoses," p. 172,
emphasis added.

[5] This is, of course, not to say that the psychoanalytical account is, or should be,
persuasive.

situation cannot conform to the old formula of the schools, especially *before* one avails oneself of Freud's explanation, the psychoanalytical explanation achieves understanding exactly by making clear the surprising way in which the child conceives this ritual to be good. Even if it is at the outer edges of intelligibility, we can see how the child (perhaps unconsciously) finds a point in this behavior, a point that is integrated in a kind of "paralogical" symbolic structure. Indeed, it might be worth noting that the Freudian explanation not only makes the act intelligible but by postulating, at least in some cases, a traumatic event and mental mechanisms that are beyond the control of the agent, the Freudian explanation also *excuses* the agent from achieving anything near full intelligibility.

The scholastic view will have a harder time trying to provide a preliminary explanation of compulsive behavior in which the agent's object of pursuit is completely unintelligible. It is worth stipulating a form of explanation that would have that character, even if the explanation is not particularly plausible. Let us define a "merely biochemical" explanation of compulsive behavior as follows: According to this understanding, the compulsions manifested by obsessive behavior have as their proximate cause certain abnormal biochemical processes, and *there is no further, or higher-level, explanation of why the agent is inclined to behave in such a manner*. This last clause ensures that there is no intelligible object of pursuit that is the object of another kind of (or perhaps a fuller) explanation of roughly the same bodily movements. Abnormal biochemical processes do not confer the right kind of intelligibility on the agent's behavior. They can at best *excuse* the agent; that is, they can explain why the agent cannot be made intelligible in those circumstances. If compulsive behavior would end at simple, mindless movements toward the object of one's obsession, there would be no reason not to simply exclude this kind of behavior from the purview of intentional explanations.

Compulsive behavior can be quite complex, however, and the pursuit of the object of one's obsession can be conducted through the kind of rational management that seems to be the subject matter of intentional explanation. Indeed, it seems that compulsions confer intelligibility on behavior in the pursuit of an unintelligible object, and this seems hard to accommodate with the scholastic view.[6] Even someone who suffers from obsessive–compulsive disorders will still typically exhibit the kind of means–end rationality in the pursuit of the object of her compulsion that seems to call for intentional explanation.

It is worth emphasizing that a merely biochemical explanation is not particularly plausible even in severe cases of OCD. Typically, a biochemical explanation of OCD will not be put forth as the full explanation of the behavior. A merely biochemical explanation would move directly from the biochemical phenomenon to the behavior in a clause such as "disregulation of the serotonergic system directly causes compulsive behavior" without any psychological mechanism intervening between the biochemical phenomenon and the behavior, or even corresponding to it. Typical explanations of OCD are not like this. Usually they postulate certain psychological mechanisms that mediate the onset of the pathological behavior. Dan Stein and Eric Hollander, for instance, argue that the neurochemical perturbations that are typical of OCD lead to an "impairment in the determination or assessment of goal-response completion." (They will impair, for instance, one's capacity to assess that one has achieved the goal of having one's hands clean after a brief period of hand-washing).[7] Moreover, there will generally be something approaching a rationalizing explanation of these obsessions (such as fear of contamination in the case of hand-washing), although the agent will often admit that the belief that supposedly explains the obsession does not make sense. (The agent will admit that constant hand-washing is not a particularly effective way to prevent the diseases that the agent is concerned about, such as, for instance, cancer.) One might see the postulated psychological mechanism in two different ways. First, one might think that this explanation helps us make the agent intelligible. In this case, one should treat the explanation of the psychological mechanism as an

---

[6] Indeed, compulsion seems clearly to be accounted for by subjectivism: We start from an end that is neither rational nor irrational to pursue, and we assess the rationality of ensuing behavior as an effective pursuit of these means. Of course, one could think that this is itself the problem with subjectivism; there *is* a difference between these actions and most other actions agents undertake.

[7] Dan Stein and Eric Hollander, "A Neural Network Approach to Obsessive–Compulsive Disorder," p. 227.

intentional explanation in the same way that we treated Freud's explanation and take the biochemical explanation underlying the phenomenon as excusing the limited intelligibility provided by the intentional explanation. Or one could think that the postulated psychological mechanism adds nothing to the intelligibility of the behavior (which I think is typically the case). Often the postulated mechanism can be seen as locating the "excusing" circumstances of the agent more precisely. So, for instance, if we learn that "obsessional problems will occur in individuals who are distressed by the occurrence of [intrusive thoughts] ... and also believe the occurrence of such cognitions indicates personal responsibility for distressing harm unless corrective action is taken," we are then locating the excusing circumstances earlier in the mental life of the agent than the intention to carry out the compulsive action.[8] But again, for the purposes of this chapter, I will assume that there is nothing beyond the biochemical explanation that can explain or make more intelligible the pursuit of these obsessive ends. Of course, having in hand an explanation of this kind, we do understand, in some sense, why the agent behaves the way she does. However, this understanding is of a different kind: It is clearly more like the understanding of how muscle contraction causes the finger to move in a certain way. At best, this sort of explanation can be an *excuse* for the unavailability of a proper intentional explanation; the biochemical story might help us understand why an otherwise normal agent has become unintelligible.

So if we assume the merely biochemical explanation of compulsive behavior, the agent's pursuit of the object of the obsession will be, in the relevant sense, completely unintelligible. However, once we understand that the agent has this inscrutable end, we can

---

[8] Paul M. Salkovskis, "Psychological Approaches to the Understanding of Obsessional Problems," p. 41. I can't resist pointing out that Salkovskis postulates among the causes of OCD certain assumptions that consequentialist philosophers ought to think would make compulsive behavior more intelligible. According to Salkovskis, "The belief that failing to prevent ... harm to self or others is the same as having caused the harm ... may be a key assumption in the generation of obsessional problems" (p. 45). Indeed, one fears that exposure to philosophy might be particularly dangerous in this regard. J. L. Rappoport, in "The Biology of Obsessions and Compulsions," p. 69, suggests that an OCD patient "becomes an ultimate skeptic who cannot credit his sense data."

explain the agent's complex behavior in pursuit of this end in what seems to be a typical intentional explanation. Let us suppose that someone puts a lot of effort into acquiring prime tickets for an expensive production of *Aida*; he works overtime, he avoids all but the most essential expenditures, and so on. When asked why he wants so much to see this production of *Aida*, he explains that he always wanted to see real elephants in an opera, and this is one of those rare occasions where real elephants will be brought to the stage. So he goes to the opera, and just as the elephants are about to make their entrance, he gets up and goes in the direction of the theater's supply closet. Suppose now we give the following explanation of the action:

(CA) Compulsive Action Explanation:
[P1] The agent wanted to wash his hands.
[P2] The agent mistook the supply closet for the bathroom.
[E] Therefore, the agent walked toward the supply closet.

Let us assume that if one asks the agent why he wanted to wash his hands, he wouldn't say things like "Oh, I just touched a *really* foul substance on the bottom of my seat" or "I've just realized that my hands were *so* dirty." Rather, the agent would simply say, "I had to wash my hands." I shall assume that, in this context, this kind of behavior is not just an instance of *akrasia*, of acting for a lesser reason, but one in which the agent himself sees no point.[9] However, the fact that the initial end is unintelligible does not seem to prevent us from continuing the explanation in the same way as we would if the agent wanted to wash his hands after eating barbecued chicken. How can the scholastic view accommodate this fact? Shouldn't it make all the difference in the world, for the scholastic view, whether the end in question is an intelligible object of pursuit or not? Shouldn't the scholastic view be committed to saying that only one of these two almost identical explanations is a proper intentional explanation?

---

[9] It might be worth noting that behavior typical of *akrasia* in some contexts would be hardly intelligible. Suppose, for instance, the same agent at the same time was told, "There is free ice cream in the lobby." If the agent darted out of his seat to get the ice cream, it wouldn't be a very satisfying explanation to say, "The agent is weak-willed; he often acts for the lesser reason."

First, I want to suggest that things are made unnecessarily difficult for the scholastic view if we grant, as we did in [P1], that the agent *wants* to wash his hands. This is obviously immediately incompatible with the scholastic view and, moreover, is not in keeping with what is typically the agent's self-understanding of the situation. Thus, if the scholastic view is correct, we should replace [P1] with a simple statement of the fact that the agent feels compelled to wash his hands. According to the scholastic view, the explanation does not start from a proper desire, from the fact that there is something that the agent wants to do, but from the fact that the agent feels *compelled* to engage in certain actions that do not serve any of his desires. So we replace [P1] with something like:

[P1*] The agent feels compelled to wash his hands.

It is important to note that there are independent reasons to prefer [P1*] over [P1]. After all, the agent does not have clean hands, or even bringing about that his hands are washed, as an aim – the compulsive agent will typically not be after very clean hands or want his hands to be clean or washed; he just keeps washing them.[10] It is exactly the perplexing character of the behavior that makes us search for pathological explanations, that leaves us unsatisfied with the mere fact of his wanting; it seems that these cases are not appropriately explained by saying that the agent just likes washing his hands or that he just feels like doing it. But once the compulsion is postulated, the desire seems explanatorily idle. Once we say that the agent is compelled to act in this manner, the action is fully explained without the addition that the agent also wanted to act in this manner. Of course, certain philosophical theories will imply that such instances of compulsion are also instances of desire if, for instance, one thinks that a desire is simply a disposition to behave. But, in this case, it is the prior commitment to a certain theory that

---

[10] Indeed, according to the fourth edition of the American Psychiatric Association's *Diagnostic and Statistical Manual of Mental Disorders*, "*by definition*, adults with Obsessive–Compulsive Disorder have at some point recognised that the obsessions or compulsions are excessive and unreasonable." The third edition defined obsessions as thoughts that "invade consciousness and are experienced as senseless or repugnant" (cited in Ian Jakes, *Theoretical Approaches to Obsessive–Compulsive Disorder*, pp. 5–6, emphasis mine).

is forcing one to accept the conclusion; obviously, the scholastic view does not have any such theoretical commitments.[11]

Having noted that [P1] should be reformulated in this way, we can now more comfortably say that there is indeed an essential difference between explanations in which the agent is shown to be in an intelligent pursuit of means to unintelligible ends and explanations in which proper desires figure as premises. As we looked into the nature of the Instrumental Principle, we argued that the Instrumental Principle was a transfer principle. Of course, what it transferred was the goodness of the end to the goodness of the means. This sort of employment of the Instrumental Principle shows a certain action to be intelligible; it shows how the agent saw a certain action as the pursuit of a good. Given that CA does not start from something that the agent regards as good, we cannot see the Instrumental Principle as performing quite the same function. However, we can still regard the Instrumental Principle as functioning in CA more generally as a transfer principle, though what it "transfers" is not goodness or intelligibility. We can say that in the intentional explanation earlier, the belief that a certain means–end relation obtains transfers the *excuse* from the premise to the conclusion. Let us say that we start from the general attribution of a pathological condition as excusing the agent. Suppose we ask someone, "Why did Martin decide to wash his hands right now?" and get the answer that "It's an obsession; he has to wash his hands all the time." One can see this kind of explanation as excusing a particular instance of behavior from the need for an intentional explanation. The explanation displays this kind of behavior as one for which the agent is not (fully) responsible; it is simply something that the agent cannot avoid doing. But the excuse should be transferred also to other instances of the behavior that were generated by the compulsion. The Instrumental Principle allows us to

---

[11] One could say that [P1*] already necessarily expresses a desire of the agent, but, for those same reasons, I think we should understand the compulsion as just the mechanism that produces the behavior. The mechanism can be intentional and thus incorporate a desire, as in the Freudian explanation, or it can be a nonintentional mechanism and thus *not* incorporate a desire, as in the biochemical explanation. This does not mean that we cannot refer to the compulsion outside a specific theoretical framework; in this case, talk of "compulsions" will be a placeholder for the appropriate theoretical explanation.

excuse the agent's behavior through the whole chain of events that are supposed to bring about the object of compulsion.[12]

There are other circumstances in which we excuse the agent's movements in a similar manner (for example, when she trips, walks in an absent-minded manner, sleepwalks, etc.). In Wilkie Collins's *The Moonstone*, Franklin Blake, the protagonist, turns out to have stolen the moonstone, an action that does not speak well of his motives and character, which, in light of other evidence, seemed unimpeachable. Later in the book, we learn that these actions were performed under the influence of a drug, and thus we "write off" these actions from our understanding of Blake's character and his motives. Seeing these movements as the irresistible effects of a drug, we discount them in our understanding of what the agent wants and his general conception of the good; we excuse Blake not only for taking the moonstone but also for all actions he undertook as means to this end. For many other occasions in which we excuse the agent's behavior, we are dealing with a quite circumscribed action. So if I hit someone who accidentally touched me with a lit cigarette, I can explain away this apparent instance of an extremely vindictive disposition by saying that it was just a reflex. Managing to steal a precious stone is a more complex behavior that might involve engaging in various preparatory acts. In this case, we need to excuse not only the action of taking possession of the stone but also the behavior that was undertaken in order to take possession of the stone. Attributing to someone the effects of a compulsive disorder is no different in this respect: Compulsive behavior can generate complex and efficient behavior in the pursuit of the object of compulsion.

Thus, in these cases, the Instrumental Principle will not be transferring "goodness" or "intelligibility" but rather "excusability." Instead of showing how it makes sense for an agent to pursue a certain end in light of the fact that it is undertaken in order to pursue other intelligible ends, it shows how one should excuse the lack of intelligibility of a certain action in light of the fact that it is

---

[12] It might be worth noting that as we excuse pathological behavior, we might need to rely on transfer principles that are substantively different from the Instrumental Principle. (We might allow, for instance, that the excuse be transferred to objects symbolically connected to the pathology.)

undertaken as a means to (or part of) a larger action for which the agent is not responsible (and whose lack of intelligibility is thus excused).[13] The principles of instrumental reasoning will guide us in paring off episodes of the agent's life that go beyond the immediate effect of the compulsion. Of course, this kind of intentional explanation performs a different function, but it is still an essential function in rendering the agent intelligible; namely, the recognition that certain areas of her behavior are excluded from the demands of intelligibility, so that we can block off specified parts of the life of the agent without affecting the possibility of our making other aspects of her life intelligible.[14]

6.2 DO CHILDREN AND ANIMALS DESIRE?

If, as seems reasonable to suppose, a notion such as "good" lies far beyond the conceptual repertoire of animals,[15] then it seems that a scholastic view cannot make room for the possibility that these animals have desires, at least not in the sense of "desires" that is relevant to deliberation and the explanation of human action.

This might appear to be a form of parochial arrogance, an ascription of some sort of angelic nature to the human species. In general, it might seem just a matter of common sense that animals have desires, that they want various things that they set out to pursue, and so forth. Perhaps more problematic yet is the fact that the account also seems to exclude attributing desires to small children. Again, it appears to be a matter of plain common sense that small children have desires. Moreover, one may argue that we cannot understand how adult human beings can have desires if we

---

[13] This is not to say that *any* actions that are means to an "excused" action are also excused.

[14] This is not to say that the existence of compulsion will leave our assessment of the rationality of the agent intact. However, the kind of irrationality that might be exhibited here is not one of pursuing ends that one ought to know should not be pursued but rather that the agent does not have rational control over some piece of behavior.

[15] Someone might deny this and think that animals and small children have somehow the concept of good. In this case, there would be no problem attributing desires to them according to the scholastic view.

do not first attribute them to children. So, for instance, Velleman argues as follows:

A young child can want things long before it has acquired the concept of their being worth wanting, or desirable. Surely, the concept of desirability – of something's being a correct or fitting object of desires – is a concept that children need to be taught. And how would one teach this concept to a child if not by disciplining its antecedently existing desires?[16]

Here we have to distinguish a number of objections, some of them more problematic than others. First, one might argue that human agents are, after all, animals like all others, equally brought about to their current genetic makeup by evolutionary forces. Moreover, human behavior and animal behavior, or at least the behavior of higher mammals, exhibit an enormous similarity. "We" all search for food, drink, and security; higher mammals show similar attachments to other beings (and especially their offspring) and even engage in what seems to be playful behavior. It now seems that the main categories that explain human behavior must also explain nonhuman animal behavior; differences here must be differences in degree, not differences in kind.

However, this argument rests on a fallacy. Because it is not controversial that human cognitive faculties are more developed than those of nonhuman animals, it seems at least possible to think, without doing any violence to the most stringent principle of continuity in nature, that this difference, no matter how minute it is in the grand scheme of things, could allow for a certain sort of understanding of human action that is unavailable even for the next step down in the cognitive ladder of the animal world. The scholastic view postulates that human action can be understood as the expression of practical reason at work – as part of a life that aspires to the ideals of rationality – and this simply might not be possible for any other animals, even if their cognitive capacities are, in many ways, not all that different from ours. But if this is true, insofar as we are interested in the categories that articulate this understanding, it should be no sign of failure that these categories cannot be extended to the rest of the animal kingdom. This is not to deny that there

---

[16] Velleman, "The Guise of the Good," p. 7.

are many similarities between human beings and nonhuman animals and that these similarities often make it tempting to attribute these categories to other animals. But even this is not surprising; because the rational is a form of the teleological, we should expect the categories of the rational to serve as a metaphor for the teleological, especially when the teleology of nonhuman animals sets ends to those beings that are quite similar to the ones that we set to ourselves by virtue of our rational nature (such as the ends that relate to survival and reproduction).

Velleman's argument to the effect that we must attribute desires to small children is importantly different. The idea is that the motivational makeup of an adult is not produced ex nihilo. Even if an adult can see the object of his desire as good, as something that is fit to be desired, this is to a large extent the product of the kind of manipulation of one's motivation involved in education. So, for instance, we need to make a child acquire a motivation to share her toys and treat others nicely before we can have an adult who conceives the well-being of others as good; we need to teach children that there are things that they *should* desire. But, as Velleman argues, if the child is not already motivated to act in certain ways, if the child does not already possess certain desires, how can we introduce the child to the idea that certain things are (or are not) fit objects *of desire*? However, this objection also seems to make an unwarranted assumption. It seems to suppose that one could only teach children by some kind of quasi-reasoning. Of course, if our model of teaching is that we *persuade* a child that certain objects are fit to be desired,[17] then it is hard to see how we could teach such a thing to anyone who did not already desire certain things. But this assumption is certainly unwarranted; we also teach children by training them to do things of which they had no previous inkling.[18] There is no reason to reject the hypothesis that children learn at the same time *to desire* and *to desire properly*. This is not to deny that in

---

[17] Of course, "persuasion" here would not necessarily be a matter of "rational" persuasion, especially given that they can't rely on a previous understanding of which objects are fit to be desired. Persuasion here would probably be effected by mere dint of authority.

[18] Compare McDowell on introducing children to the space of reasons. (If I am correct, this will include enabling them to desire.) See his *Mind and World*, Lecture VI.

teaching children to desire we exploit the teleological character of their behavior and general similarities between children's and adult's behavior. However, it is unclear why this should on its own pressure us to attribute to children a system of desires. If we think of the vocabulary of desires, judgments about the good, and so forth as some of the categories of intentional explanation and deliberation, and if we accept that an agent who deliberates and can be the subject of intentional explanations must be an agent to whom the ideal of rationality can be attributed, we need not think that these similarities force us to ascribe desires to very young children.[19] That is, we can conclude that the fact that children cannot have a concept of the "good" is not a reason to withdraw our commitment to the scholastic view but a reason to think that their behavior does not yet aspire to the ideals of rationality and thus that their behavior is not subject to the categories of deliberation and intentional explanations.[20] This is not to deny that the process of being brought into the purview of rationality is a gradual process and that it will often be difficult to determine when a child has entered this stage. But the existence of a grey area does not necessarily speak against the existence of a distinction. In fact, the existence of a grey area might help support an argument that the application of the categories of intentional explanations to children and lower animals is merely metaphorical.

Moreover, the existence of the grey area explains a problem that might seem intractable in this context: When we deal with computers or artifacts, we immediately recognize that our use of the intentional categories is metaphorical. But this is obviously not true in the case of children and animals; few of us have any pre-philosophical disposition to treat the application of intentional categories to adult human beings, children, and animals as anything but univocal. But this is understandable in light of the fact that the

---

[19] It might be worth noting that children do seem to acquire some kind of concept of good at quite an early age. Although I have not found psychological research on this subject, my anecdotal evidence suggests that by the age of two they typically do possess some such concept.

[20] This is not unlike Wilfrid Sellars's point that children, although exhibiting some of the same discriminating capacities as adult human beings, cannot be said to know anything until they can inhabit "the logical space of reasons," until they can give and ask for reasons. See his *Empiricism and the Philosophy of Mind*.

move from childhood to adulthood is gradual and there is no clear moment at which we can say that our use of intentional vocabulary changes from being merely metaphorical to literal. We can imagine computers becoming gradually more and more like human beings and going through the same learning process, so that your new home PC moves gradually from being capable of performing the same functions that your existing computer performs up to the point that it lacks no capacity that a human being has. I would hazard a guess that if this were to happen, we would also have problems determining when intentional language is used non-metaphorically in the case of computers, and we might even be tempted to regard our use of intentional language in its early stages of "development" as nonmetaphorical.[21]

These points are only intended to shake one's confidence (at least to some extent) that the attribution of desires to small children and animals is just as unproblematic as the attribution of phenomenal states such as pain and pleasure. But having said all that, I must confess that I find it hard to accept that this is all there is to the difference between the seemingly correct and unguarded way in which we talk in intentional terms about higher mammals and small children as opposed, for instance, to the obviously metaphorical, often ironical way in which we attribute beliefs and knowledge to artifacts in sentences such as, "The thermostat doesn't know that there is a fireplace in the living room, and so it thinks that the whole house is warm." It seems that this is a distinction that philosophy has an obligation to preserve rather than revise in our ordinary understanding of small children and animals. Although I am not particularly confident that our ordinary understanding of animals and small children is all that coherent, given the strength of the intuition that babies and brutes want various things, it is worth trying to see if we can accommodate these putative desires within the scholastic framework. And fortunately, I think that the scholastic view can do better than merely explain how tempting it is to speak figuratively in these cases. In the rest of this section, I'll try to show

---

[21] Of course, the fact that the teleological nature of artifacts is provided by design rather than by nature also helps to explain why we would be tempted not to consider the latter as metaphorical.

that the scholastic view can allow that animals and small children have desires. Even though these are not paradigmatic cases of desire for the scholastic view, they will still turn out to be real desires.

When discussing obsessive behavior, we noted that the Instrumental Principle could allow us to excuse behavior of the agent that was not an immediate expression of the obsession. Excluding episodes of the life of the agent in this manner would allow us to see the rest of his behavior as intelligible and at the same time allow us to explain the agent's obsessive behavior as something over which the agent did not have full control. To do this, we didn't need to count the object of the agent's obsession as a desired object, and this was something with which obsessive agents would typically agree.

However, we can imagine things being different. Suppose we detect in a certain being a great deal of complex behavior that seems capable of being explained as if it were guided by instrumental principles and rational control of the environment. We can imagine that as we move up the chain of instrumental reasoning, we do not arrive at anything that is intelligible or that the agent sees a point in doing. We see that he repeatedly engages in a whole array of different activities that effectively bring about bizarre outcomes, such as holding on to saucers of mud for a certain period of time and putting green books on rooftops. Suppose that we also find that the agent is either incapable of providing an answer or sees no need to provide an answer to the question of why he is acting as he does. We can think that an articulate individual like this when asked this question would answer, "For no reason. I just find myself pursuing those things."[22] How would we describe such a case? So far, we have described beings that have rather brute behavioral dispositions. For some, this will seem enough to attribute desires or motivation to the agents in question. However, it is important to note that this certainly does not tell the whole story about when, and to what extent, we are tempted to ascribe desires to agents. As I argued earlier, we seem to resist ascribing desires at least to human agents when we can't see the point of the activity. But leaving this point aside, we should also note that whether we will be tempted to call them

---

[22] This would not be the same as the answer "for no particular reason" or as being unable to articulate further why one sees this as important. See chapter 1.

"desires" will depend, to a large extent, on what else we find out about them. For instance, we might want to ask what happens when things don't go as expected and the agent faces something like a failure. Let us call one of these beings Larry. As Larry is "working" to procure a saucer of mud, let's suppose he hits a snag. Where there used to be mud, there is nothing now, and it's now too late to look for mud somewhere else (at least in the sense that we have never observed Larry to search for mud if there was no hope of finding mud within a certain amount of time). We can imagine a few different scenarios. In one scenario, Larry throws his saucer violently to the ground and makes some loud noises. In a second scenario, Larry might just continue on in a dejected manner and be somewhat less focused now on the next task. (Larry now overlooks some green books that he would typically put on a rooftop.) Finally, we can imagine that Larry does nothing of this sort; he seems hardly to notice whether he gets hold of the saucer of mud or not. When Larry fails to hold on to a saucer of mud, he simply goes on in the same way. In fact, there is no noticeable difference in the continuation of Larry's life whether he succeeds in these bizarre tasks or whether he fails.

Now I take it that our temptation to assign desires to Larry will be severely diminished in the last case. In the last case, it seems that we would say that getting saucers of mud, putting books on rooftops, and so forth are simply the kind of things that Larry does. On the other hand, if we encounter what seems to us to be signs of frustration and sadness, rather than just pursuit of an end, we will be more tempted to say that these were things that Larry wanted. Part of the difference, I shall propose, is that it is easier to make sense of a certain conception of "living well" for those beings when we have a conception that things *matter* to those beings.[23] Given our assumption that they see no point in what they are doing, there is no reason *why* these things matter to those beings; they simply do. The more we are confident that these dispositions to behave are in tune with the possibility of this being's life going better or worse, the more we are confident that this being *has* certain ends (and not merely that

---

[23] As John Haugeland puts it, "The problem with artificial intelligence is that computers don't give a damn." See his *Having Thought: Essays in the Metaphysics of Mind*, p. 60.

ascribing those ends to this being can be instrumental in predicting its behavior). Of course, signs of frustration and sadness are not the only ways in which we could be tempted to attribute ends: the possibility of attributing ends similar to our own, such as avoidance of pain, pursuit of nourishment, and so on, would play a similar role. The more a disposition to behave resembles intentional actions, the more we are entitled to say that a being pursues something *as if it were good* (although it does not *represent* it as good). One can make the point more generally in terms of the formal end of practical reason. As we said earlier, to say that the good is the formal end of practical reason implies that this is the end that ought to guide us in moving from prima facie attitudes (and all-out attitudes) to (new) all-out attitudes. The more we see evidence that postulating something as being good for the agent allows us to see a whole array of complex behavior as organized in the same way as it would be for an agent who took such objects to be good, the more we are entitled to attribute to the agent practical attitudes. This is more true if we can see the agent's signs of frustration and recognition of failure, signs that the agent is behaving as if bringing about a certain object was an *ideal* of practical reasoning. In fact, I take it that we'll be even more inclined to attribute desires to Larry if we can recognize a distinction between prima facie and all-out attitudes. Let us assume, for instance, that Larry always pursues saucers of mud at a determinate time. But now, as he is searching saucers of mud, he sees some green books lying next to a house, and a ladder that is tall enough to climb to the rooftop. Suppose he gets off his path, starts going in the direction of the house, but "gets a hold of himself" and goes back to the pursuit of mud while still, from time to time, throwing glances at the ladder and the books. It would now seem even more tempting to say that he wants to put the green books on the rooftop but sticks with the pursuit of his desire for the saucer of mud.

Let us say that beings that pursue things as if they were good in this way but do not represent them as good have *merely given ends*. We can go further and say that for beings with merely given ends, it is part of their nature to *take* certain things to be good[24] even if they

---

[24] Of course, this does not mean that the behavior in question must be instinctual or unlearned. It might be part of their nature, for instance, that they imitate behavior

are incapable of representing them as good. What counts as their taking them to be good, as we said earlier, is the fact that we can see their actions as being *guided* by a certain ideal. In particular, we can say that the more plausible it is to attribute to a being moves between various prima facie and all-out practical attitudes that resemble acceptable moves in the practical realm, the more we are justified in taking the agent to be guided by the formal end of practical reason (i.e., the good), *even if the agent cannot represent anything as good*. It is worth noting that this is no different from how we attribute beliefs to beings that do not have a concept of truth. In this case, we think that we have to think that the being *takes* a certain content to be true even in the absence of the capacity to represent certain things as true.

Let us call beings that can only have merely given ends "natural agents." Of course, I want to suggest that small children and animals are natural agents in this sense. Once we attribute to these agents the formal end of practical reason, we can say that some objects of their pursuit play roles in their lives similar to those they would play if they were represented as good. These objects are objects that, in this proposal, natural agents conceive to be good, even if they do not have as the content of any of their representations that a certain object is good. But the scholastic view only requires that practical attitudes be ones in which the object is conceived to be good; it does not require that the attitude contain a representation of the content "*X* is good." Thus the scholastic view can say that natural agents have real desires and other practical attitudes.

However, it seems hard to attribute to natural agents in any way a *general conception of the good*, and it is worth examining if this will not generate difficult problems for this attempt to account for their practical lives within the scholastic framework. Although these agents do not have a general conception of the good, it seems to make sense to say that they (or their lives) can be, or fail to be, happy. Let us say now that when things go as well as possible for a natural agent, the agent does well or is happy.[25] Now if we stick to

of other beings and thus by nature they take to be good whatever other beings around take to be good.

[25] Of course, it is more plausible to think that their happiness comes in degrees. But I will just stick with the simplifying assumption that their happiness is an on/off

the cases of the natural agents we know, small children and certain animals, they are incapable of representing in any way the content of this ideal of a life going as well as possible. They are not going after a life they judge to be good; they simply pursue the ends they happen to have in a particular situation. So they do not in any way take the happy life as a whole to be a good life, and so we cannot say that natural agents desire their happiness as such. This, however, does not strike me as particularly counterintuitive. I can't see any pretheoretical reason to think that we need to attribute to animals and small children a general desire for happiness. What about the things they pursue as (constitutive or instrumental) means to their happiness, or as means for their given ends? Here I would like to follow a lead from Kant. Just before Kant introduces the old formula of the schools, he criticizes those who take the source of good (for human reason) to be pleasure as follows:

A philosopher who believed that he had to put a feeling of pleasure at the basis of practical appraisal would have to call *good* that which is a *means* to the agreeable.... The practical maxims that would follow from the above concept of good merely as means would never contain as the object of the will anything good in itself but always only good *for something*; the good would always be merely the useful and that for which it is useful would lie outside the will.... There would be nothing immediately good, and the good would have to be sought, instead, only in the means to something else.[26]

Of course, Kant is criticizing conceiving the good in this manner, but he is not claiming that this is an incoherent view; it simply does not allow for the possibility of something that is *immediately* good.[27] It is important to note that Kant takes "pleasure" to stand for the state one is in when one's given ends are realized, when one's life goes as it is supposed to go.[28] Thus "pleasure" itself is not conceived

---

matter because I can't see how this added complication would make any significant difference to the account.

[26] Kant, *Critique of Practical Reason*, pp. 58–59.

[27] I discuss Kant's view on those issues in more detail in my "Speculative Mistakes and Ordinary Temptations: Kant on Instrumentalist Conceptions of Practical Reason."

[28] "Pleasure *is the representation of the agreement of an object or of an action with the* subjective *conditions of life*" (Kant, *Critique of Practical Reason*, 9n).

as good but is just the realization of a given end. But although pleasure is not good under this conception, Kant allows that means to those ends would be good. I take it that Kant allows for this possibility because a given end sets a *practical* problem for reason: to find the means to something that I find myself pursuing. As reason answers this problem, we can say that it represents something as worth pursuing *given that* one is pursuing a certain end. This is to say that it represents something (such as, say, eating nuts) as good for something else (ultimately, always pleasure). If this is correct, we can say that the lack of a general conception of the good has similar implications in the case of natural agents. Natural agents do desire the means to their happiness, even if they do not desire their happiness. But I find this to be exactly what one would want to say about natural agents. It seems irresistible to attribute to a cat the desire to eat the tuna on the plate, to the baby the desire to play with the ball. But it is certainly a stretch to say that the cat or the baby want to be happy.

Understood this way, no doubt the intentional explanations of natural agents are derived from our understanding of rational human agents. Although they begin from our understanding of them as pursuing some things "as if they were good," we could not understand this if we did not already have a conception of pursuing something as good. However, as the examples of the bizarre beings discussed earlier should have made clear, this is not at all surprising: We will be more tempted to ascribe intentional states to those agents the more their behavior approximates ours in important respects. Perhaps more importantly, to the extent that intentional explanations are possible for small children and animals, they can neither be made fully intelligible nor is there a general normative ideal for them as the one implicitly represented in a human being's general conception of the good. In this way, these intentional explanations must be limited or partial in relation to the explanation of human actions. This is also not surprising given that the range of available explanations of human actions is much wider and richer than that available for explaining the behavior of brutes and babies. As long as this difference does not prevent us from attributing desires to these beings, it should not be the source of any embarrassment for the scholastic view.

6.3   PURSUING THE BAD

We have been looking into cases in which the agent pursues certain things that she does not consider either good or bad. However, we should also look at another possibility, the possibility that an agent will be attracted by some prospect *simply because it is bad*. One might think that the scholastic view is committed to a too optimistic characterization of human nature, overlooking the fact that perversity and rebellion are also part of our humanity. It seems that agents give weight to desires that are quite perverse, and even desires that the agent would *recognize*, sometimes rather gladly or glibly, to be perverse. If even in the life of the average agent we find much that the agent does not conceive to be good, things look even worse when we direct our gaze to less sympathetic characters. After all, as Velleman points out, we need to account not only for the average agent but also for "those agents who are disaffected, refractory, silly, satanic, or punk.... [One] hope[s] for a moral psychology that has room for the whole motley crew."[29]

It is important not to fall into a verbal dispute. As we pointed out earlier, "good" is no doubt said in many ways, and in some of those it would be ludicrous to say that we desire only what we conceive to be good, especially if "good" has some moralistic connotations. It is not enough then to find moments in one's life when one says that one desires the bad, for we need to see whether there is any more general reason to think that we cannot say that we desire only what we conceive to be good, especially when we think of the "good" as the practical analog of the "true."[30] Moreover, as pointed out in chapter 1, a scholastic view allows for the possibility that we desire what we know to be bad; that is, it is perfectly possible that one desires what upon reflection one judges to be bad. However, the scholastic claim is that *in desiring an object* one conceives it to be good.

---

[29] Velleman, "The Guise of the Good," p. 3.

[30] Velleman does not think that desire can be the practical analog of belief, and thus it cannot aim at the good in the way that belief aims at the truth. However, as we pointed out in chapter 1, desire should not be considered the practical analog of truth but rather of an appearance. Once we note this point, the disanalogies that Velleman finds between belief and desire shouldn't serve as grounds to object to the proposal that desire involves *conceiving* something as good.

Velleman thinks that any view like the scholastic view will fail to make sense of certain possibilities of agency. One example of this kind of impossibility will be a satanic agent:

If Satan ever loses sight of the evil in what he now desires, if he ever comes to think of what he desires as really good, he will no longer be at all satanic; he'll just be another well-intentioned fool. The ruler of Hell doesn't desire what he wrongly thinks is worthy of approval; he desires what he rightly thinks isn't.[31]

The idea of such a satanic agent seems perfectly coherent; this would be an agent who is *guided* by the badness of certain ends rather than by their goodness. There is, however, a classic alternative to this description of satanic agency, a description that is fully compatible with the scholastic view. This is the description offered by Anscombe that examines the famous expression uttered by Milton's Satan, "Evil be thou my good." According to Anscombe, when Milton's Satan utters "Evil be thou my good" he is not saying something meaningless because we can provide, in her terms, a "desirability characterization" of evil in the way that Satan upholds it. According to Anscombe,

One can go on to say 'And what's the good of its being bad?' to which the answer might be condemnation of good as impotent, slavish, and inglorious. Then the good of making evil my good is my intact liberty in the unsubmissiveness of my will.[32]

Velleman is aware of this response, but he thinks that this does not do justice to the devil because in this case Satan "remains, at heart, a lover of the good and the desirable – a rather sappy Satan."[33] I take it that, according to Velleman, we will not do full justice to the structure of Satan's desire if we attribute any kind of *mistake* to Satan. Satan is supposed to be a wholly perverse agent, and one can be wholly perverse only if one is clear-minded about what one is doing. Any attribution of mistake will render the agent confused rather than perverse.

---

[31] Velleman, "The Guise of the Good," p. 18.
[32] Anscombe, *Intention*, p. 75.
[33] Velleman, "The Guise of the Good," p. 19.

It is important to avoid several confusions here. The first is to conflate good and morally good. Perhaps Satan's judgment is that he makes what is *morally* bad his good *simpliciter*. In this sense, Satan's being a lover of the good might not be sappy at all; it might be, indeed, as fully perverse as possible. In this view, Satan does not need to lose sight even for a moment of the fact that what he does is *morally* evil, and he might even be guided by the fact that the action is an instance of moral evil. It is then unclear that we should characterize Satan as being guided by a more general conception of the bad. It seems foreign to our understanding of Satan to conceive of him as proceeding in the same way with respect to other values: if he, for instance, turns down ice cream on the grounds that ice cream is good and he will only eat something that is bad.

Of course, it might turn out (and hopefully it will) that what is morally good is good *simpliciter*, in which case we would have to see Satan as making a mistake, a practical mistake. And indeed we can think that this way of answering Velleman forces us into a dilemma: On the one hand, we can think that what is morally good is also in fact good (and ought to be judged so by all agents). In this case, we haven't advanced much in our response to the problem because we still need to characterize Satan as making a mistake and thus as confused rather than perverse. On the other hand, we can think that the morally good is *not* something that is in fact good. We would then solve this problem, but at the price of making morality at best an optional good and at worst an illusion. So the scholastic view can only avoid this problem by accepting some kind of error theory about morality.

Does the scholastic view really face this dilemma? It is true that if we accept that what is morally good is good *simpliciter* and something that everyone ought to (or will, if they think rightly) judge to be good, there will be no escape from equating Satan's perversity with some kind of mistake. But this follows from the nature of this claim about the morally good, *whether or not one accepts the scholastic view*. Indeed, it is worth noting that it is a straightforward consequence of accepting some form of moral cognitivism, or at least any form of moral cognitivism that is coupled with some kind of motivational internalism, that one needs to view Satan as making a mistake. No doubt, some forms of moral cognitivism might allow that correct moral judgment will generate motivation, but not necessarily motivation that can overpower other motivations. But any kind of moral cognitivism that implies that, at least in some cases, a fully rational and knowledgeable agent will judge that acting morally is the best action available to the agent (or the one the agent has the most reason to do) will have to represent Satan either as making a mistake (by being less than fully rational or lacking a piece of knowledge) or as being akratic (for lacking motivation to choosing what he knows to be the best option). Because it seems even more counterintuitive to attribute *akrasia* to Satan than a lack of knowledge or failures of rationality, it seems that this kind of problem will plague *any* version of moral cognitivism.

Of course, one might be glad to take this consequence as an added bonus in an argument against internalist moral cognitivism. But the problem is that this simply begs the question against moral cognitivism because if one accepts moral cognitivism, one will probably embrace one of two options. One can, on the one hand, accept a Socratic form of moral cognitivism, in which case all moral failures are similar to theoretical errors and perversity would always be a kind of theoretical ignorance (or at least no more culpable than theoretical ignorance). In this case, it would be correct to say that Satan would turn out to be something like a "well-intentioned fool," deserving instruction. However, if we accept the Socratic view, this consequence will come as no surprise; this is exactly what the view is putting forward, and, if one can make a case for the Socratic view, one would hope that regarding Satan this way would no longer appear implausible. The other (and perhaps more common) option for the cognitivist is to *equate* perversion with some kind of practical or evaluative mistake. In this picture, the difference between the well-intentioned fool and the evil person would be understood in terms of the different kind of mistakes they make, one theoretical in nature and the other practical in nature, and perhaps in terms of certain different features of these different kinds of mistakes – one might think that one is culpable, whereas the other is not.[34]

---

[34] This I take to be Kant's view. The well-intentioned fool lacks *Klugheit* (cleverness) and the evil person lacks *Weisheit* (wisdom). For a discussion of the latter concept in Kant, see Stephen Engstrom, "Kant's Conception of Practical Wisdom."

I think there are two sources of resistance to treating perversion in this way, but both are ultimately misguided. The first is the view that this does not respect an important intuition about responsibility for evil. In the law, we generally think that someone is culpable only if they satisfy a knowledge condition; those who do not have the requisite moral knowledge, such as children and the mentally incapacitated, are excused from responsibility. And this kind of knowledge condition seems to extend more generally to responsibility for immoral and perverse actions. However, there is no doubt that Satan satisfies the knowledge condition as required by law. The knowledge condition does not require that one have the understanding of moral (and positive) commands that the virtuous (or civically virtuous) person has. To be responsible, one must be capable of *determining* what is morally good or evil in a particular circumstance; that is, one must be capable of *understanding* the perspective of the virtuous person and know which judgments in a particular situation would be warranted by the perspective of the virtuous person. One is not required in any way to *endorse* the perspective or *make* the judgment; correctly endorsing the virtuous perspective upon reflection and making the evaluative judgment warranted from this perspective is in a cognitivist view what distinguishes the virtuous person from the perverse, and thus the distinguishing "marks" of the virtuous person are items of knowledge. However, the knowledge condition on responsibility is neutral on the question of whether these distinguishing marks are themselves candidates for knowledge.

The second source of resistance is the thought that, if we understand perversion this way, we might not do full justice to the fact that Satan is *guided by the bad*. But it might be worth emphasizing that we rarely think of Satan and other evil characters as guided by the bad *simpliciter*. We do not expect Satan not to plan ahead because planning ahead is what prudence recommends, and thus good, and Satan only pursues what is bad. Even less do we expect Satan to punch himself in the nose or to drink spoiled milk simply on the grounds that these activities are bad and Satan enjoys pursuing the bad. Once we keep this in mind, it seems Anscombe's discussion of Satan fits at least Milton's Satan. What Milton seems to accomplish is to exact from us a certain kind of sympathy for the devil, to put us at a point of view from which we can see, or be caught in the illusion, that Satan's ends are desirable. This is indeed how art and more ordinary circumstances of life can often succeed in making evil an intelligible – as opposed to an inscrutable – tendency of human nature by presenting evil in, for instance, all its glory and glamour, in all its courage and daringness, in sum in such a way that it can appear to be good.[35]

---

[35] I have said nothing about the possibility that our intuitions about Satan are not to be relied on as an oracle. It is unclear at least that human beings could exhibit this sort of commitment to evil. Kant, for instance, thought that human beings could not have what he called a "diabolical will," a will that takes the moral law as a counterincentive. See his *Religion within the Bounds of Reason Alone*.

7

Evaluation and Motivation Part Company?

The Problem of Akrasia

The scholastic identification of desiring and conceiving to be good, of motivational and evaluative attitudes, faces a challenge from cases of *akrasia*. In cases of *akrasia*, agents are not motivated in accordance with comparative evaluations. An akratic agent will think that *A* is better than *B* yet pursue *B*. In these cases, the agent's motivational states seem not to fall in line with his evaluative states.

It is not completely uncontroversial that *accidie* and *akrasia* are indeed possible, at least if described as cases in which the agent's motivation does not correspond with his evaluative judgments. However, denying this possibility seems like denying the phenomena; we at least *seem* to confront instances of these kinds of behavior often enough. The existence of phenomena that correspond to these descriptions of *akrasia* seems to be a major argument against the scholastic view in the context of intentional explanations and in favor of separatist views, views that allow motivation and evaluation to come completely apart.[1] The aim of this chapter is to show not only that the scholastic view has the right tools to account for *akrasia* but also that it accounts for the phenomena better than separatist views.

7.1 THE PROBLEM WITH *AKRASIA*

In the *Protagoras*, Socrates says that most people

---

[1] Similar things can be said about *accidie*, but this will be the subject matter of the next chapter.

maintain that there are many who recognize the best but are unwilling to act on it.... Whenever I ask what can be the reason for this, they answer that those who act in this way are overcome by pleasure or pain.[2]

This popular view seems to describe precisely the possibility of *akrasia*. Both Protagoras and Socrates find this view untenable. Socrates shows that it is untenable by first identifying pleasure with the good. He then presents the following *reductio* of this popular view:

Suppose we now say that a man does evil though he recognizes it as evil. Why? Because he is overcome. By what? We can no longer say by pleasure because it has changed its name to good. Overcome we say. "By what?" we are asked. By the good, I suppose we shall say. I fear that if our questioner is ill-mannered, he will laugh and retort: What ridiculous nonsense for a man to do evil, knowing it is evil and that he ought not to do it, because he is overcome by good.[3]

The scholastic view does not say much about pleasure. But we can just as well say that the akratic agent is overcome by certain desires, including the desire for pleasure. And here the same *reductio* would seem to go through when we replace "pleasure" with "desire" in the preceding quotation. Indeed, even if we accept that akratic agents are overcome by the prospect of pleasure, it must be the case that if pleasure can overcome the agent in this way, this must be because the agent desires it, and if the agent desires it, then the agent has to conceive of it as good. And once we make this inference, it seems hard to avoid the conclusion that the scholastic view would have to treat the popular view, and thus the possibility of *akrasia*, just as harshly as Socrates does. But *akrasia* seems to be an extremely common phenomenon. All of us have found ourselves yielding to temptation, procrastinating, eating beyond healthy limits, and even abandoning the greater good for the sake of pleasure.

The separatist view, on the other hand, seems to have no problem accounting for *akrasia*. If we accept that motivation and evaluation can part company, there seems to be no problem in saying that the akratic agent is motivated by what he does not judge to be the best; we can describe the usual phenomenon in this seemingly natural

---

[2] Plato, *Protagoras*; 352e.
[3] Plato, *Protagoras*; 355c.

way without contradicting ourselves. However, this apparent straightforward separatist solution creates some difficulties that we will be in a better position to assess later. We can have a preview of these problems if we think about a different, somewhat less common phenomenon: compulsion. I might be compelled to do something by other people, or I might be compelled to do something by my own desires, my urge getting the better of me. So a drug addict might be incapable of resisting the strength of his urge, and in a moment of madness I might indeed be *incapable* of overcoming the strength of my desire for ice cream. As Aristotle says, "When nature is the cause, no one would call the people akratic."[4] There seems to be a difference between *akrasia* and compulsion. Aristotle says that *akrasia* is "blameworthy and base," and though we might find this language too strong,[5] we do conceive of an akratic person as a free and responsible agent (or at least this is what makes the issue of *akrasia* puzzling, for there is no difficulty understanding that we might lose control of our bodily movements). Indeed, we rarely find that the claim "I was too weak to resist temptation" is enough to excuse the agent from all, if any, blame. On the other hand, an agent acting under compulsion is not to blame for her actions; if my desires, working "behind my back," drive me to an action despite myself, I am no more free than in cases of external compulsion. At any rate, I will try to show here that the scholastic view can explain the possibility of *akrasia* with the understanding that *akrasia* is not the same as compulsion.

Here is how I will proceed with respect to *akrasia*. In section 7.2, I briefly examine Davidson's effort to resolve the problem without abandoning a scholastic view; this attempt turns out to face some serious problems. In section 7.3, I examine whether a separatist view fares any better. It turns out that attempts to explain the possibility of *akrasia* in terms of a gap between evaluation and motivation have a difficult time distinguishing *akrasia* from compulsion; moreover, I argue that they seem plausible only as long as we think that the possibility of *akrasia* is peculiar to practical reason – if we deny the possibility of theoretical *akrasia*. Because there is no

---

[4] Aristotle, *Nicomachean Ethics* (trans. by T. Irwin), p. 186 (1148b30).
[5] Aristotle himself qualifies this claim later, saying that the akratic agent is not base but "half base." (*Nicomachean Ethics*, 1152a15–20.)

equivalent split between evaluation and motivation in theoretical reason,[6] if we find that *akrasia* is also possible in the theoretical realm, we have a good reason to think that the separatist strategy cannot be a satisfactory account of the phenomenon. In section 7.4, I argue that we can find in Descartes' *Meditations* a characterization of theoretical *akrasia*; indeed we can find (perhaps unexpectedly) in the *Meditations* the basic resources to account for this phenomenon: a distinction between direct and oblique cognitions and a distinction between primary and reflective cognitions. In section 7.5, I argue that a similar account of *akrasia* can be extended to the realm of practical reason in conformity with the old formula of the schools.[7]

7.2 DAVIDSON ON *AKRASIA*

Davidson presents the problem of *akrasia* as the conjunction of the following principles, which are at the same time individually plausible and apparently inconsistent:

(P1) If an agent wants to do x more than he wants to do y and he believes himself to be free to do either x or y, then he will intentionally do x if he does either x or y intentionally.

(P2) If an agent judges that it would be better for him to do x than to do y, then he wants to do x more than he wants to do y.

(P3) There are incontinent actions.[8]

Principle (P2) clearly commits Davidson to a scholastic view. Davidson does think that we can interpret "want" and "judges it to be better" in such a way as to make (P2) false, but he assumes that

---

[6] This is not to say that there is no such thing as a motivated belief, a belief that is motivated by a certain desire. I will be ignoring these cases of motivated belief. Apart from these cases, there is little sense to be made of a parallel distinction between motivation and evaluation (more on this later). However, I will argue that, even if we ignore these cases, theoretical *akrasia* is possible.

[7] I will not try to explain the possibility of what David Pears calls "underivative brazen *akrasia*." (See his "How Easy Is *Akrasia*?" On this issue, see also Al Mele's "Pears on *Akrasia* and Defeated Intentions.") I believe that there is no difficulty in assimilating these cases to momentary changes of mind or compulsion, depending on the case, but discussing this issue would lead us astray. I will here assume that "underivative brazen *akrasia*" is impossible. This assumption is also implicit in Davidson's early account of *akrasia*. (See his "How Is Weakness of the Will Possible?")

[8] Davidson, "How Is Weakness of the Will Possible?" p. 23.

there is at least *some* plausible interpretation of these expressions that makes the combination of (P1) through (P3) paradoxical. Davidson's solution to the paradox is well known, and I will present only a brief sketch of it here.[9] He argues that judgments of the form "*x* is better than *y*" that we make when deliberating about an action are always prima facie judgments relative to some consideration, in the same way that judgments of probability are always relative to a certain body of evidence. Let us consider the plight of the Orthodox Jewish smoker whose religion forbids him from lighting a cigarette Friday night but who feels the urge to smoke and ends up acting on it. According to Davidson, he would make the following judgments:

(a) From a religious perspective, not smoking appears better than smoking.
(b) From a "hedonistic" perspective, smoking appears better than not smoking.

But of course this is not all there is to the way that the Orthodox Jew sees things. He probably also thinks that on reflection the religious perspective should be the one endorsed:

(c) From a reflective perspective, not smoking is better than smoking.

But when he acts, he needs to make an all-out judgment. He needs to decide which is better *simpliciter*, to smoke or not to smoke. Because he acts on his desire to smoke, he makes what Davidson calls an "all-out" judgment, as follows:

(d) Smoking is better than not smoking.

Judgments (c) and (d) characterize the Orthodox Jew as an akratic agent because he acts against his judgment of what is best, all things considered. But (c) and (d) do not contradict each other because the first is conditional whereas the second is an all-out judgment. Principles (P1) and (P2) do imply that if the agent judges *x* to be better than *y*, then the agent will do *x* rather than *y*, but only if "better than" is being used in an unconditional sense. This is compatible with the agent finding *y* better than *x* all things considered, and thus being weak willed.

[9] I have changed Davidson's terminology to make it consistent with mine.

However, this solution does not seem very satisfactory. Davidson is committed to saying that one acts from the all-out judgment but one chooses as one's all-out judgment what was a prima facie judgment overridden by better claims to the good. One is struck by the mystery of how one could succumb to such an obvious mistake. If we follow Davidson's own analogy with judgments of probability, the akratic person is like the person who knows that the *New York Times* published an announcement that the presidential elections would take place today and believes that this is an erroneous report but still goes to the local polling place. Why would anyone make such an obvious mistake? Davidson is certainly aware of this problem; he presents his solution to it in the following sentences:

> If r is someone's reason for holding that p, then his holding that r must be, I think, a cause of his holding that p. But, and this is what is crucial here, his holding that r may cause his holding that p without r being his reason; indeed the agent may even think that r is a reason for rejecting p.[10]

So, in the case of the Orthodox Jew, though he did not hold that the reasons from the point of view of sensuous pleasure were good ones, these reasons nonetheless caused him to hold that it was better to smoke. But adopting this solution would amount to giving up some of the ambitions of the scholastic view presented here. After all, this solution does postulate a gap between the agent's motivation and his evaluations. The capacity of a reason to motivate the agent is, in this picture, independent of his endorsing or rejecting the reason. The fact that the desires that lead the agent to act can be said to be reasons actually has no role to play in explaining why the agent chose this particular action – as opposed to any other that can be rationalized by her beliefs and desires – because the action is not determined by the agent's assessment of the reasons. But if this is so, Davidson's characterization of akratic action does not distinguish it from acting on compulsion; the agent judges a certain course of action best, but some contrary desires take charge of the agent.[11]

---

[10] Davidson, "How Is Weakness of the Will Possible?" p. 41.

[11] For further criticisms of Davidson's views on *akrasia*, see, inter alia, William Charlton, *Weakness of Will*, chapter 7; and Irving Thalberg, "Questions about Motivational Strength."

Davidson's view is thus neither very satisfactory nor one that can be endorsed by the scholastic view.

7.3 SEPARATIST ACCOUNTS OF *AKRASIA*

Perhaps the best attempt at accounting for *akrasia* by means of a separatist view can be found in Alfred Mele's work. Mele tries to explain the phenomenon of *akrasia* as a case in which the strength of motivations does not correspond to the strength of evaluations; what the agent judges best is not what the agent is most motivated to do.[12] The separatist account, however, seems simply to assimilate *akrasia* to cases of compulsion.Let us take cases of compulsion that seem to be interestingly different from cases of *akrasia*. A case of compulsion would be a case in which an agent has a certain urge that he is powerless (or mostly powerless) to counter. The examples of compulsive disorders from the previous chapters would be a case in point, but examples of addicts, kleptomaniacs, and others also seem to fall under this category. It seems natural to describe these cases as cases in which a certain urge causes the agent to behave in ways she wishes she would not. In what ways are cases of *akrasia* described by the separatist different from cases of compulsion?[13] Can a separatist account distinguish between compulsion and *akrasia* or show how akratic actions can be free?

I do not have an argument that will show that there is *no* separatist account of *akrasia* in which *akrasia* turns out to be a free action. I will just look at Mele's account, and I will try to argue that it fails. I know of no other separatist account of *akrasia* that does better than Mele's in this regard. Thus, I hope to establish that it is far from obvious that there is any satisfactory account of *akrasia* within the separatist framework. The next section will give further reasons to suspect that there is no such account. The following sections will show that there *is* a satisfactory account of *akrasia* within the scholastic view.

[12] See his *Irrationality*. For another separatist account, see John Heil's "Minds Divided."

[13] Note that if the separatist is willing to grant that cases of *akrasia* are just cases of compulsion, *akrasia* would not pose any further threats to the scholastic views beyond the ones discussed in the last chapter. However, separatists typically agree that *akrasia* is not a case of compulsion. See Al Mele, "Akratics and Addicts."

Mele aims to show that, within his account, *akrasia* can be free, and thus that his account does not reduce *akrasia* to compulsion. According to Mele, the akratic agent may still be free because the fact that an agent is motivated to pursue what he takes to be a lesser good does not rule out the possibility that the akratic agent is still capable of exercising self-control. The agent might still be free to engage in a certain action that will make the strength of motivation equal the strength of evaluation. Thus, if the agent is free to exercise self-control, the agent's choice of the akratic action must be regarded as free; it is not true in these cases that the agent had no choice but to act as he did.

However, this seems to push the problem one step further. We now need to ask why the akratic agent failed to engage in self-control, and the same questions about weakness of the will should resurface. In order to see that this appeal to self-control does not work, it is worth examining Mele's view in more detail, especially his attempt to answer a similar criticism raised by Watson.[14]

According to Watson, if an agent chooses freely not to exercise self-control, the agent must have changed his judgment. That is, if the agent could have exercised self-control in such a way that he would choose *A* over *B*, and yet decides not to do it, then it could no longer be true that the agent still holds *A* to be better than *B*. It is exactly this point that Mele contests:

Perhaps to choose not to implement a *choice* would be to abandon the choice; but it does not follow that one who chooses not to exercise self-control in support of one's better judgment no longer holds that *judgment*. We may, without obvious contradiction, describe a case in which an agent judges that all things considered it is better to do *A* than *B*, but due in part to his taking his reasons for doing *A* to be only slightly more weighty than his reason for doing *B*, decides to indulge himself and to refrain from exercising self-control in support of *A*. In such a case, the agent may think his doing *B* to be *permissible*, even though he judges *A* to be better; and he may self-indulgently opt for the lesser alternative.[15]

---

[14] For Watson's version of the criticism, see "Skepticism about Weakness of the Will." Mele's response can be found in his "Is Akratic Action Unfree?" and *Irrationality*, section 2.2.

[15] Mele, *Irrationality*, p. 28.

According to Mele, Watson has failed to show that the person who chooses not to exercise self-control in a way that makes it possible for her to choose A over B has thereby given up her judgment that A is better than B. Mele describes a case in which an agent thinks that his moral qualms about striptease clubs provide him with a "slightly better reason, all things considered, not to enter the clubs than to enter them,"[16] but he also experiences a certain desire to enter one of the clubs. He has a "desire-eradicating device" that he could use to do away with this desire, thus making sure that he would stay away from the clubs. According to Mele, however, there is nothing self-contradictory about imagining that the agent will choose not to use his desire-eradicating device while still judging that, all things considered, it is better not to enter the club. It is clear why Mele chooses a case in which the agent thinks there is only a "slightly better reason" to take a certain course of action and why he stipulates that the agent will think that "his doing B is permissible." It is much harder to make the case if we assume that the agent thought that A was overwhelmingly better than B or that B was not permissible.[17] I will first examine why Mele will face problems if he tries to provide an example of this kind. This will help us understand why Mele's response to Watson is unsatisfactory even in the case he describes.

---

[16] Mele, *Irrationality*, p. 28.

[17] It is not clear what "worse but permissible" could mean in this context. We can say that an option A is morally permissible but worse than B from a moral point of view. But this is tightly connected with the possibility of supererogatory actions. The concept of supererogation is difficult enough in the realm of ethics. (For doubts about its applicability, see Shelly Kagan, "Does Consequentialism Demand Too Much?") It is even harder to understand how an action can be better, all things considered, yet supererogatory (all things considered?). To say that B is morally better than A but that A is permissible implies that doing A is not immoral. Mutatis mutandis, we would expect that the akratic action would *not* be irrational. In what sense, then, are we still speaking of *akrasia*? In what sense can we then say that option A was better than B, all things considered, if it is not irrational to choose B? Perhaps although choosing B is not irrational it is more rational to choose A. But Mele surely owes us an explanation of what it means to say that choosing A is more rational than choosing B and yet it is not irrational to choose B. At any rate, because Mele gives no explanation about what it means to say that an option is permissible in this context, I will assume that it adds no content to the claim that one option is only slightly better than another.

Let us assume that Joe lives in a dictatorship. The dictators are after his sister, who is the head of an underground guerrilla group, and Joe knows that they will show no mercy toward her. The government offers Joe a million dollars to turn her in and he refuses because he finds it abominable to trade his sister's life for a few bourgeois comforts. The government explains to Joe that the offer will still stand for 48 hours and that they will bring to his home tonight a suitcase full of cash, hoping he will have changed his mind by then. They will open the suitcase in front of him and wait for his answer. Joe knows he cannot resist such a vivid display of hard currency. Fortunately, he can avoid facing this irresistible temptation by just putting a sign on the door that says, "Joe does not live here anymore." Not being very bright, the government agents will turn around and never come back.

Could Joe choose not to put a sign on the door and yet retain his judgment that he should not turn in his sister? Now it seems that the answer is "no," and that is the reason Mele did not choose an example like this. If we rest satisfied with this point, it would already be the case that Mele's position has to give up a lot because typical cases of *akrasia* do not involve our choosing against our judgment that something is "slightly better" or choosing to do something that we consider to be in any interesting way "permissible." So, Mele would have shown that only a small subset of akratic actions are free, and this would already amount to giving up a lot of the phenomenon. However, the correct answer to the question about Joe is not "no" but "yes." Instead of making things better for Mele's position, however, this fact just helps us illuminate why his reply to Watson is unsatisfactory even in the case he describes.

There is a clear reason why it is hard to imagine that Joe could fail to choose to exercise self-control and not change his judgment. Suppose he still makes this judgment and also judges that he cannot give in to his desire for cash without exercising this form of self-control. But as long as Joe is minimally logically competent[18] and is otherwise indifferent about posting or not posting the sign on the

---

[18] If he is not, we have a different kind of problem, similar to the case in which Joe does not realize that exercising self-control would let him act according to his best judgment. I'll discuss this case later.

door, he must conclude from the fact that it is better to save his sister's life than to accept the money that it is better to post the sign than not to post the sign. So we can safely conclude that, as long as Joe is not overcome by tremendous stupidity, he cannot maintain the original judgment that *A* is better than *B* (that saving his sister's life is better than accepting the money) and also judge that it is better not to exercise self-control (that not posting the sign is better than posting it). However, he *can* fail to exercise self-control while still maintaining his original judgment. We can imagine that as Joe is about to post the sign he starts imagining all the wonderful cars he could drive, the wonderful places he could visit, the wonderful house he could buy if he had a million dollars – none of which, of course, compensates for the loss of his sister. We can imagine that despite not changing his reflective judgment, he falls into temptation and does not post the sign.

In this case, however, Joe exhibits another instance of akratic behavior. Because Joe accepts the judgment that, all things considered, it is better to exercise self-control, if he doesn't do it, he will be acting against his best judgment. And it should now be clear that the possibility of exercising self-control could not, in this case, help us to explain how the akratic agent was free. If the answer is "because he was free to exercise self-control," it must be true that when the agent does act akratically, when he does not exercise self-control, he is still free to exercise self-control. But if his failure to exercise self-control itself involves *akrasia*, we cannot assume that he was free to exercise self-control unless we explain how *akrasia* can be free action.[19]

---

[19] In responding to this objection, Mele argues that we need not assume that the explanation for the failure of self-control was *akrasia*. There might be a different explanation for such failure. (See his "Akratics and Addicts.") However, this reply faces a problem. Let us assume that event *E* explains the failure of self-control. Then we face a dilemma. Either *E* is an action that the agent could have chosen not to perform or it is not. Suppose it is. Then either the desirability of performing *E* changed the balance of reasons regarding the exercise of self-control or it did not. If it did, then the agent acted freely, but not akratically, because she chose the option she considered to be best. If the desirability of performing *E* did not change the balance of reasons, then performing *E* was itself akratic because the agent then chose what she judged not to be the best option. Now if *E* is not at all an action that the agent chose not to perform, then, of course, her failure to exercise self-control is not a free action, and it could not thus make a difference to the question of whether the akratic action itself is free.

The same analysis applies to the case Mele discusses, and we should not get confused by the fact that the agent judges the reason to be only "slightly better." If he thinks that not going to the striptease show is better than going and he is otherwise indifferent about using the desire-eradicating device, as long as he maintains his original judgment and is minimally logically competent, he must conclude that it is better to use the desire-eradicating device (given that he judges it to be a necessary, painless means to the option he judges to be better). Of course, he still might not use it, but this would be a case of going against his best judgment because he must judge that, all things considered, it is better to use the device. As we said, however, if his failure to exercise self-control is due to *akrasia*, it cannot help us understand how akratic action can be free.

7.4 DESCARTES AND THEORETICAL *AKRASIA*

If we think that *akrasia* is a phenomenon that has no parallel in the realm of theoretical reason, it is natural to look at unique features of practical reason to account for *akrasia*. Thus, it might be tempting to look for the source of *akrasia* in a sort of motivational breakdown because there is no similar form of breakdown in theoretical reason. In this section, I want to examine Descartes' views on the relationship between the will and the intellect; specifically, how they show us that there is a theoretical counterpart to the phenomenon of *akrasia*. I shall also argue that we can find in Descartes' work the resources to account for this possibility. In the following section, I will show how to extend this account to practical reason within the framework of the scholastic view.

The possibility of theoretical *akrasia* comes up most clearly in Descartes' *Meditations* when we try to carry the sceptical lessons of the first Meditation into the later Meditations. At the end of the first Meditation, Descartes expresses the problem as follows: "My habitual opinions keep coming back, and despite my wishes, they capture my belief, which is as it were bound over to them as a result of long occupation and the law of custom."[20]

---

[20] Descartes, *Meditations* AT VII, 22.

This is not very far from how an akratic agent could describe his failed attempts to follow his reflective perspective. But what makes those "habitual opinions" come back, flouting the skeptical arguments of the first Meditation? Why can't the agent's "wish" be easily fulfilled in light of the doubts raised against his habitual opinions? In other words, why aren't the skeptical arguments enough to make sure that old habits will not capture his belief?

I think the answers to these questions can best be seen by looking at a distinction implicit in Descartes' reexamination of these doubts in the Third Meditation. When Descartes conceives of the possibility of radical doubt, he notes that whenever he contemplates thoughts such as "$2 + 3 = 5$" he cannot fail to assent to them. As he says:

When I turn to the things themselves which I think I perceive very clearly, I am so convinced by them that I spontaneously declare: let whoever can do so deceive me; he will never bring it about that I am nothing so long as I continue to think I am something; ... or bring it about that two and three added together are more or less than five, or anything of this kind in which I see a manifest contradiction.[21]

The possibility of skeptical doubt depends on the possibility of not "turning to the things themselves"; that is, not turning my attention to those truths that I cannot doubt when I contemplate them while still retaining them in the mind somehow. I take it that Descartes is here drawing a distinction between oblique and direct cognition.[22] There is a way in which I conceive of two plus three equaling five such that this thought presents itself to me as impervious to doubt, a thought in which I grasp not only *that* two plus three equals five but *how* it is so.

We can say, roughly, that a direct cognition is a representation of an object or claim through which one clearly understands (or seems to understand) *why* the object is as one represents it, or *how* it is that

---

[21] Descartes, *Meditations*, AT VII, 36.
[22] I do not intend to use the word "cognition" here as an achievement noun, so it does not follow from the fact that I have a cognition that presents an object as X on the grounds that Y that the object is in fact X or that Y constitutes good grounds for accepting that the object is X. My cognition might in some way be delusory.

this claim is true.[23] An oblique cognition is a representation of a claim or an object that is not a direct cognition but one through which one understands (or seems to understand) *that* there are reasons to accept that the object is as one represents it, or that the claim is true. We can think of an oblique cognition as standing proxy to one or more direct cognitions. A direct cognition carries with it the explicit justification of what the cognition represents as true. So, a mathematical proof of a theorem is a direct cognition of this theorem because it not only presents the theorem as true but also presents the reasons for holding this theorem to be true. But if I later remember having proven this theorem to be true, without remembering the proof itself, my cognition is oblique. It represents not *the* reason for holding the theorem to be true but that *there is* a reason to hold this theorem to be true, a reason that this cognition does not make available to me. Of course, there is a sense in which my memory itself is a reason for my accepting the truth of the theorem, but it is a reason for *accepting* the theorem, not a reason *why the theorem is true*; my memory could not be part of the proof of the theorem. In the same way, if I trust the judgment of reputable physicists on matters of quantum mechanics, my cognitions of the matter are oblique; they stand proxy not to a direct cognition that *I* have ever had available to me but nonetheless stand proxy to a direct cognition.

In both direct and oblique cognitions, we deal with the same proposition, but we conceive of this proposition in different ways. We can also see that this distinction is important in motivating Descartes' intuitionism. Descartes insists that we should try, as much as we can, to entertain several steps of a derivation at once.[24] This insistence can be seen as manifesting not a bizarre mistrust in the powers of memory but rather a realization that this is what true understanding partly consists in. The mathematician who does not see the whole proof of a proposition within a single intuition knows *that* it is so and even *that it must be so* but does not know *how* it is so and *how it must be so*.

---

[23] This does not mean to say that one can say anything more than "I see it!" to justify why the object is as she represents it.

[24] See Rule 11 of "Rules for the Direction of the Mind" (AT X, 407).

Oblique cognitions seem to be especially important in reflective judgments because reflective judgments might have to weigh considerations that are not clearly commensurate. By looking at two objects at more or less the same distance, I can determine, in most cases, which object is larger just by looking at them. But the situation is more complex if I have to examine, for instance, incompatible claims of my sensory cognitions of an object and my more theoretical understanding of a physical object. Suppose, for instance, I see what seems to be an object floating in the air in flagrant violation of the laws of gravitation. When one asks whether the claims of our theoretical understanding of physical objects should be valid or whether the claims of sensory perceptions should be valid, one is not just struck by each of these cognitions and put in the position of waiting to see which of them would incline the will one way or the other. I have to consider how I should take each idea, when and how I should take my sensory perceptions at face value, the reliability of my clear and distinct perception (or my theoretical beliefs about the nature of the object), and so forth. In order to settle the competing claims of those cognitions, we need to rely on oblique cognitions such as, "The fact that I have a sensory cognition of the state of a physical object is a reliable but not infallible guide to the state of this object (it should count as some evidence for the claim that the object is in this state but not as conclusive evidence)." In cases of conflict of cognitions from different cognitive sources, our reasoning might involve not only the presentation of these cognitions to the mind but primarily the representation of the *fact that we are in the possession of these cognitions* and of our reflective views on the relative weight that we should accord to these cognitions. We can now reserve the term "reflective cognition" only for those cognitions that evaluate the relative weight of a certain cognition, such as the following: "The fact that I have a sensory cognition of the state of a physical object is a reliable but not infallible guide to the state of this object (it should count as some evidence for the claim that the object is in this state but not as conclusive evidence)." I will call a "primary cognition" any cognition that is not reflective. All reflective cognitions are oblique, but not all oblique cognitions are reflective. Those reflective cognitions are elements of our reflective perspective, a perspective from which one ultimately will form one's "reflective

judgment" or "all-things-considered judgment." Reflective judgment and all-things-considered judgment are in this view, just as in
Davidson's, conditional judgments; they simply express how things
appear from the reflective perspective, not necessarily the agent's
all-out attitude toward a certain content. Of course, a fully rational
and reflective agent will form her all-out attitude in accordance with
her reflective judgment; after all, all-things-considered judgment
expresses how a reflective agent thinks she *ought* to settle the
incompatible claims of different sources of cognition. A reflective
judgment will be based on reflective cognition and thus on oblique
cognitions. Note that this is not a claim about empirical psychology
or phenomenology but a claim about what must be involved in our
capacity to adjudicate the claims of incompatible cognitions.
Because each cognition presents the object as corresponding to
this cognition, we cannot settle this question through, so to speak,
the eyes of the cognitions themselves but only as we reflect on the
significance of having these cognitions.

Notice that, as Descartes himself points out, as long as our primary cognitions present us with obvious and sufficient grounds to
endorse their content, as long as they are in Descartes' terms clear
and distinct, we should not expect our situation to be any different
from that of the ideal agent; there will be no clash between our all-
things-considered judgment and our all-out attitude regarding the
content in question. If we are dealing with our cognition of, say, the
fact that two is larger than one, we should expect that the clarity and
distinctness of the primary cognition will suffice to guarantee
unproblematic assent to its content. But if, as a result of an abstruse
derivation, the will has to rely upon oblique cognitions, the will
might end up making the wrong judgment. If, when going through
the reasoning of the First Meditation, all that I carry from it is the
thought *that* I had reasons for doubting the existence of the external
world, I might not withhold my judgment accordingly (though I
might accept that I ought to withhold judgment). If I (or "my will" in
Descartes' words) compare this mere recollection with the ideas of
sensory perception – which provide me, at least apparently, with
primary cognitions that represent this world – I might find the latter
convincing while still agreeing that I ought to be convinced by the
former (and this might in practice be the fate of every skeptic). If

this happens, we have a case of theoretical *akrasia*. Note that theoretical *akrasia* is possible not only when we are confronted with an argument that arguably we have good reasons to be suspicious of anyway, such as the dream argument. A similar phenomenon is possible, for instance, when we are confronted with an instance of the gambler's fallacy. Even knowing perfectly well that past coin tosses will not affect future ones, it is hard to shake the feeling that, after repeated tosses of a fair coin have landed tails, it will likely land heads on the next toss. And sometimes we might even "give in to temptation." I might be unable to resist the feeling that I am less likely to win the lottery if I bet on consecutive numbers, even if I know that it ought to make no difference to my chances.

This brings us back to a point I made earlier. The more clearly and distinctly I understand the grounds for a certain truth, the less I am prone to this sort of theoretical *akrasia*. Descartes' advice in Rule Eleven that we should keep as much of a proof in mind as possible is all the more important if we realize that this clear understanding of a proposition can also prevent us from slipping into this form of theoretical *akrasia*. At any rate, it is important to note that the fate of the skeptic is not unlike the fate of the akratic agent. In the same way, we can say that the Orthodox Jewish smoker thinks that he ought to be convinced by his reflective perspective, but he is actually convinced by the judgment from the hedonic perspective.

It is worth noting that Descartes provides himself with a device against theoretical *akrasia* that performs a role parallel to similar devices against practical *akrasia*. At the end of the First Meditation, Descartes assumes that there is an evil demon trying to deceive him. In this way, the upshot of the First Meditation can be surmised in a direct cognition. The evil demon here has a function similar to the various devices that help us exercise self-control. The evil demon performs the same function for the meditator that the conspicuously displayed autopsy photos of the lungs of a heavy smoker perform for the person trying to quit smoking.

It is important to distinguish what I have been calling theoretical *akrasia* from another much-discussed phenomenon: self-deception. Mary gives Joe all the indications, short of just saying it, that she considers him a bore. She yawns while he speaks, she avoids his company at parties, and she makes no effort to feign interest in his anecdotes. Joe thinks very highly of Mary's judgment, and it would be devastating to him to believe that she finds him a bore; he certainly wants to go on believing that she finds his company invaluable. Despite all evidence, Joe believes that Mary does not consider him a bore.

We can make the distinction clear by pointing out that theoretical *akrasia*, as I understand it, is a shortcoming wholly within theoretical reason. Its description involves no reference to the desires, values, or practical judgments of the agent. Self-deception involves the interference of practical reason; Joe's desires are determining the formation of an irrational belief. One is not motivated in any way to find the gambler's fallacy persuasive; it would be quite surprising to find out that one has a stake in that issue. Yet, one finds it persuasive even if one acknowledges that one ought not to find it persuasive.

7.5 EXTENDING THE ACCOUNT TO PRACTICAL REASON

It is easy to see that we can also distinguish between oblique and direct cognitions in the practical realm. When I set myself to eat gumbo in full awareness of how gumbo tastes because I desire gumbo by virtue of its taste (from the perspective of "gastronomic pleasure"), the way in which gumbo appears good to me is no doubt a direct cognition. But when I set myself to eat gumbo because my cousin told me that gumbo is really good, the way in which gumbo appears good to me is an oblique cognition. This is perhaps even clearer if my cousin recommends that I develop friendships (something, say, I had never tried to do before), and I trust him to know what is good for me. Here, too, the way in which friendship appears good to me amounts to an oblique cognition.

The reflective perspective in practical reason is what we described in chapter 2 as the agent's general conception of the good. And in the same way as in theoretical reason, when I reflect on the various appearances of the good, I form a general conception of the good by means of oblique cognitions. I have to assess whether the fact that something appears "so good" from a gastronomic perspective is something to which I should attach much importance.

For instance, when I recall the thrill of watching a mystery movie and imagine myself reliving this experience, I am, as it were, in the grips of an evaluative perspective in which watching such a movie appears to be good. However, when evaluating what I should do tonight, I have to weigh the claim of this perspective against other incompatible claims. When reflecting on this option, I weigh that watching a movie is desirable because of this thrill, but in doing so I do not necessarily see *how* the thrill makes it desirable; I am no longer judging what is good from the perspective of desires for thrills. My general conception of the good here is based on oblique cognitions. What I judge to be more or less valuable will be grounded on considerations such as, "The fact that I find *X* pleasant is a reliable but not infallible guide to the fact that *X* makes some positive contribution to my good." As I recognize reflective appearances as authoritative, I recognize that my all-out judgments *should* always be in tune with my general conception of the good. But here, just as in the case of theoretical *akrasia*, the less clear my grasp is on the reflective cognitions, the more prone I will be to form all-out judgments that short-circuit my general conception of the good and arise directly from certain appearances of the good. Let us now examine this claim in more detail.

Let us return to our Orthodox smoker. He judges that:

(a) From a certain perspective, smoking is better than refraining from smoking.
(b) All things considered, refraining from smoking is better than smoking.

As we said earlier, Davidson correctly points out that (b) is compatible with the all-out judgment that it is better to smoke. But we argued that though Davidson's account of *akrasia* could make these statements compatible, it could not explain the frequency of instances of their conjunction in free action.

The root of this difficulty is that Davidson's account is oblivious to the fact that when we move from judgments of the form of (a) to judgments of the form of (b), something gets lost. In order to make judgments of the form of (a), we have to step back from the perspectives under which judgments of the form of (a) are made, from the perspective from which smoking appears to be good. If we lose sight of this, we will be bound to think that (b) makes (a) irrelevant – at this point (a) could have no bearing on the agent's action if he can follow his judgment. After all, (b) seems to do away with any plausibility that (a) might have. But (b) loses sight of the way in which things appear when we are "in the grips" of the relevant perspective; it at most *takes into account* the fact that they appear this way.

So, for instance, Walter might see his desire to avenge himself against his rival who got the poetry prize he coveted so much as arising from ungrounded emotions. After all, Walter thinks that to the extent that desire for revenge makes sense, it ought to be directed against those who wronged him, those whom he might legitimately resent. But Walter cannot take seriously the thought that someone who got a poetry prize he coveted indeed has wronged him. However, the primary cognition remains, and the reflective cognition might not have the same immediacy or clarity as the first cognition.

So in the same way that convincing myself that the sun is bigger than the Earth does not thereby change the way the sun looks to me when I step out of my house, the judgment that he ought not to try to avenge himself does not do away with the original appearance of the good. A certain appearance of the good that I believe I ought to accept might fall short of immediately providing me with an all-out judgment in at least two ways. I might understand that I should pursue a certain course of action but have very little insight as to why. This could happen if I were told by someone I trust that a certain course of life is worth pursuing (she explains to me, for instance, how one feels much better when one stops eating animal products) or if I were convinced by complex considerations that I ought to become a vegetarian. But it might also fall short of immediately providing me with an all-out judgment if I can see why I ought to endorse this appearance of the good but cannot clearly grasp the alternative appearances as illusory or overridden.

This is similar to a situation in which a *reductio* makes it clear to us that a certain proposition cannot be true but we do not understand what is wrong with the reasons we took to support this proposition. Again, we can think about the fate of skepticism at the end of the First Meditation in the same terms. The remembrance of having good reasons to doubt all of one's beliefs tells us that what our senses convey to us ought to be doubted. But the conviction that this was shown is an oblique cognition, whereas the presentation of objects by the senses is immediately clear. And if my understanding of this argument is unclear and vague, I might not be persuaded by such an argument but still retain my conviction that I ought to be. Similarly, realizing that the gambler's fallacy is a poor form of reasoning does not necessarily dissolve the temptation to avoid betting on last week's winning number, and this temptation is greater the less clear my grasp of the structure of the fallacy is. So I will probably be persuaded differently by instances of the gambler's fallacy if I were just assured by a friend that this is a fallacy, or if I have merely a vague understanding of how the principle guiding my choice is an instance of the gambler's fallacy. And if this is the case, I might find myself saying things such as, "I understand that this is a fallacious reasoning, but it just does not seem possible that these numbers will come up again."[25]

Turning back to the akratic person, we may say similarly that the akratic agent's understanding that *A* is better than *B* is a reflective appearance of which she might have only a vague or oblique understanding. And in the same way that someone who has read the First Meditation might believe that he ought to be persuaded by the argument while not actually being persuaded by it, the akratic agent believes that he ought to be persuaded by his reflective understanding but is not persuaded by it. And this amounts to saying that the akratic agent acts against his own recognition that all things considered he should act otherwise.

When Walter vividly imagines that person holding with pride the award he so coveted, he can see the *point* of hating that person and taking revenge. Walter knows indeed *that* he ought not to take revenge, but his desire for revenge might stem from a perspective whose inadequacy he only vaguely understands right now. Walter might see *why* he should take revenge in a way that he cannot see why he should refrain from doing so. Or Walter might see *that* he

---

[25] One might think that if a person does not bet consistently with the belief that these are instances of the gambler's fallacy, then, at least when it comes to the time of betting, he does not have available (at least at that moment) the understanding that this is a fallacious form of reasoning. But the same goes for practical *akrasia*. One can always claim that the agent who acts against her best judgment no longer has available her reflective understanding that, say, *A* is better than *B*. There is no more reason (at least no more pretheoretical reason) to deny the phenomenon in one case than in the other.

should not take revenge but not clearly see *why* he shouldn't – the
plausibility of the desire for revenge is still there. Of course, Walter
could, so to speak, wise up. His understanding of the grounds for
the inadequacy of his desire for revenge could become more and
more clear to him, in the same way that the inadequacy of one's
distant perceptions is quite apparent to an adult human being; it
actually requires some effort for a mature human being to
acknowledge that, in a sense, the stars in the sky "look small" rather
than just distant. In the ideal case, Walter will become virtuous in the
Aristotelian sense of "virtuous,"[26] and he will no longer be prone to
akratic behavior. His understanding that there is nothing to be said
for this perspective will become flawless, and his desire for revenge
will be lost. Walter would not see revenge as good from any perspective, and so, according to our scholastic view, desire for revenge
would not in this case be one of his desires. What the virtuous agent
accomplishes is that his all-out judgment no longer needs to rely on
oblique cognitions because there are no longer any perspectives that
make temptation appear good to him in any way. Because those
things that could be objects of temptation do not appear to be good
to this ideally virtuous agent, a reflective perspective is idle: It
does not need to compare or weigh the claims from different
perspectives.

Perfect virtue is certainly not easy, and it is likely impossible. It is
no surprise that we devise methods that are similar to Descartes' evil
genius: a direct cognition that can mimic the function of perfect
understanding. One might look at a lovely picture of one's family to
stay away from a gambling table or keep large-sized clothes that one
used to wear in order not to indulge again in old eating habits. Of
course, these strategies are just the same strategies that come under
the heading of self-control and that are invoked by those who
ascribe *akrasia* to a gap between motivation and evaluation. Self-
control would be a way to line up one's motivation with one's evaluation. But in the view that I am defending, self-control should be
understood as a way of getting one's evaluation attuned with one's

---

[26] The virtue in question, for Aristotle, is temperance. According to Aristotle, "The
continent and the temperate person are both the sort to do nothing in conflict with
reason ... ; but the continent person has base appetites, and the temperate person
lacks them." (*Nicomachean Ethics*, 1151b–1152a).

conception of how one ought to evaluate. It is not a process of garnering motivation but of finding a clear and obvious way to present something that one abstractly and perhaps vaguely conceives to be good all things considered – in the ideal case, finding a direct cognition that can substitute for an oblique one. This is in fact a better account of how we generally conceive of these strategies. We can compare the examples given earlier with the example of a pill that would create an irresistible craving to do the right thing. The pill does not make it vivid to me how much better it is to do the right thing but just creates in me what one could describe as a "surd" form of craving for, for instance, saying "no" to any form of bribery, or a surd form of revulsion to accepting bribery.[27] If we accept the account of self-control according to which self-control aims at garnering further motivation that will match a fixed evaluation of the options, taking the pill would be a form of self-control like any other; it does indeed garner motivation that will make me act according to my evaluation. Undoubtedly, given my tendencies toward *akrasia*, I could decide to take the pill. However, it would be odd to describe this as an exercise of self-control. Quite the contrary, it would seem to be a case in which I despair of exercising self-control and let myself be dragged by my passions, and, in light of this fact, try to make sure that they will at least drag me in the right direction.

The possibility of virtuous agency makes it clear that according to this account of *akrasia*, akratic behavior always involves a form of cognitive failure. It is important to note, however, what sort of cognitive failure this is, so that we can see that the account does not rule out the possibility of "clear-eyed *akrasia*." Consider an akratic agent and a virtuous agent who is not prone to *akrasia*. Let us assume that according to both their general conceptions of the good *A* is better than *B*. The difference between the akratic agent and the virtuous agent is not a difference about the *content* of what they conceive to be best, all things considered. They both accept that *A* is better than *B* all things considered. Also, they both agree, as broadly

---

[27] A classic fictional example of this sort of revulsion is the revulsion developed by the central character of the movie *A Clockwork Orange* toward violent crimes.

rational agents, that one ought always to follow the reflective perspective. So the akratic agent endorses both the following:

(a) From a reflective perspective (all things considered), A is better than B.

(b) I ought to accept the judgments from a reflective perspective. (I ought to follow the judgments that are warranted by my general conception of the good.)

Endorsement of (a) and (b) should certainly suffice, insofar as the agent is rational, to issue in the same all-out evaluative judgment as the virtuous agent; that is:

(c) I shall pursue A rather than B.

Indeed, as one would expect from any account of *akrasia* that does *not* deny the phenomenon, the puzzle is why the agent, insofar as she is still a free agent, does not act exactly like the virtuous agent. Insofar as one holds a scholastic view, this puzzle will come together with the puzzle of why the akratic agent, unlike the virtuous agent, does not endorse (c),[28] and, of course, through the course of this chapter, I have been aiming at dispelling this puzzle.

It is important to note that this account preserves the truth of most of the statements that we would make to describe an akratic agent. It is true, under the scholastic account, that the akratic agent acted against her best judgment (she acted in conflict with her general conception of the good) and that she did what she knew she should not have done (she knew her all-out judgment should have been in line with her general conception of the good), and she acted in a way she knew to be irrational (she accepted an all-out judgment she knew she should not have accepted). But does it preserve *everything* we ordinarily say about weakness of the will? Does it preserve the simple judgment that the akratic agent chose B, even though she judged that A was better than B? It depends on whether by "judging that A is better than B" we mean the all-things-considered judgment, the judgment that is warranted by one's general conception of the good, or the all-out judgment. The

---

[28] The same is true, for instance, of Davidson. In his account, the akratic agent always accepts the all-out judgment that corresponds to the action. See his "How Is Weakness of the Will Possible?"

scholastic account, of course, can accommodate only the former. The question is whether we are required to use the latter interpretation to save the phenomenon. The fact that we can preserve all the ordinary judgments given earlier using the former interpretation suggests that the answer is "no." The former interpretation still allows us to describe the agent as freely choosing what she knows she ought not to choose, and this is the essence of the puzzling phenomenon of *akrasia*.[29]

Of course, it might be the case that in a certain philosophical account of the phenomenon, one needs to accept the former interpretation. It is important not to confuse the phenomenon and its putative accounts, hard as it is to keep them apart. One cannot demand that a philosophical account will preserve all the features attributed to it by putative philosophical accounts. One should keep this in mind when considering whether, under this account, clear-eyed *akrasia* is really possible. One might say that there is, after all, a cognitive difference between the akratic agent and the virtuous agent. So, isn't only the virtuous agent really clear-eyed?[30]

But, as I said earlier, the difference between the akratic agent and the virtuous agent is not a difference in their acceptance of the

---

[29] Charlton (*Weakness of the Will*, p. 124) points out, in criticizing Davidson's account of *akrasia*, that the akratic agent will not agree with Davidson's characterization of her. The akratic agent will deny making the unconditional judgment that the course of action he undertook was the best one. Michael Bratman makes a similar point in "Practical Reasoning and Weakness of the Will." However, the distinction between an unconditional or all-out judgment and an all-things-considered judgment is part of the philosophical lore. It is not a distinction that one is ordinarily aware of but rather depends on a particular theory about the nature of practical reason. The fact that an agent claims that she does not consider the action she undertakes better than the one she does not cannot settle whether she is expressing her all-things-considered or unconditional judgment. Insisting that we interpret it as the latter is already the result of adopting a certain philosophical position on the matter.

[30] Of course, I am not the first one to propose that understanding the akratic agent in a way that involves some cognitive failure preserves the phenomenon. Aristotelian accounts of *akrasia* will typically attribute to the agent some cognitive failure. Norman Dahl, for instance, in his *Practical Reason, Aristotle and Weakness of the Will*, tries to show that "Aristotle did allow genuine cases of weakness of the will" (p. 140) while providing an interpretation of his account of *akrasia* that "a person cannot act contrary to full and complete knowledge of how one ought to behave" (p. 189). See especially Part II of Dahl's book and also John McDowell's "Comments on 'Some Aspects of Rational Aspects of Incontinence' by T. H. Irwin."

content of the all-things-considered judgment but rather in their understanding of its *grounds*. So the akratic agent knows all there is to know in order to choose the correct course of action. The akratic agent *knows exactly what he ought to do* but doesn't do it; this is an appropriate description of the phenomenon that the scholastic account preserves. Indeed, the lesser grasp of the grounds of the reflective judgment of the akratic agent, as compared with the virtuous agent, does not, by itself, make an agent akratic – it just makes him *prone* to *akrasia*. The strong-willed agent does not succumb to this temptation.

One can think of the akratic agent as someone who has a desire whose presentation of an object wins over his reflective understanding of the good, as someone who is so persuaded by the desire that he no longer accepts that the general conception of the good presents the better reasons, though he accepts that he ought to be persuaded by his general conception of the good. The akratic fails to act in accordance with a valid practical principle, what Davidson calls "the principle of continence,"[31] that, at least in typical cases of *akrasia*, the agent knows to be valid. Moreover, the agent exhibits theoretical understanding of his practical failures; he knows that a rational agent would not have acted as he did. In other words, he knows that his actions should be determined by his general conception of the good rather than by rejected appearances.

[31] Nomy Arpaly has presented a series of examples challenging the validity of this principle. However, Arpaly herself recognizes that principles of continence would have to appear in a kind of "manual" of how an agent ought to behave rationally (even if it is not always the correct principle to follow from a God's-eye view). So even if Arpaly's argument is cogent, known violations of the principle will be cases in which the agent recognizes that he falls short of the ideal of rationality. See Arpaly's "On Acting Rationally Against One's Best Judgment" and her *Unprincipled Virtue*.

8

Evaluation without Motivation?

The Problem of Accidie

Accidie seems to be a phenomenon in which evaluation and motivation come completely apart, the kind of phenomenon that could only be explained by a separatist view. Someone who suffers from *accidie* supposedly still accepts that various things are good or valuable but is not motivated to pursue any of them. This phenomenon seems harder to accommodate within the framework of the scholastic view than *akrasia* because here there is not a different (even if lesser) good that motivates the agent. At any rate, our way of explicating *akrasia* by means of the scholastic view does not seem to have any straightforward application to the cases of *accidie*; it is quite implausible to say that an agent who is in the state of *accidie* is somehow persuaded by an appearance of the good of, say, "staying put."

I will try to show in this chapter how one can account for *accidie* within the scholastic view. This account will depend on defining a relation I call "conditioning," a relation that may obtain between certain states of affairs and evaluative perspectives. Roughly, an evaluative perspective is *conditioned* by a state of affairs if and only if whether the objects that appear to be good from this perspective should be allowed into one's general conception of the good depends on whether that state of affairs obtains. I will argue that the person suffering from *accidie* takes certain evaluative perspectives to be conditioned by certain states of affairs. Whether the dejected agent is rational or not will depend on whether it is rational to accept this relation called conditioning.

We will proceed as follows. Section 8.1 describes more precisely what I take *accidie* to be and the problem that this kind of phenomenon seems to generate for scholastic views. Section 8.2 introduces the relation of conditioning and argues that it is indeed plausible to think that relations of conditioning play an important role in practical reason. In particular, following Kant, I try to show that it is a plausible way of understanding the relation between virtue and the value of our own happiness. Section 8.3 generalizes this notion of conditioning and tries to show how the generalized notion has widespread application. Section 8.4 uses the generalized notion to present a scholastic account of *accidie*.

8.1   THE PROBLEM WITH *ACCIDIE*

Accidie is among the phenomena that Michael Stocker finds obviously inexplicable by a scholastic view. After all, the agent who suffers from *accidie* manifests a lack of motivation that could not be understood as a shift in the agent's evaluations – in what the agent conceives to be good. Stocker describes the problem this way:

> Through *accidie*, ... through general apathy, through despair, ... and so on, one may feel less and less motivated to seek what is good. One's lessened desire need not signal, much less be the product of, the fact that, or one's belief that, there is less good to be obtained or produced.... Indeed, a frequent added defect of being in such "depressions" is that one sees all the good to be won or saved and one lacks the will, interest, desire or strength.[1]

Stocker's apt description of the dejected person seems to pose a particularly difficult challenge to the scholastic view. The person in a state of *accidie* is not rejecting a particular conception of the good in favor of other conceptions of the good that might be tempting in other ways. The dejected person seems simply to lack the will to do *anything* she finds good or valuable, however generously we conceive of goodness or value; she seems to be unmotivated to act *from any conception of the good*. It would indeed be odd to conclude that in some sense, however attenuated, she conceives inaction to be good, and thus it is hard to avoid the conclusion that there is a purely

---

[1] Stocker, "Desiring the Bad," p. 744.

motivational element in intentional action that is independent of
evaluative considerations.

It is worth putting forth the following tentative characterization of
the dejected agent, or the agent who suffers from *accidie*. We can say
that the dejected agent is an agent who, for some period of time, is
not motivated to do anything in particular, or someone who has very
little motivation to pursue ends that she herself would recognize that
she would pursue if she were not in a "dejected state." However, she
also denies (sincerely) that she no longer understands the value or
importance of the things that she does not pursue; she does think
that it is in her power (at least in some sense) to pursue these things;
and she does not think that she is pursuing anything of greater
importance at the moment. Moreover, we have no reasons, or at
least no prima facie reasons,[2] to think that her self-description is
systematically mistaken. Persons in a state of *accidie*, under this
description, might range from the "average" person who sometimes
lacks the motivation to get out of bed or engage in meaningful
activities to some cases of clinical depression.[3] If this is an accurate
description of the dejected person, it seems hard to deny that for
instance, he conceives, of his own health as being good but just does
not desire to pursue it.

8.2   CONDITIONING AND VALUE: HAPPINESS AND VIRTUE

We have already seen that the way we move from appearances of the
good to a general conception of the good is not always straightforward. One might, on reflection, revise the value of the object that
appears to be good, draw various inferences about what must be
good if a certain appearance is of something that is actually good,
deem the appearance illusory, or conclude that the object is good
only insofar as it indeed appears to be good or that it might be
permissible but not obligatory to conclude that the object is good,

---

[2] Of course, we might end up having theoretical reasons to conclude that her self-
description is mistaken.
[3] Certainly not all cases of clinical depression can be described in this manner or pose
any particular threat to scholastic views. In many cases, patients simply "don't care"
about anything in such a way that it would be hard to say that they still value
anything. See the DSM-IV entry on Major Depressive Disorders.

for example. However, I want to introduce here a different relation between an evaluative perspective and a conception of the good, the relation of *conditioning*. We can define this relation tentatively as follows: A certain perspective is conditioned by X if what appears to be good from this perspective could only be correctly judged to be good if X obtains.[4] I think the clearest statements of such a relationship obtaining appear in Kant's discussion of the relationship between happiness and virtue. I will thus start by looking into Kant's account of this relation. I will outline the way in which Kant understands the relationship and try to show that this is a plausible understanding of how one can come to see the value of one's happiness as dependent on one's character. I will then try to generalize this relation in two ways. I will show that the relevant relation can hold a number of conditions and evaluative perspectives and also that there are less stringent relations between certain conditions and evaluative perspectives of which this kind of relationship will be just a particular case. I will then argue that we can make a plausible case for understanding cases of *accidie* as particular instances of a general relation of conditioning.

So this detour through Kant's views serves various purposes. First, it will help us to understand the nature of the relation of conditioning. Second, it will help us defuse the charge that we are introducing an ad hoc modification to the scholastic view in order to accommodate *accidie*. If I am correct, *accidie* is a particular case of a relation that obtains in various other contexts. Finally, the relation between virtue and happiness as Kant understands it displays the relation of conditioning in a setting in which no irrationality is involved. This will help us in understanding what kind of irrationality may or may not be displayed in *accidie*.

Kant famously argued that a relation like this obtains between virtue and happiness and that a virtuous disposition is what makes one worthy of being happy. Kant often describes the relationship between virtue and happiness from the point of view of an impartial spectator who cannot be pleased by a disproportion in the unhappiness of the virtuous person or the happiness of the vicious

---

[4] See the more precise definition in section 8.3.

person.[5] This claim implies at least that if one's ends are evil, they should not be satisfied, and thus to that extent the person should be unhappy; the object of the happiness of the evil person is often itself morally objectionable.[6] No doubt, when one imagines a vicious person being happy, one will include in the conception of his happiness the satisfaction of evil ends (such as, for instance, the schadenfreude of seeing other people humiliated). These are certainly ends that an impartial spectator could not consider to be good. However, this doctrine also implies something about how a virtuous person conceives of happiness brought about by (or conjoined with) evil, *even when there is nothing untoward about the object of one's happiness.* This point might be clearer if we move from "an impartial spectator" to the virtuous agent's own conception of the worth of her happiness when brought about, or accompanied, by evil. How would a virtuous agent conceive of possible cases in which she could obtain something genuinely valuable through immoral means?

Suppose Isabel can spend a weekend in New York (which she very much wants to do), but only if she betrays her friend Ralph. (Suppose Ralph's enemies offer the trip in exchange for breaking Ralph's confidence.) No doubt, the fact that the weekend can be obtained only by this means does not affect the fact that Isabel's representation of vacationing in New York is the representation of a genuine form of value. However, one might say the value of loyalty overrides the value of any other enjoyment afforded by such a vacation. This is certainly true, but this seems to fail to capture appropriately what it would be for Isabel (a virtuous person for our purposes) to betray Ralph because what Isabel imagines when she sees herself in New York at the expense of her friend is not just that she settled for a lesser good. It seems plausible that Isabel will see her stay in New York as not worth having at all rather than as something that would be a second best to staying loyal to her friend.

It would certainly be wrong to say that when Isabel represents herself spending time in New York because of an immoral act,

---

[5] See, for instance, Kant's *Critique of Practical Reason*, Ak. VI, 110.
[6] See Kant's examples of what an immoral person would want in *Critique of Practical Reason*, Ak. VI, 481.

something changes in the content of the representation; it is not the case that she now represents New York as noisy, chilly, and consumerist, or that she suddenly remembers that crowded places can be unpleasant. We would naturally describe this situation as a case in which Isabel is so disgusted with herself that she would not enjoy her trip. However, we must be careful here because it is not the case that we would merely be making a psychological prediction. Isabel would find her character wanting if she realized that her happiness was brought about by evil, but she would nonetheless have no problem enjoying herself. She would probably not think that if she succumbed to temptation, she should at least try to find some kind of therapy that would allow her to enjoy the trip. What would be lacking here is not the capacity to appreciate the good, as might be the case if someone were to face an exquisite dessert after having had too much of the main course. The problem is not in what is available in New York or with Isabel's sensibilities; the problem is just that the trip was made possible by those means.

Of course, one might say that the fact that Isabel cannot enjoy the trip because she was saddened by the fate of her friend can be fully accounted for by the fact that she recognizes that the betrayal is a much greater loss than anything that can be gained by it. Again, this fails to capture the situation. No doubt, the trip might not be enough *to compensate her for* the fate of her friend, neither in the sense that she will think that overall it all worked out for the best nor in the sense that the trip will suffice for her to check the "yes" box after the question "Are you happy?" in a welfare survey. But if her happiness is not *conditioned* by her disposition not to betray her friend, there is no reason that she could not enjoy the trip; after all, the fate of her friend would not make it the case that she would be *indifferent* to the prospect of a weekend in New York. Her friend's well-being and her being in New York would just make two independent contributions to her well-being. It is worth comparing Isabel with the person who just before embarking for her trip to New York learns that a good friend has been fired from his job. It might be the case that the person would have gladly given up her trip if it could have saved her friend's job. But it would be perfectly reasonable in these circumstances for her to continue as planned, thinking that, given that nothing will be gained by staying home, she might as well enjoy the trip (even if her friend's loss of a job would be enough for her not to check the "yes" box in the welfare survey).[7]

Suppose now that Isabel, in a moment of weakness, does betray her friend. In an important sense, Isabel still sees the value of spending time in New York at the same time that she cannot judge this to be good. If asked "Don't you think that enjoying art is one of the greatest things in life, and that it's just wonderful to take walks in Central Park?" she might respond that she does agree with those things. She can say all those things and still refuse to go to New York because she thinks that her betrayal of her friend makes this end no longer worth pursuing. If we recall the distinction between "good" and "valuable" from chapter 1, we can say that although Isabel finds going to New York not to be good under these conditions (and thus not worth pursuing), she does find it valuable. After all, she would find going to New York something that is worth pursuing (and thus good) if she could travel there without having to engage in vicious behavior, and she certainly wishes she could travel there without engaging in vicious behavior. This means that, according to the account of valuing presented in chapter 1, she does find value in going to New York. Thus we can say that even when Isabel no longer thinks that her trip is worth pursuing, she still retains her understanding of the value of engaging in such a trip. As one might have guessed, this point will be crucial in allowing us to understand how the agent who suffers from *accidie* still values, in at least some sense, the things he does not pursue.

8.3 GENERALIZING CONDITIONING

If we talk about virtue being the condition of happiness in the sense that no worth will be attached to happiness when conjoined with a disposition that is not virtuous, we had better have relatively low thresholds for virtue because minor failings certainly will not, and should not, do all that much damage to how I conceive the worth of my happiness. A few trivial lies, a broken promise to my

---

[7] Of course, he might find that it is his duty to stay and support his friend. But it is easy to assume that no such duty obtains, if, for instance, the friend goes back home (and home is miles away) to cope with the situation or decides to spend the next few weeks in isolation.

grandmother to visit her more often, and my occasional dumping of a recyclable bottle in the nearest garbage bin will not make the prospect of going to New York seem much less worthy of pursuit to me. This is not just a fact about the uncaring beings we are but seems perfectly justified: Only an extremely gloomy person would be incapable of enjoying life as a result of some minor vices. A relaxed notion of conditionality can make room for an attitude toward the relation between virtue and happiness that falls in between these two cases. Let us distinguish between the following:

> *Strong Conditionality.* C strongly conditions an evaluative perspective for an agent A if and only if, for every O conceived to be good from that perspective, A should judge O to be good only if C obtains.
>
> *Weak Conditionality.* C weakly conditions an evaluative perspective for an agent A if and only if, for some O conceived to be good from that perspective, A should judge O to be of lesser value if C does not obtain than if C obtains.

So we can think of an interpretation of Kant's claim that the highest good is happiness *in proportion* to virtue that makes it into a plausible requirement on conceptions of the good if we allow that at most only the absence of a thoroughly vicious disposition strongly conditions our happiness (or the evaluative perspectives from which we consider various elements of our happiness to be good). Although there is nothing here that approximates mathematical exactitude in the calculation of proportionality, we may say that one's ethical disposition is relevant to how we conceive our happiness to be good, and, of course, the worse the vice, the less we should see our happiness as desirable.

It is important to note that conditionality cannot be incorporated into the evaluative perspective itself. It is not the case that when we learn that the worth of our happiness suffers these bruises from our disposition, we should conclude that being virtuous is part of the good that one enjoys when one goes to, say, the Rockies. It would be ludicrous to suggest that as I see the beautiful landscape, I am appreciating something like the mereological sum, or the "organic whole," of my virtue (such as it is) and the beauty that surrounds me.[8] What I enjoy is just the beauty itself; that is what constitutes this

---

[8] My discussion of conditioning, and especially this point, is obviously indebted to Korsgaard's paper "Two Distinctions of Goodness."

happy aspect of my existence. Whatever relation there is between my virtue on the one hand and my enjoyment and its worth on the other, it can't be a part–whole relation. It is important to note that I am not raising a general criticism against the idea of an organic unity here. I have suggested in chapter 3 that the possibility of this kind of enjoyment can be better understood in different terms once we accept a wider notion of a mental state. But let us leave this aside and assume that the best account of aesthetic goods relies on a notion of an organic good. I take it that part of the appeal of this account would be the fact that *both* our experience and the object seem to be involved in describing what we find valuable in aesthetic goods. But nothing like that is true of the New York example. Suppose Isabel has now gone to New York by unimpeachable means and that she is now fully enjoying a stroll in Central Park. Would it be plausible to say that what Isabel appreciates is the organic whole formed by the stroll in Central Park combined with her virtue? Certainly Isabel could be enjoying the stroll in Central Park without any thought of her virtue whatsoever. If Isabel were asked to describe what she finds so good about strolling in Central Park, no matter how articulate she was, she would never mention her virtue. Moreover, suppose a completely vicious person is walking alongside Isabel and is undisturbed by the effect that his lack of virtue ought to have on his appreciation of this activity. He strolls along having more or less the same reactions that Isabel does. Trying to appeal to the notion of an organic unity would have the implausible conclusion that Isabel and this vicious person are enjoying two very different kinds of values.

Are these relations of conditioning more general? If we accept Kant's proportionality requirement, we can think that the contribution that an element in a certain evaluative perspective makes to a conception of the good can be *affected* by a certain condition without fully depending on it. That is, even if being *thoroughly* vicious might make one's happiness not worth having, more common human vicious dispositions can affect the worth of one's happiness without rendering it an object that can no longer be judged to make any contribution to the good.

Furthermore, there is no reason to think that what conditions an evaluative perspective has to be a disposition to act, or anything for which the agent is responsible. The representation of the pursuit of one's happiness after a tragic event will share many of the features of the representation of this pursuit conjoined with the awareness of a vicious disposition. Moreover, certain conditions might not have such a general impact on one's conception of happiness. The loss of a loved one might dampen one's appreciation for sports but make one's commitments to other people all the more important. Finally, Kant's conception makes one's happiness depend on a very specific condition. However, one could think that the general structure of the relation of conditioning does not require anything that specific. One might have just a vague conception that "the way one's life is going" cannot leave one's conception of what is worth pursuing untouched.

On the other hand, there might be more specific relations of conditioning. Suppose that as I was growing up I spent time around my grandfather's hometown, where I would often go fishing, sometimes with him. I might find that after the death of my grandfather (say from natural causes when he was already advanced in his years) I can no longer see much point in fishing in that area, or even fishing itself, anymore. It might not be the case that I liked fishing just because I was doing it, at least at times, with my grandfather. However, even if fishing there is very good, the prospect of driving there and fishing without my grandfather might seem meaningless. It need not be the case that I find these memories painful; quite the opposite, I might cherish my memories of those days. It is just, as one might say, not the same without him there (although the sense of "its not being the same" can't be that one no longer understands the point of fishing; one might still otherwise be an avid fisherman and recognize that this was a prime spot for fishing). It is natural to say that the value of fishing in this area was conditioned by my grandfather's being around.

Of course, this shows that conditioning judgments need not have, as might be the case for the relation between virtue and happiness, objective purport in the second dimension.[9] I might not find that other people need to have the same attitude toward fishing in that area or anything else in relation to my (or their) grandfather's being

[9] See chapter 4.

alive. In fact, it might not even be the case that I would find myself wanting if this relation were to fail to obtain in my case. I might consider the counterfactual situation in which I still value fishing in that area despite the loss of my grandparent as a case in which my evaluative outlook would be different but not necessarily defective. Moreover, relations of conditionality can also be much more frivolous than anything I have presented so far. One might think, for instance, that certain goods are conditioned by one's age: One might think that it does not become a middle-aged man to rollerblade around town or for a young fellow to have tea and cookies in the afternoon. It is important to note that the relation of conditioning here should not be understood in causal terms; it is not the case that certain capacities of appreciation might malfunction if certain conditions are not present. There are certainly cases of such things, as when a headache prevents me from enjoying a movie that I would otherwise appreciate. The condition here is a justificatory condition. In the absence of these conditions, the move from certain appearances to an all-out attitude would be *unwarranted*.

8.4 CONDITIONING AND *ACCIDIE*

It should be obvious by now that I think that the best way for a scholastic view to accommodate *accidie* is by means of this relation of conditionality. We can say that the agent in a state of *accidie* takes certain evaluative perspectives to be conditioned by certain states of affairs that do not obtain. In extreme cases, *all* evaluative perspectives are taken by the person suffering from *accidie* to be conditioned and to be such that the particular condition does not obtain.[10] But what could this condition be? The account does not need to be committed to a particular condition or to assume that the same condition will apply to every case. However, it would be plausible to think that the condition will have something to do with the agent's own state of mind or with his assessment of himself. Some ways in which we could express the violation of the condition on the evaluative perspective would be the following: "Given that I feel this way," "Given the kind of person I am," "Given that my life has

---

[10] As will become clear, this needs elaboration.

turned this way," or "Given all that has happened around me," for example. No doubt, all of these are vague characterizations of why conditions on evaluative perspectives do not obtain, but, as we said earlier, there is no need to think that only precisely characterized states of affairs can serve as conditions on evaluative perspectives.[11] One can say that although the dejected agent judges certain things to be valuable, he thinks that some of the facts we gave constitute a violation of a condition of his evaluative perspective and thus a violation of a condition of their being good or worth pursuing.

How plausible is it to see the dejected agent as being committed to taking a certain evaluative perspective to be conditioned by something? It does explain many aspects of the phenomenon. First, we need not claim that the depressed agent, for instance, has completely lost touch with the value of the things he does not pursue and thus deny his own assessment of his situation. Doing justice to this assessment is important not just because of philosophical squeamishness about overriding an agent's report of his state of mind. As Stocker points out in the passage quoted in Section 8.1, we cannot very well describe the awful predicament of the person suffering from *accidie* if we do not ascribe to him a certain appreciation of the values in question. Part of the predicament, as Stocker describes in the same passage, "is that one sees all the good to be won or saved and one lacks the will." We also do not need to postulate newly acquired desires or evaluative perspectives counteracting the usual course of the old evaluations. As we said, it is not as if *accidie* was the result of sudden heightened sensitivity to the value of staying put. Finally, we need not see *accidie* as the result of a surd lack of "oomph" on the part of our evaluations, as the result of something completely external to how the agent views the world, as would be required by a separatist view.

However, not all seems to fall so neatly into place. It seems that *accidie* does not take the form of any particular judgment, and it is

---

[11] Although sometimes a more specific condition could be seen to be at work in clinical depression. See, for instance, the following description in DSM-IV under the heading "Major Depressive Episodes": "The sense of worthlessness or guilt associated with a Major Depressive Episode may include unrealistic negative evaluations of one's worth or guilty preoccupations or ruminations over minor past failings."

certainly not necessarily connected to the awareness that a certain fact renders much that is valuable no longer worth pursuing. But even if there were such a fact, the agent who suffers from *accidie* might resist the claim that she thinks that the fact conditions the value. After all, the depressed person often tries to work against her depression in an apparent recognition that the value is still worth pursuing.

As I said earlier, the relation of conditionality does not preclude the possibility that what conditions a certain evaluative perspective is rather vague. If my proposal is correct, we should see the agent who suffers from *accidie* as being *committed* to a certain relation of conditionality. The proposal does not require that the agent be able to immediately describe or even assent to the attitude ascribed to her. The conditions of adequacy of the explanation are given by whether it can help make the agent intelligible, or, in certain cases, whether it helps us better place the origin of a certain lack of intelligibility in the behavior of the agent. Nonetheless, distinguishing various forms of *accidie* in light of this account can help us see the extent to which the scholastic view can explain the agent's view of her situation. Moreover, these distinctions will also help us see the extent to which the scholastic view can take *accidie* to be a form of irrationality.

On this account, we can distinguish at least three kinds of agents suffering from *accidie*: the full-blown, the hesitant, and the inconsistent.[12] In the first case, the agent's commitment to the absence of a condition that makes a certain value worth pursuing will be stable and not challenged by any of her other practical commitments; that is, the agent simply accepts that a general condition of value does not obtain. This is not to say, of course, that there is nothing that the agent considers regrettable about her situation; it would be hard to describe the case as a case of *accidie* if the agent were completely content with her situation. Rather, what she finds regrettable in this case is the fact that the condition does not obtain: that she is the kind of person she is, that things came down this way, and so on. In the full-blown case, the agent is not inconsistent, nor does she fail to

---

[12] Here, of course, it is a matter of conceptual space. I am not arguing that we do in fact find abundant cases of all three kinds.

act in accordance with how she thinks she should act. This does not mean that there is nothing amiss with her from a practical standpoint. We might think that at least in some cases it would not be completely warranted, for instance, for an agent to think that various pleasures are no longer worth having on account that, for instance, she finds (perhaps also without justification) that she has failed so miserably in her life. But insofar as these are judgments that she fully endorses, whatever her cognitive failings, her practical attitudes are consistent.

Indeed, an agent who engaged in vicious behavior in the past but now, on account of accepting some kind of Kantian view of the relation between virtue and happiness, does not find her happiness worth pursuing, would be suffering, on this account, from full-blown *accidie*. If one accepts the Kantian view in question, there would be nothing wrong with her attitudes; her happiness would, in this view, indeed not be worth pursuing.[13] It might also be worth remarking that the fact that this agent turns out to fall into our classification of *accidie* is *not* an unwelcome consequence. Suppose, for instance, an agent in this predicament let a good opportunity to significantly improve her happiness pass by. Her explanation for passing it up could be something like "Of course it is a good thing when people are happy, and, of course, I see the value of having all those things. However, after what I have done I can't just live like anyone else." Just as with other cases of *accidie*, she would still be capable of appreciating the value of those things that would make her happy, but she would be incapable of finding them good; that is, she would be capable of seeing that if certain desirable conditions were to obtain, her happiness would be worth pursuing, but given that these conditions do not obtain, her happiness cannot be judged to be good.[14]

But the full-blown case need not be the only case of *accidie*. Another possibility is that the agent will waver between the view that the value is not worth pursuing and the view that the value is worth

[13] I am not sure that the view this agent endorses is properly Kant's view. Insofar as she recognizes her past as vicious and no longer acts in this manner, it is unclear to what extent she is still vicious and whether her happiness is worth pursuing or not.

[14] It might be worth noting again here the DSM-IV description quoted earlier on of the importance of self-evaluations of guilt in "Major Depressive Episodes."

pursuing, as well as other intermediate positions allowed by the weaker notion of conditionality. Again, depending on the more substantive views one has on the adequacy of various relations of conditionality, one might consider different forms of *accidie* as cases if not of irrationality then some other kind of cognitive shortcoming.[15]

But one can also be divided, as it were, in relation to the very judgment of conditionality. That is, one might think that one ought to judge that nothing conditions the value that one fails to pursue but yet find oneself judging otherwise. In this case, I think the agent suffering from *accidie* is much like the akratic agent, who does not have his reflective understanding of how he ought to judge lined up with the way he judges. And just as with akratic behavior, the agent in this case would be manifesting a form of irrationality. That is, just like the akratic agent, the inconsistent dejected agent manifests the irrationality of judging or acting in a way that we ourselves recognize to be unwarranted.

But here it might seem that one could raise a new objection because if the agent recognizes that he ought to judge that the value is still worth pursuing, and that nothing about him or the world around him makes it the case that there is some unmet condition on the relevant evaluative perspective, then what could be missing? What we said in the case of *akrasia* should hold here, too. Given the nature of reflective appearances, all things considered, evaluative attitudes must rely on oblique cognitions and thus it is possible that we will be persuaded by a cognition that we recognize should not persuade us.

One might argue that this account still falsifies the agent's self-understanding; after all, in this view, the person suffering from *accidie* does not accept the all-out judgment that she should act in the relevant ways. At best, in the case of the "divided" dejected agent, she recognizes that this is a judgment she *ought* to make. And this, one might claim, is not enough to make sense of the phenomenon. We should answer this objection the same way we answered a similar objection in the previous chapter. The lines

---

[15] One could also think that wavering and hesitation are themselves marks of an irrational disposition.

between the phenomenon and our philosophical understanding of it start to fade. Any understanding of the phenomenon must preserve the obvious fact that the agent suffering from it takes himself to be in a predicament, and this predicament should be understood in terms of the fact that the agent recognizes that he has no motivation to promote ends that he recognizes to be valuable. But this phenomenon is preserved in our account by the fact that something that under normal conditions is valuable cannot be incorporated into one's conception of the good because of undesirable circumstances. And in the case of the divided agent, the predicament is made worse by the fact that the very judgment of conditionality is recognized by the agent to be one that she ought not to make.

I have not argued that the scholastic view is the only view capable of accounting for *accidie*. My aims have been more modest; I hope to have shown that the scholastic view can account for *accidie*. In general, the case I have presented for the scholastic view has been a "possibility" result. I wanted to show that the scholastic view could accommodate a wide spectrum of intuitions and commonsense judgments about the nature of practical reason and intentional explanations in some cases better than rival accounts, and in some cases at least as well. However, the result should not be underestimated. If my arguments work, the scholastic view can give a plausible, intuitive, and unified account of practical reason and intentional explanation, and it can also present theoretical and practical reason as a unified rational capacity guided by two different formal ends: the true and the good. This should certainly suffice to show that the scholastic view should not be eliminated as a candidate for our favorite theory of practical reason and should also lead us to suspect that it might very well be the leading contender.

Bibliography

Ackrill, J. L. "Aristotle on Eudaimonia." In *Essays on Aristotle's Ethics*, edited by A. Rorty, 15–34. Berkeley: University of California Press, 1980.

Adams, Robert. "Scanlon's Contractualism: Critical Notice of T. M. Scanlon, *What We Owe to Each Other*." *Philosophical Review* 110 (2001): 563–586.

Ainslie, Donald. "Character Traits and the Humean Approach to Ethics." In *New Essays in Moral Psychology*, edited by Sergio Tenenbaum. Amsterdam: Rodopi, 2006.

The American Psychiatric Association. *Diagnostic and Statistical Manual of Mental Disorders DSM-IV-TR (Text Revision)*. Washington, D.C.: American Psychiatric Publishing, 2000.

Anderson, Elizabeth. *Values in Ethics and Economics*. Cambridge, Mass.: Harvard University Press, 1993.

Anscombe, G. E. M. *Intention*, 2nd ed. Ithaca, N.Y.: Cornell University Press, 1963 (1st ed., Oxford: Basil Blackwell, 1957).

Aristotle. *Nichomachean Ethics*. Translated by T. Irwin. Indianapolis: Hackett, 1985.

Arpaly, Nomy. "On Acting Rationally Against One's Best Judgment." *Ethics* 110, no. 3 (2000): 488–513.

Arpaly, Nomy. *Unprincipled Virtue*. New York: Oxford University Press, 2004.

Audi, Robert. *Practical Reasoning*. New York: Routledge, 1989.

Audi, Robert. *The Architecture of Reason: The Structure and Substance of Rationality*. New York: Oxford University Press, 2001.

Audi, Robert. *The Good in the Right: A Theory of Intuition and Intrinsic Value*. Princeton, N.J.: Princeton University Press, 2004.

Augustine. *Confessions*. Oxford: Penguin Books, 1961.

Blackburn, Simon. "Practical Tortoise Raising." *Mind* 104 (1995): 695–711.

Brandom, Robert. *Making it Explicit*. Cambridge, Mass.: Harvard University Press, 1994.

Brandom, Robert. "Actions, Norms and Practical Reasoning." In *Varieties of Practical Reasoning*, edited by Elijah Millgram, 465–479. Cambridge, Mass.: MIT Press, 2001.

Brandt, Richard. *A Theory of the Good and the Right*. New York: Oxford University Press, 1984.

Bratman, Michael. "Practical Reasoning and Weakness of the Will." *Nous* 13 (1979): 153–171.

Bratman, Michael. *Intention, Plans, and Practical Reason*. Cambridge, Mass.: Harvard University Press, 1987.

Bratman, Michael. *Faces of Intention: Selected Essays on Intention and Agency*. New York: Cambridge University Press, 1999.

Bratman, Michael. "Davidson's Theory of Intention." In Bratman, *Faces of Intention*, 209–224, 1999.

Bratman, Michael. "Two Faces of Intention." *Philosophical Review* 93 (1984): 375–405.

Brewer, Talbot. "The Real Problem with Internalism about Reasons." *Canadian Journal of Philosophy* 32, no. 4 (2003): 443–474.

Brewer, Talbot. "Virtues We Can Share: Friendship and Aristotelian Ethical Theory." *Ethics* 115 (2005): 721–758.

Broome, John. "Normative Requirements." In *Normativity*, edited by Jonathan Dancy, 78–99. Oxford: Basil Blackwell, 2000.

Broome, John. "Are Intentions Reasons? And How Should We Cope with Incommensurable Values?" In *Practical Rationality and Preference: Essays for David Gauthier*, edited by Christopher Morris and Arthur Ripstein, 98–102. Cambridge: Cambridge University Press, 2002.

Buss, Sarah. "Appearing Respectful: The Moral Significance of Manners." *Ethics* 109 (1999): 795–826.

Chang, Ruth. "Introduction." In *Incommensurability, Incomparability, and Practical Reason*, edited by Ruth Chang, 1–34. London: Harvard University Press, 1997.

Charlton, William. *Weakness of Will*. New York: Basil Blackwell, 1988.

Chekhov, Anton. *Uncle Vanya*, translated by Michael Frayn. London: Methuen, 2005.

Clark, Philip. "Velleman's Autonomism." *Ethics* 111 (2001): 580–593.

Cohen, G. A. "Facts and Principles." *Philosophy and Public Affairs* 31 (2003): 211–245.

Collins, Wilkie. *The Moonstone*, edited by John Sutherland, New York: Oxford University Press, 2000.

Dahl, Norman O. *Practical Reason, Aristotle, and Weakness of the Will*. Minneapolis: University of Minnesota Press, 1984.

Dancy, Jonathan. *Moral Reasons*. Cambridge, Mass.: Blackwell, 1993.

Dancy, Jonathan. *Practical Reality*. Oxford: Oxford University Press, 2000.

D'Arms, Justin, and Dan Jacobson. "Anthropocentric Constraints in Human Value." In *Oxford Studies in Metaethics*, vol. 1, edited by Russ Shafer-Landau. Oxford: Oxford University Press, 2006.

Darwall, Stephen L. *Impartial Reason*. Ithaca, N.Y.: Cornell University Press, 1985.

Davidson, Donald. "Actions, Reasons, and Causes." In Davidson, *Essays on Actions and Events*, 3–20. Oxford: Clarendon Press, 1980.

Davidson, Donald. "How Is Weakness of the Will Possible?" In Davidson, *Essays on Actions and Events*, 21–42.

Davidson, Donald. "Intending." In Davidson, *Essays on Actions and Events*, 83–103.

Davidson, Donald. "Mental Events." In Davidson, *Essays on Actions and Events*, 265–283.

Davidson, Donald. "On the Very Idea of a Conceptual Scheme." In Davidson, *Inquiries into Truth and Interpretation*, 183–198. New York: Oxford University Press, 2001.

den Hartogh, Govert. "The Authority of Intention." *Ethics* 115 (2004): 6–34.

Descartes, Rene. *Meditations*. In Descartes, *The Philosophical Writings of Descartes*. New York: Cambridge University Press, 1991.

Dreier, James. "The Structure of Normative Theories." *The Monist* 76 (1996): 22–40.

Dummett, Michael. "What Is a Theory of Meaning (II)." In Dummett, *Seas of Language*, 34–93. New York: Oxford University Press, 1996.

Dworkin, R. M. "Hard Cases." In Dworkin, *Taking Rights Seriously*, 81–130. London: Duckworth, 1977.

Engstrom, Stephen. "Kant's Conception of Practical Wisdom." *Kant-Studien* 88 (1997): 16–43.

Evans, Gareth. *The Varieties of Reference*, edited by John McDowell. New York: Oxford University Press, 1982.

Foot, Philippa. "Utilitarianism and the Virtues." *Mind* 94 (1985): 196–209.

Foot, Philippa. *Natural Goodness*. Oxford: Clarendon Press, 2001.

Foot, Philippa. "Morality as a System of Hypothetical Imperatives." In Foot, *Virtues and Vices*. New York: Oxford University Press, 2002.

Freud, Sigmund. "Further Remarks on the Defence of Neuro-Psychoses." In *The Standard Edition of the Complete Psychological Works of Sigmund Freud*, vol. 3, ed. and trans. by J. Strachey, 162–185. London: Hogarth Press, 1952.

Gauthier, David P. *Morals by Agreement*. Oxford: Clarendon Press, 1986.

Gert, Joshua. *Brute Rationality*. New York: Cambridge University Press, 2004.

Greenspan, Patricia. "Conditional Oughts and Hypothetical Imperatives." *Journal of Philosophy* 72 (1975): 259–267.

Griffin, James. *Well-Being: Its Meaning, Measurement, and Moral Importance*. New York: Oxford University Press, 1989.

Griffin, James. "Against the Taste Model." In *Interpersonal Comparisons of Well-being*, edited by Jon Elster, Gudmund Hernes, and John E. Roemer, 45–69. New York: Cambridge University Press, 1991.

Hampton, Jean. "On Instrumental Rationality." In *Reason, Ethics and Society*, edited by J. B. Schneewind, 84–116. Chicago: Open Court, 1996.

Hampton, Jean. *The Authority of Reason*, edited by Richard Healey. New York: Cambridge University Press, 1998.

Harman, Gilbert. *Change in View: Principles of Reasoning*. Cambridge, Mass.: MIT Press, 1986.

Harsanyi, John. *Rational Behavior and Bargaining Equilibrium in Games and Social Situations*. New York: Cambridge University Press, 1977.

Harsanyi, John. "Morality and the Theory of Rational Behavior." In *Utilitarianism and Beyond*, edited by Amartya Sen and Bernard Williams, 39–53. New York: Cambridge University Press, 1982.

Haugeland, John. *Having Thought: Essays in the Metaphysics of Mind*. Cambridge, Mass.: Harvard University Press, 1998.

Hausman, Daniel. "The Impossibility of Interpersonal Utility Comparisons." *Mind* 104 (1995): 473–490.

Heath, Joseph. "Foundationalism and Practical Reason." *Mind* 106, no. 423 (1997): 451–473.

Heil, John. "Minds Divided." *Mind* 98 (1989): 571–583.

Herman, Barbara. "Leaving Deontology Behind." In Herman, *The Practice of Moral Judgment*, 208–242. Cambridge, Mass.: Harvard University Press, 1993.

Hobbes, Thomas. *Leviathan*, edited by C. B. Macpherson. London: Penguin Books, 1985.

Hornsby, Jennifer. *Simple Mindedness: In Defense of Naive Naturalism in the Philosophy of Mind*. Cambridge, Mass.: Harvard University Press, 1997.

Hubin, Donald C. "What's Special about Humeanism." *Nous* 33 (1999): 30–45.

Hume, David. *A Treatise of Human Nature*, edited by David Norton. New York: Oxford University Press, 2000.

Hurka, Thomas. "Virtuous Acts and Virtuous Dispositions." *Analysis* 66 (2006): 69–76.

Hutcheson, Francis. *An Essay on the Nature and Conduct of the Passions and Affections: With Illustrations upon the Moral Sense*, edited by Aaron Garrett. New York: Liberty Fund, 2002.

Jakes, Ian. *Theoretical Approaches to Obsessive–Compulsive Disorder*. New York: Cambridge University Press, 1996.

Kagan, Shelly. "Does Consequentialism Demand Too Much?" *Philosophy and Public Affairs* 13 (1984): 239–254.

Kagan, Shelly. *The Limits of Morality*. Oxford: Clarendon Press, 1991.

Kamm, Frances. "Toward the Essence of Nonconsequentialism." In *Fact and Value: Essays on Ethics and Metaphysics for Judith Jarvis Thomson*, edited by Alex Byrne, Robert Stalnaker, and Ralph Wedgwood. Cambridge, Mass.: MIT Press, 2001.

Kant, Immanuel. *Religion within the Limits of Reason Alone*, edited by Theodore Meyer Greene and Hoyt H. Hudson. 1st Harper Torchbook ed. New York: Harper Torchbooks, 1960.

Kant, Immanuel. *The Metaphysics of Morals*, edited by Mary Gregor. New York: Cambridge University Press, 1996.

Kant, Immanuel. *Critique of Pure Reason*, translated by Paul Guyer and Allen Wood. New York: Cambridge University Press, 1997.

Kant, Immanuel. *Critique of Practical Reason*, edited by Mary Gregor. New York: Cambridge University Press, 1997.

Kolodny, Niko. "Why Be Rational?" *Mind* 114 (2005): 509–563.

Korsgaard, Christine M. "Kant's Formula of Humanity." In Korsgaard, *Creating the Kingdom of Ends*, 106–132. New York: Cambridge University Press, 1996.

Korsgaard, Christine M. "Two Distinctions of Goodness." In Korsgaard, *Creating the Kingdom of Ends*, 249–274.

Korsgaard, Christine M. *The Sources of Normativity*. New York: Cambridge University Press, 1996.

Korsgaard, Christine M. "The Normativity of Instrumental Reason." In *Ethics and Practical Reason*, edited by Garett Cullity and Berys Nigel Gaut, 215–254. New York: Clarendon Press, 1997.

Korsgaard, Christine M. *Locke Lectures*, http://www.people.fas.harvard.edu/~korsgaar/, 2002.

Lavin, Douglas. "Practical Reason and the Possibility of Error." *Ethics* 114 (2004): 424–457.

Lewis, David. "Desire as Belief." *Mind* 97 (1988): 323–333.

Mackie, J. L. *Ethics: Inventing Right and Wrong*. New York: Penguin Books, 1977.

MacMahon, Christopher. "The Paradox of Deontology." *Philosophy and Public Affairs* 20 (1991): 350–377.

McDowell, John. "Comments on 'Some Aspects of Rational Aspects of Incontinence' by T. H. Irwin." *Southern Journal of Philosophy* 27 (supp.) (1988): 89–102.

McDowell, John. *Mind and World*. Cambridge, Mass.: Harvard University Press, 1994.

McDowell, John. "Singular Thought and the Extent of Inner Space." In McDowell, *Meaning, Knowledge, and Reality*, 228–259. Cambridge, Mass.: Harvard University Press, 1998.

McDowell, John. "Are Moral Requirements Hypothetical Imperatives?" In McDowell, *Mind, Value and Reality*, 77–94. Cambridge, Mass.: Harvard University Press, 1998.

McDowell, John. "Might There Be External Reasons?" In McDowell, *Mind, Value and Reality*, 95–111.

McDowell, John. "Values and Secondary Qualities." In McDowell, *Mind, Value and Reality*, 131–150.

McDowell, John. "Functionalism and Anomalous Monism." In McDowell, *Mind, Value and Reality*, 325–340.

Mele, Al. "Pears on *Akrasia* and Defeated Intentions." *Philosophia* 14 (1984): 145–152.

Mele, Al. "Is Akratic Action Unfree?" *Philosophy and Phenomenological Research* 46 (1986): 673–679.

Mele, Al. *Irrationality*. New York: Oxford University Press, 1987.

Mele, Al. *Self-Deception Unmasked*. Princeton, N.J.: Princeton University Press, 2001.

Mele, Al. "Akratics and Addicts." *American Philosophical Quarterly* 39, no. 2 (2002): 153.

Mill, J. S. *Utilitarianism*. Indianapolis: Hackett Publishing, 1981.

Millgram, Elijah. *Practical Induction*. Cambridge, Mass.: Harvard University Press, 1997.

Misak, Cheryl. *Truth and the End of Inquiry*. New York: Oxford University Press, 2004.

Moore, G. E. *Principia Ethica*. Buffalo, N.Y.: Prometheus Books, 1988.

Nagel, Jennifer. "The Empiricist Conception of Experience." *Philosophy* 75 (2000): 345–376.

Nagel, Thomas. *The Possibility of Altruism*. Oxford: Clarendon Press, 1970.

Nagel, Thomas. *The View from Nowhere*. New York: Oxford University Press, 1986.

Nozick, Robert. *Anarchy, State, and Utopia*. New York: Basic Books, 1974.

Nozick, Robert. *The Nature of Rationality*. Princeton, N.J.: Princeton University Press, 1993.

Parfit, Derek. *Reasons and Persons*. Oxford: Clarendon Press, 1984.

Pears, David. "How Easy Is *Akrasia*?" *Philosophia* 11 (1982): 33–50.

Pettit, Philip. "Consequentialism and Respect for Person." *Ethics* 100 (1989): 116–126.

Pettit, Philip, and Michael Smith. "Backgrounding Desire." *Philosophical Review* 99 (1990): 565–592.

Plato. "Protagoras." In *The Collected Dialogues of Plato, Including the Letters*, edited by Huntington Cairns and Edith Hamilton, translated by W. K. C. Guthrie. Princeton, N.J.: Princeton University Press, 1971.

Quinn, Warren. "Actions, Intentions and Consequences: The Doctrine of Doing and Allowing." In *Morality and Action*, edited by Philippa Foot, 149–174. New York: Cambridge University Press, 1993.

Quinn, Warren. "Actions, Intentions and Consequences: The Doctrine of Double Effect." In Foot, *Morality and Action*, 175–193.

Quinn, Warren. "Putting Rationality in Its Place." In Foot, *Morality and Action*, 228–271.

Railton, Peter. "Moral Realism." *Philosophical Review* 95 (1986): 163–207.

Railton, Peter. "Naturalism and Prescriptivity." In *Foundations of Moral and Political Philosophy*, edited by Fred D. Miller and Jeffrey Paul. Oxford: Blackwell, 1990.

Railton, Peter. "On the Hypothetical and Non-Hypothetical in Reasoning about Belief and Action." In *Ethics and Practical Reason*, edited by Garrett Cullity and Berys Nigel Gaut, 53–80. New York: Oxford University Press, 1997.

Railton, Peter. "Taste and Value." In *Well-Being and Morality: Essays in Honour of James Griffin*, edited by Roger Crisp and Brad Hooker, 53–74. New York: Oxford University Press, 2000.

Rappoport, J. L. "The Biology of Obsessions and Compulsions." *Scientific American* 260, June (1989): 11–12.

Rawls, John. *A Theory of Justice*. Cambridge, Mass.: Belknap Press of Harvard University Press, 1971.

Rawls, John. "Two Concepts of Rules." In Rawls, *Collected Papers*, edited by Samuel Freeman, 20–46. Cambridge, Mass.: Harvard University Press, 2001.

Rawls, John. "Kantian Constructivism in Moral Theory." In Rawls, *Collected Papers*, 303–358.

Raz, Joseph. "The Moral Point of View." In *Reason, Ethics and Society*, edited by J. B. Schneewind, 70–83. Chicago: Open Court, 1996.

Regan, Don. "Why Am I My Brother's Keeper?" In *Reason and Value: Themes from the Moral Philosophy of Joseph Raz*, edited by Jay Wallace, Philip Pettit, Samuel Scheffler, and Michael Smith. New York: Oxford University Press, 2004.

Regan, Donald H. "The Value of Rational Nature." *Ethics* 112, no. 2 (2002): 267–291.

Rosati, Connie. "Internalism and the Good for a Person." *Ethics* 106, no. 2 (1996): 297–326.

Salkovskis, Paul M. "Psychological Approaches to the Understanding of Obsessional Problems." In *Obsessive–Compulsive Disorder: Theory, Research, and Treatment*, edited by Richard P. Swinson, Martin M. Anthony, S. Rechman, and Margaret A. Richer, 33–41. New York: Guilford Press, 1998.

Sayre-McCord, Geoffrey. "The Metaethical Problem." *Ethics* 108 (1997): 55–83.

Scanlon, Thomas. *What We Owe to Each Other*. Cambridge, Mass.: Harvard University Press, 1998.

Schapiro, Tamar. "Three Conceptions of Action in Moral Theory." *Nous* 35, no. 1 (2001): 93–117.

Scheffler, Samuel. *The Rejection of Consequentialism: A Philosophical Investigation of the Considerations Underlying Rival Moral Conceptions*, 2nd ed. Oxford: Clarendon Press, 1994.

Schroeder, Mark. "The Scope of Instrumental Reason." *Philosophical Perspectives* 18 (2004): 337–364.

Schroeder, Mark. "Teleology, Agent-Relative Value, and 'Good,'" unpublished manuscript.

Schueler, G. F. *Desire: Its Role in Practical Reason and the Explanation of Action*. Cambridge, Mass.: MIT Press, 1995.

Schueler, G. F. "How Can Reason Be Practical?" *Critica* 28, no. 84 (2000): 41–62.

Schueler, G. F. *Reasons and Purposes: Human Rationality and the Teleological Explanation of Action*. New York: Oxford University Press, 2003.

Sellars, Wilfrid. "Some Reflections on Language Games." In Sellars, *Science, Perception and Reality*, 321–358. Atascadero, Calif.: Ridgeview Press, 1963.

Sellars, Wilfrid. *Empiricism and the Philosophy of Mind*. Cambridge, Mass.: Harvard University Press, 1997.

Smart, J. J. C. *Utilitarianism: For and Against*, edited by Bernard Arthur Owen, Williams. Cambridge: Cambridge University Press, 1973.

Smith, Michael. *The Moral Problem*. Oxford: Blackwell, 1995.

Smith, Michael. "In Defense of *The Moral Problem*: A Reply to Brink, Copp, and Sayre-McCord." *Ethics* 108, no. 1 (1997): 84–119.

Sobel, David. "On the Subjectivity of Welfare." *Ethics* 107 (1997): 501–508.

Stampe, Dennis. "The Authority of Desire." *Philosophical Review* 96 (1987): 335–381.

Stein, Dan, and Eric Hollander. "A Neural Network Approach to Obsessive–Compulsive Disorder." *Journal of Mind and Behaviour* 15, no. 3 (1994): 223–238.

Stocker, Michael. "Desiring the Bad: An Essay in Moral Psychology." *Journal of Philosophy* 76 (1979): 738–753.

Sumner, L. W. *Welfare, Happiness, and Ethics*. New York: Oxford University Press, 1999.

Sussman, David. "The Authority of Humanity." *Ethics* 113, no. 2 (2003): 350–367.

Swanton, Christine. "Profiles of the Virtues." *Pacific Philosophical Quarterly* 76 (1995): 47–72.

Tenenbaum, Sergio. "Realists without a Cause: Deflationary Theories of Truth and Ethical Realism." *Canadian Journal of Philosophy* 26, no. 4 (1996): 561–590.

Tenenbaum, Sergio. "The Judgment of a Weak Will." *Philosophy and Phenomenological Research* 49, no. 4 (1999): 875–911.

Tenenbaum, Sergio. "Ethical Internalism and Glaucon's Question." *Nous* 34 (2000): 108–130.

Tenenbaum, Sergio. "Speculative Mistakes and Ordinary Temptations: Kant on Instrumentalist Conceptions of Practical Reason." *History of Philosophy Quarterly* 20, no. 2 (2003): 203–223.

Tenenbaum, Sergio. "Accidie, Evaluation, and Motivation." In *Weakness of Will and Practical Irrationality*, edited by Sarah Stroud, 147–171. Oxford: Clarendon Press, 2003.

Tenenbaum, Sergio. "Direction of Fit and Motivational Cognitivism." In *Oxford Studies in Metaethics*, vol. 1, edited by Russ Shafer-Landau. Oxford: Oxford University Press, 2006.

Tenenbaum, Sergio. "The Conclusion of Practical Reason." In *New Essays on Moral Psychology*, edited by Sergio Tenenbaum. Amsterdam: Rodopi, 2006.

Thalberg, Irving. "Questions about Motivational Strength." In *Actions and Events: Perspectives on the Philosophy of Donald Davidson*, edited by Ernest LePore and Brian P. McLaughlin. Oxford: Basil Blackwell, 1988.

Thompson, Michael. "Naïve Action Theory," unpublished manuscript.

Thomson, Judith Jarvis. *The Realm of Rights*. Cambridge, Mass.: Harvard University Press, 1990.

Van Fraassen, Bas C. *The Scientific Image*. Toronto: Oxford University Press, 1980.

Velleman, David. "Brandt's Definition of 'Good'." *Philosophical Review*, 97 (1988): 353–371.

Velleman, David. "The Guise of the Good." In Velleman, *The Possibility of Practical Reason*, 92–122. New York: Oxford University Press, 2000.

Velleman, David. "What Happens When Someone Acts?" In Velleman, *The Possibility of Practical Reason*, 123–143. New York: Oxford University Press, 2000.

Velleman, David. "The Possibility of Practical Reason." In Velleman, *The Possibility of Practical Reason*, 170–199.

Vogler, Candace A. *Reasonably Vicious*. Cambridge, Mass.: Harvard University Press, 2002.

Wallace, Jay. "Explanation, Deliberation, and Reasons." In Wallace, *Normativity and the Will*, 63–70. New York: Oxford University Press, 2006.

Wallace, Jay. "Normativity, Commitment, and Instrumental Reason." In Wallace, *Normativity and the Will*, 82–120.

Watson, Gary. "Free Agency." *Journal of Philosophy* 72 (1975): 205–220.

Watson, Gary. "Skepticism about Weakness of Will." *Philosophical Review* 86 (1977): 316–339.

Watson, Gary. "Free Action and Free Will." *Mind* 96 (1987): 145–172.

Wedgwood, Ralph. "The Aim of Belief." *Philosophical Perspectives* 16 (2002): 267–297.

Williams, Bernard. "Internal and External Reasons." In Williams, *Moral Luck*, 101–113. New York: Cambridge University Press, 1981.

Williams, Bernard. *Ethics and the Limits of Philosophy*. London: Fontana Press/Collins, 1985.

Williams, Bernard. "The Point of View of the Universe: Sidgwick and the Ambitions of Ethics." In Williams, *Making Sense of Humanity and Other Philosophical Papers, 1982–1993*, 153–171. New York: Cambridge University Press, 1995.

Williams, Bernard. "Acting as the Virtuous Person Acts." In *Aristotle and Moral Realism*, edited by Robert Heinaman. Boulder, Colo.: Westview Press, 1995.

Williamson, Timothy. *Knowledge and Its Limits*. New York: Oxford University Press, 2000.

Wolf, Susan. "Moral Saints." *Journal of Philosophy* 79 (1982): 419–439.

Wollheim, Richard. "Desire, Belief and Professor Grünbaum's Freud." In *The Mind and Its Depths*. Cambridge, Mass.: Harvard University Press, 1993.

Yaqūb, Aladdin. *The Liar Speaks the Truth: A Defense of the Revision Theory of Truth*. New York: Oxford University Press, 1993.

Zangwill, Nick. "Direction of Fit and Normative Functionalism." *Philosophical Studies* 91, no. 2 (1998): 173–203.

Index